Youth in
Contemporary
Society

Youth in Contemporary Society

Edited with an introduction by

DAVID GOTTLIEB

University of Houston

 SAGE PUBLICATIONS   *Beverly Hills/London*

Portions of this volume appeared in the September 1971 issue of Youth and Society
(Volume 3, Number 1), published by Sage Publications, Inc.

For information address:

SAGE PUBLICATIONS, INC.
275 South Beverly Drive
Beverly Hills, California 90212

Printed in United States of America

International Standard Book Number 0-8039-0167-4

Library of Congress Catalog Card No. 72-84050

FIRST PRINTING

1 6/75 Beckert Tglr 1000

Contents

Editor's Introduction

Too often, social science inquiry and the availability of funds for research are intimately interwoven. As a result, most often it is only when the government or a private foundation declares some aspect of human behavior to be a social problem that funds are made available for empirical inquiry. Such certainly appears to be the case with the study of youth behavior. While social scientists did some research on youth behavior prior to the last few years of the 1960s, it was not until college student activism, youthful drug use, and the emergence of what has been identified as the new "youth culture" that the literature grew by leaps and bounds. One apparent explanation for this increased concern centers upon the fact that the youth involved were the sons and daughters of the middle class—the children of those who do the research, write the books, operate the mass media, and determine social policy. For example, we know that long before grass came to suburbia there were thousands of ghetto youth who were victims of heroin, a drug far more harmful than marijuana. Long before middle-class college students began to drop out there were many less than affluent students who were being pushed out of American high schools. For years, prior to the time that college students questioned the relevancy of American higher education, others had questioned the meaning and value of our educational process. Yet, it was not until our own children began to question, rebel, and show overt signs of alienation that we, social scientists particularly, began to take the problem seriously.

A major purpose of this book is to attempt to identify how different kinds of youth will be reacting to different aspects of the social system in the years ahead. More specifically, each of the authors was asked to speak on the following:

What is the current status of youth with regard to the issue with which you will be dealing?

What attitudes and behaviors can we anticipate in this decade?

Given how we now deal with youth, what outcomes might we anticipate? What will be the effect upon youth? What will be the effect upon social institutions which deal with youth?

If you like, what recommendations would you make? What are the social policy or programatic implications?

Each author was selected on the basis of his interest and professional work with a specific segment of the youth population or a specific issue area. Needless to say, each author recognized the difficulty of attempting to predict or anticipate future trends. Still, each of the authors was willing to participate in this project, since each recognized the need for a future-oriented approach. Hopefully, the materials contained herein will be of value to those who study the young, those who have the day-to-day responsibility for youth socialization, and those who are responsible for the development of youth policy.

—David Gottlieb

1

BLACK BRAINPOWER
Characteristics of Bright Black Youth

DONIVAN J. WATLEY

Until fairly recently, little attempt has been made to study empirically the characteristics of "bright blacks"—those considered most academically able. Events of the past decade, however, have spotlighted the black American and his problems—large-scale poverty in the midst of the world's wealthiest nation, unequal educational opportunities, racial discrimination in a country known for its democratic principles, and the like.

Who are bright blacks? The main purpose here is to discuss some of the characteristics of academically able blacks, and to consider their educational ambitions and their future careers. But "Who are they?" also inherently involves the matter of how they can best be identified.

THE SEARCH FOR BRIGHT BLACKS

The current crisis over civil rights, fair employment, and equal educational opportunity is supported by the fact that some racial and other minority groups are underrepresented in the various levels of the educational, occupational, governmental, and socioeconomic structure—indeed, some have been arbitrarily excluded because of color. It is important in considering "underrepresentation," however, to distinguish between clear prejudice because of one's skin color, sex, and other such characteristics, and that which is due to the fact that some individuals or groups for a variety of complex reasons may be currently less qualified on some set of selection criteria that theoretically applies to everyone. Although in practice these two reasons are entangled to the extent that they really cannot be entirely separated, at least one kind is more willful, while the other is more subtle. The advantage of this distinction is that it brings clearly to light the problem of test performance and selection.

Blacks score on the average about one standard deviation below the average of the white population in tested IQ (Dreger and Miller, 1960; Shuey, 1966; Jensen, 1969). It is estimated that 15% of the Negro population exceeds the white average on tests of this type. The top universities draw students from the top quarter of the white distribution on entrance tests, but only about 5% of the blacks today get scores this high. Correcting for the proportions of Negroes in the total population, this means that there is only about one black to every thirty Caucasians in the top quartile of test scores (Humphreys, 1969). Judging from the Coleman Report (1966), Negroes also score about one standard deviation below the average for whites and Orientals on tests of scholastic achievement. This difference holds up fairly consistently across grades 1 through 12. What does all of this mean?

The "human resources" push of the late 1950s and early 1960s had already set in motion a well-oiled procedure for selecting top academic talent. Thus, an obvious first step was applying this machinery to the task of identifying the most talented students from so-called culturally disadvantaged groups like blacks and providing them the means to attend college. This temporary device is intended to help blacks gain admission into the mainstream of national life. "The truth," said Stalnaker (1965: 142-143), "is that few Lincolns, few young Horatio Algers, and relatively few young people from culturally disadvantaged groups like Negroes actually win scholarships offered in open competition." He goes on to say: "Scholarships are usually awarded because of some outstanding positive characteristics a student has, not because of a weakness, a deficiency, inadequate preparation, or the scarring which basic deprivation is apt to leave." In addition to the identification of bright blacks, a second approach has been that of attempting to develop through better instruction college-calibre students from among those groups that traditionally have been educationally undernourished and underdeveloped.

But we find here an apparent clash between the "development of talent" and "equality of everyman" interests. Critical events of the middle to late 1960s seemed to produce a rapid and marked change of emphasis from "human conservation" to one of concern for every man's right to be educated. These two interests—"talent development" and "equality"—are not basically in conflict, however, when equality of everyman means in part that every man has a right to equal opportunity. Even with equal opportunities, it is obvious, nevertheless, that everyone is not equally talented in given areas. Years of "opportunity" will not make a halfback with average ability run with the skill of Gale Sayers.

Although the equal educational opportunity crisis was in preparation for many years, "it occurred in the spring and summer of 1968 and established the academic year of 1968-1969 as the time when most institutions moved the problems of the disadvantaged near the top of their lists of urgent problems" (Kendrick and Thomas, 1970: 152). Following McGrath (1966), Kendrick and Thomas go on to point out (1970: 153) that

American higher education, historically heterogeneous, but usually designed for some selected population, is now asked to provide a useful experience for most young people, including those who can not afford to pay the bills, are not "prepared for college," do not have "college ability," and do not arise from the backgrounds that have provided even the self-made men of earlier times.

Despite the new emphasis, the search by colleges for "bright blacks" has continued unabated. But this approach alone is not, and never has been, enough. The "talent development" and "equality" emphases are both needed, although crisis states can make them appear to be in opposition to each other. Educational opportunity for everyman does not remove the responsibility of identifying the "best" people to do the jobs that have to be done and developing their skills to the level that the jobs can be done effectively. Nor, in fact, is the search for talent any less important when a long-term view is taken. Interestingly enough, the question of the number of test-bright but non-college-going youth to be found in disadvantaged populations still remains largely unanswered.

But the current tidal wave of interest in equality of educational opportunity has brought with it a rash of protests against all forms of ability-testing of disadvantaged groups. It is argued that, since the validity of such tests is highly questionable for disadvantaged students, the results are used to make unfair judgments. Thus, there is considerable talk now about throwing out current selection tests for disadvantaged groups altogether. The wisdom of this move is debatable, however, in the case of identifying academically oriented, achieving blacks. Thus far, the weight of the evidence shows that tests like the Scholastic Aptitude Test (SAT) of the College Entrance Examination Board predict first-year college performance as well for blacks as for whites (e.g., Hills et al., 1963; Boney, 1966; Stanley and Porter, 1967; Kendrick and Thomas, 1970; Stanley, 1970), although Clark and Plotkin (1963) provide a note of caution about using such tests with blacks.

John Gardner (1961: 47) notes that scholastic ability tests are, after all, *"designed to do an unpopular job."* Since a great number of whites as well as blacks never make it into Princeton, Caltech, MIT, or Rice, hostility toward tests is really no respecter of color. It is not the tests themselves that are to blame, however, since they presently represent only one of the best means now available for predicting success in colleges. If ability tests really do predict as well for blacks as for whites, and if colleges continue to evaluate students as they have been, the traditional scholastic potential indices should continue to have some value for predicting the bright black's performance in college.

Of course, the fabric and structure of a college can change, or it can remain pretty much the same. But if an academically difficult college, for example, keeps its programs basically unchanged and attempts to deal with the problem of educational equality by going in search of certain skin colors to fill some quota, one can probably expect additional problems if many of those admitted are seriously unqualified academically. Such a situation seems to invite frustration, and the path from frustration to aggression has been well documented. The tensions on college campuses are already running high over a variety of problems (e.g., the war in Indochina and environmental pollution), the racial question being only one among many that greatly bother young people today.

At this juncture, colleges are faced with the difficult task of helping to create an American society where there is truly both freedom and equality. What student selection policies are best designed to fulfill this objective? A growing number believe that the answer is open admissions. Others strongly disagree. One of the reasons is that there is strong disagreement of the meaning of "equality" and how to bring it about. Moreover, where there is freedom, people soon become unequal in important ways, because some are more talented or motivated or dedicated than others.

Although, in the long run, democracy at work does not in principle provide quotas because of someone's sex or skin color, it seems reasonable nevertheless that temporary handicaps can be useful in breaking a monotonous and vicious chain of events among the so-called "disadvantaged" groups. The granting of earmarked scholarships is one way of doing this.

NOMINATIONS VERSUS TEST PERFORMANCE

In a nationwide talent search for bright blacks, what strategy works best to identify the ablest academic brainpower? To what extent are scholastic ability tests of significant value? The three most commonly used ways of identifying "brains" of academic promise are standardized tests, scholastic performance, and teacher recommendations. In practice, these three can be reduced to two, test performance being contrasted with school nominations, which takes into consideration both grades and teacher ratings. Are blacks identified by the first route different from those found by the second? Are those who obtain high tests scores *and* who are nominated by school officials unlike those who obtain a high score only (no nomination) or those who are nominated only with no accompanying test score?

Data relevant to these questions have been collected for participants in the National Achievement Scholarship Program (Blumenfeld, 1969). The aim of NASP is to identify and to provide scholarship aid to outstanding Negro students. Students entered the 1967 Achievement competition through either school nomination, a high scholastic ability test score, or both. Entering students were then placed into four categories: (1) nominated but no ability test information; (2) nominated and a low test score; (3) nominated and a high test score; and (4) no nomination but a high test score. Interestingly, the members of group 3 differed from group

2 in much the same way that bright whites differ from their white peers who do not score as well on tests: both their fathers and mothers were better educated, they had higher educational aspirations, they came from larger high schools where fewer blacks attended, more books were available in their high school libraries, and fewer of them attended public schools. The thing that seemed to characterize the nominated but low test scorers was the drive to excel academically; the percentages making the National Honor Society or the Dean's List were just as great as the percentages for group 2. About two-thirds of them were women. Except that the group 4 members did not do as well academically, they had much in common with the members of group 3, both scoring much higher on ability tests on the average than groups 1 or 2. In fact, groups 3 and 4 were very much alike when they were contrasted to groups 1 and 2: their parents were better educated, they attended larger high schools enrolling fewer blacks, and so forth. Group 4–high test score but no nomination–appeared to consist of individuals of academic promise who came mostly from good schools and who were overlooked for nomination because of the stiff competition from their own classmates. On the whole, those who entered the Achievement competition by nomination only (group 1) tended to have a broad range of personal characteristics and to have come from a great variety of schools; generally, they seemed to be less advantaged in their socioeconomic and educational background.

These results provide evidence, then, that the blacks who score highest on ability tests differ from their peers in much the same way that bright whites differ from their lower-scoring white peers. Thus, if one's aim is to identify the cream of the academic crop among blacks who now appear to have the best chance of successfully competing academically with bright whites, test scores are an invaluable aid in finding them. Almost 80% of those chosen by a selection panel for 1967 Achievement scholarships could have been identified for consideration in the competition by the test alone. And those who are chosen for scholarships do well in college, including many of those attending the most prestigious campuses (Burgdorf, 1969; Borgen, 1970). Additional comparative analyses are anticipated on the college performance of blacks who entered the scholarship competition by the nomination and test routes. Importantly, the focus of attention here is on bright blacks who are highly motivated to achieve academically. Many blacks do not share the characteristics, ambitions, or interests of these high academic achievers.

BRIGHT BLACK ACHIEVERS

We really do not know what *pure* ability is, although the debate over the relative roles of genes and environment in the origin and development of human ability still goes on. Nevertheless, that some people perform certain tasks more skillfully or accurately than others is unmistakable. Yet observing someone in the midst of his mental cogitation does not provide much information concerning the mechanics of how he does it. Thus mental ability is pinned down at all only in terms of someone's functional definition of it—the ways that it seems to manifest itself.

The emphasis here is on bright academic achievers—those blacks who score highest on a scholastic aptitude test and who obtained exceptionally high grades in high school. The data reported here come primarily from research conducted with blacks who have participated in the National Achievement Scholarship Program. About three-quarters of the winners of Achievement awards score at or above the ninetieth percentile on scholastic ability test norms for high school juniors. In conducting an annual nationwide talent search, the National Merit Scholarship Qualifying Test (NMSQT) is administered on a voluntary basis to juniors in high schools that enroll approximately 95% of all eleventh-grade students in the United States. Achievement finalists and scholars are selected within a number of geographical regions.

THEIR CHARACTERISTICS

How is the bright academic achiever perceived by others? Prior to Sputnik 1, common stereotyping had the bright, achieving white pegged as someone strange, puny, sickly, and bespectacled. The emphasis on brainpower and continuing research has since contributed to a drastic change in this distorted image. The current image of the "bright black" likely depends upon whose opinion is asked. Looking at research results, how can we describe him at this point?

Socioeconomic Status

Like the white "brain," the bright black achiever tends to come from a family of higher socioeconomic status than his less test-bright, lower academically achieving black peer—his parents have a larger income, they have completed more education, and his father is more likely to hold a professional or skilled job. The families of winners of 1965 Achievement scholarships, for example, had a median income ($8,300) substantially larger than that ($6,000) of those who were finalists in the Achievement competition. The correlation of .24 between the selection test scores of all finalists, including the scholarship winners, and family income is about the same as those that have been reported for various white groups (Roberts and Nichols, 1966). About 15% of all finalists in the 1966 program reported family incomes of $10,000 or higher, but it is important to appreciate that a quarter of these bright blacks reported family incomes of less than $4,000 (Blumenfeld, 1966). A few had no earned income at all. Interestingly, the relatively low correlation (.24) between test scores and family income did hold up even for Southern blacks, although the restricted economic opportunities for Negroes there might have been expected to affect this relationship. Although one's status in the competition for Achievement scholarships was related to family income, relatively speaking the incomes of blacks still tended to be far below those of National Merit Scholarship winners and finalists (Roberts and Nichols, 1966). About 77% of the families of students reaching the Merit finalist level in 1964 earned $8,000 or more (Nichols, 1965). Almost two-thirds of the Merit scholars have fathers earning substantial incomes from either owning their own businesses or working in the professions, although, of course, not all of them draw big salaries or have big incomes (Watley, 1969). Bayer and Boruch (1969) report data which highlight this same income differential for black and nonblack freshman students who entered college in 1968. Thus, for financial reasons alone, attendance at prestigious colleges is beyond the reach of most bright blacks without substantial financial support.

As would be expected, therefore, high test scorers are more frequently found in ethnic groups where high social, educational, economic, and professional attainments are found. Jews and Scandinavians, for example, produce more than their share of test-bright children, while Negroes, Mexicans, and American Indians produce fewer. It is interesting, nevertheless, that many of the differences noted between high and low test-bright whites (e.g., attitudes, interests, personality characteristics) do not wash out when students of different ability levels are matched on socioeconomic-type variables like family income and father's education (Nichols and Davis, 1964; Astin, 1964). Thus, while having an economically favorable home environment is surely relevant to test performance (Shuey, 1966), many other factors seem to be related to high test performance.

About 18% of all 1966 Achievement finalists had fathers who worked in professional occupations—those requiring college or graduate training (e.g., engineer, physician). But 43% had fathers who did factory work, pumped gas, worked as laborers, and so forth. Another 11% did skilled work requiring a specialized period of training (e.g., policeman, printer). Almost none of them were employed as salesmen or did clerical work like bookkeeping or bank telling. Very few did technical work like drafting or computer programming. About 58% had mothers who worked outside the home, 18% of whom were reported to hold professional-level jobs such as teacher. Another 8% worked as housekeepers, cooks, maids, and so on, and 7% held some type of clerical position. Importantly, the jobs parents held and their incomes depended to some extent upon the part of the country in which they resided. Those from the upper Midwest and East, for example, were quite a bit better off financially than those in any other part of the country. Proportionally speaking, blacks fill many more jobs at the unskilled and semi-skilled levels than whites do, a fact which Bayer and Boruch (1969) point out in their investigation of entering black and nonblack college freshmen. Still, the black parents who send their children to college are better off financially on the average than those who do not (McGrath, 1965; Fichter, 1967), and the parents of Achievement finalists tend to have higher incomes than the parents of the typical black college freshman.

As one would expect, the fathers of Achievement scholars also have completed more education than the fathers of the average black freshmen. In fact, they have significantly more years of formal education than the fathers of a representative sample of college graduates (Nichols and Davis, 1964), although this difference does not hold up when the fathers of all Achievement finalists are considered. Finalists' fathers do, however, have more education than the fathers of graduates of predominantly Negro colleges (Fichter, 1967). Although slightly lower, the amount of education completed by Achievement scholars' fathers compares favorably with the formal schooling of the fathers of finalists for National Merit Scholarships (Roberts and Nichols, 1966). It is relevant also that the fathers of Achievement scholars and finalists from the upper midwestern and western states have more education than those from the other regions of this country, and that they have far more education than that reported by the 1960 U.S. Census for Negro men aged 45-64—84.3% were reported to have completed the eighth grade or less.

The same relationships were found for the mothers of Achievement participants as were found for the fathers: the higher a student's position in the competition, the more education completed by the mother, and mothers from the upper midwestern and eastern states had more education than those from other geographic regions. A particularly interesting point is that the mothers of Achievement participants have slightly more formal education than the fathers do. In fact, the mothers of Achievement scholars have considerably more education than the mothers of a representative sample of college graduates, and they have finished about as much as that reported by the mothers of Merit finalists. It is relevant in this connection that the Achievement scholars and finalists report many more books in their homes than did the high school seniors participating in Project Talent (Flanagan et al., 1964), the medians for the two groups being 130 and 74.

Unlike the white middle-class culture, where the father-as-breadwinner is expected to have more education than the mother, there is now some evidence that while in general the Negro mother is more apt to be the breadwinner (e.g., Doddy, 1963; Edwards, 1963), the parents of educated blacks are approximately equally educated. For their national sample of college freshmen, Bayer and Boruch (1969) report, for example, that while 20% of the black fathers and 23% of the black mothers had at least some college, the comparable percentages for the nonblacks were 44 and 37. Fichter (1967) reports that 13% of the fathers of 1964 graduates of predominantly Negro colleges had finished college and that 14% of the mothers had done so.

It appears that even now the educated and achievement-oriented black, like his white counterpart, has things in mind for his children that the poorly educated, lower-class Negroes do not. This point is emphasized by Fichter (1967: 48) in his study of graduates of predominantly Negro colleges:

the better educated Negro parents have provided certain advantages for their children. They undoubtedly anticipated their children's higher education and saw to it that they took the college preparatory curriculum in high school. In this regard, the upper class Negro students have a high school curriculum proportionately similar to that of the white students . . . The economic, occupational, and educational status of Negro parents obviously has a great influence on the academic aspirations and experiences of their children. In contrast, it is remarkable that any of the children of lower class Negro parents ever manage to attend and finish college.

In recent years, there has been a growing interest in the role of language in the development of intellectual processes, particularly regarding the influence of patterns of language and the interaction of a child with his environment. Researchers now attempt to trace backward from the school years into the preschool years, hoping to uncover clues as to how the acquisition of language patterns occurs (Dreger and Miller, 1960). The thought and work of Vygotsky and Piaget in particular have had considerable impact on those working in this area, although it is still too early to see clearly what the benefits of this activity will be.

Pettigrew (1964) maintains that just "being Negro" has in the past implicitly carried with it attitudes which have affected how blacks view themselves, the effect of which has been to derogate the Negro in a way that has influenced his intelligence and achievement performance. "No wonder that the child," says Gray (1964: 7), "who finds his pre-primers and primers full of golden haired boys and girls, with business-suited and brief-cased fathers, happy housewife mothers, and cocker spaniels, begins to believe that something is wrong with his brown skin, his father-absent home, and his yellow pup." As educational and economic opportunities are opened to blacks, and as our text books are changed, perhaps this problem can be rectified. "The Negro's principal immediate problem," observed Jerome Holland (1969: 171), "is that he is *poor,* because prejudice against his color has denied him equal economic and educational opportunities."

Hometown

About 60 to 70% of the Achievement scholars and finalists come from a central city of 10,000 or more, the great majority of which are from cities of at least 100,000. Another 10 to 20% come from the suburbs of large cities. Although the U.S. Bureau of the Census (1965) reports that about 30% of the nonwhite population enrolled in high schools in 1960 is classified as "rural," 10% or less of the Achievement scholars and finalists are from the "farm or open country." Interestingly, although about 80% of the finalists in the National Merit Scholarship Program come from either a central city of 10,000 or more or from a suburb, relatively more of them lived in the suburbs than did the Achievement scholars and finalists. As one would expect, the black winners come more frequently from the inner cities than do the whites. Using a national sample of freshman entrants to college in 1968, Bayer and Boruch (1969) report that 8% of the blacks come from the suburbs of large cities, while the comparable percentage for nonblacks was 23.

About 44% of the Achievement scholars and finalists report having lived in the same town or cities all their lives. Another 22% said that they had resided in their present communities at least five but less than ten years.

Family Characteristics

The median number of siblings reported by Achievement scholars and finalists is two (Roberts and Nichols, 1966; Blumenfeld, 1966). But about 30% have four or more. They frequently are the first-born of the family: 64% were first-born of two-child families, 43% were born first of the three-child families, and 35% were born first of the families with four children. These frequencies deviate significantly from chance expectancies, a tendency which has also been found for National Merit winners and finalists. About 11% of the bright blacks were only children.

In contrast, the families of Achievement scholars and finalists tend to be larger than those reaching the finalist stage in the Merit program. The median number of siblings reported by the bright whites was about one, and only about 5% had four or more children in the family besides themselves.

Another important factor in the lives of young people is family stability. About 74% of the parents of Achievement scholars and finalists were reported to be living together. This percentage of intact families is probably higher than that found among nonwhites in the general population. The Census Bureau report for 1960 reveals that only about 66% of all nonwhite children under 18 were living with both parents, although this statistic is not directly comparable because Achievement students were all about 17 or 18 years old. And Fichter's study of graduates of predominantly Negro colleges found that about one-third of them came from homes broken by death, desertion, separation, divorce, or some combination of these problems before they had reached the age of 16. With college freshmen, Froe (1964) reports that the percentage of broken homes among the whites was only 14 but was 32 for the blacks. Moreover, he says that these same data indicate a greater tendency for separation of parents to occur during the early or formative years of the black child than is the case for parents of the white child.

Are bright blacks religious? Very few of the Achievement scholars and finalists—2% of the boys and 1% of the girls—say that they were raised with no religious background. Some 4% of the boys and 3% of the girls claimed to accept no particular religious doctrine just prior to the time they entered college, although only about 60% of the boys and 70% of the girls reported that they often took part in church or Sunday school activities. Still, these bright blacks appear to be more active in formal religions than the brightest of the whites in the Merit program. Of the Merit finalists, about 5% of each sex indicate that they were reared in no religion, but 18% of the males and 11% of the females reported just before entering college that they then had no religious preference. Moreover, many scholars give up their religious identification after entering college (Watley and Kaplan, 1970), and the women are just as apt to relinquish their religious faiths as are the men. Only about a quarter of the men and a third of the women report seven to eight years after entering college that they attend church as much as 40 times a year. In contrast, Fichter (1967) found that only 1% of the graduates of predominantly black colleges reported being raised in no religious background, and that only 2% of the graduates of public institutions and 5% of the private college graduates claimed to accept no religious doctrine.

Activities: What Do They Do?

What does a bright black, aged 17 or 18, do with his spare time?

Interestingly, 21% of all female Achievement finalists, including scholars, report that they never date, and another 32% say that they have one date or less a month; 27% date two or three times a month. Thus, since altogether about 80% seldom or never go out with boys, it appears that they are not frequent daters. And the dating pattern among bright black boys appears to be similar to that of the girls, although fewer of them—13%—report that they never have dates. However, 33% have one date or less a month.

What do they do? On the average, 70 to 75% of each sex report that they watch TV 4 to 10 hours each week, around 15% watching more. As one would expect, their studies are **very** important to them, and they tend to give a lot of time to their schoolwork and to outside reading. During the school year, about a third of each sex estimate that they spend 15-19 hours each week studying, and another third study 20 hours or more. In addition to schoolwork, about 40% of each sex spend another 5 hours or more each week doing outside reading. Interestingly enough, however, over half the boys found some time to work for pay outside the home during the school year, about a quarter of them working more than 10 hours a week. About a third of the girls did outside work for pay, but most of them worked only a few hours each week.

About a third of each sex spent some time working in a civil rights organization or with a political action group of some sort. They engaged in a wide variety of other activities—some wrote poems, some collected stamps, some of the boys worked on cars, and so on. Only 12% of the boys and 11% of the girls said they definitely belonged to a close group of friends that did most things together.

It has been said (Nichols and Astin, 1966; Watley and Kaplan, 1970) that a crucial feature which sets the bright, achieving Merit scholar apart from the average student is the burning desire to achieve and to excel. Not only is he achievement-oriented, but he is highly industrious and persevering. It appears that test-bright, achieving blacks possess these same qualities.

Achievements

The Achievement scholars are, by and large, superior academic performers in high school. Over half the 1965 scholars, for example, graduated in the ninety-ninth percentile in their classes, and 78% of the males and 83% of the females finished in the ninety-fifth percentile or better. However, slightly over 10% of the scholars did graduate below the ninetieth percentile, indicating that other factors were taken into consideration in their selection. Perhaps it is worth noting, however, that high school rank can itself be a deceiving statistic. For example, in a class much smaller than 100, the top student cannot attain the ninety-ninth percentile, and 18% of the scholars came from classes of less than 100 (Roberts and Nichols, 1966). Moreover, many came from very large, predominantly white schools where there is strong competition for academic recognition.

Scholars and finalists tend to have many achievements and awards which involve some recognition of quality of performance (Blumenfeld, 1966). Besides academic awards, those mentioned most frequently by the male blacks are connected with leadership in school government or some type of organization. About half have writing accomplishments in the form of published articles or essays, and about a quarter have published poems or stories (including those that have appeared in school publications). They do not appear to be overly involved in dramatics, and they have even less interest in art. Around 40% report having earned a varsity athletic letter.

Among the females, virtually all have academic awards, and the great majority have held influential positions in student government and in other organizations. Fewer of them than males have won science research recognition, but more of them have been awarded for their community service work, and slightly more have won recognition for writing. Like the males, relatively few have won awards in drama, art, or debate.

PERSONAL GOALS: BRIGHT BLACKS VERSUS BRIGHT WHITES

Are the personal life goals of bright blacks different from those of test-bright whites? Comparisons are made here between the views of Merit finalists and Achievement finalists. In some cases, what they regard as *essential* life goals are similar, but in other areas their views are markedly different.

Virtually all these blacks regarded becoming a mature and well-adjusted person as an essential goal, while only about three-quarters of the bright white males held this goal in such high esteem. Furthermore, almost all blacks stated that finding a real purpose in life is essential, a point on which 97% of the white women agreed but one on which 20% of the white men did not. Rather marked differences were found between blacks and whites of both sexes on each of the following, in each case the blacks considering the goal more essential: being happy and contented, helping others in difficulty, becoming an authority on a special subject, doing something to make their parents proud of them, becoming a community leader, following a formal religious code, being well-read, keeping up with political affairs, being well-liked, being a good parent, being successful in a personally owned business, and keeping in good physical condition. Interestingly, more black males than white males consider it essential to make a technical contribution to science, but more whites want to make a theoretical contribution.

One gets the picture of a group of blacks with very high goals indeed. Moreover, they seem to have a strong sense of obligation to others as well as to their own success. Apparently, they seek personal gains for themselves—and their expectations are high—but these somehow seem to involve others. One black male scholar, a junior in college, sized up the matter this way:

> If the black students in college now do not take it upon themselves to return and devote their talents to the black

community, total and equal citizenship may "take a long time coming." We in college now seem to be the best prepared and in the best position to accomplish this operation.

Another black, a sophomore, said it like this:

> My goals in life have changed only slightly. I am still very optimistic about eventually making some worthwhile contribution to my family, the black race, America, and the world at large . . . I received a splendid opportunity for advancement in this society and my present plans are to do all I can to aid the many more who are left behind.

Most blacks seem to sense now that a crucial turning point has been reached in America, and many bright blacks apparently believe that they have a special and important role to play. One Achievement scholar, who was on the Dean's List and president of the Afro-American Society at an Ivy League college, reflected this view: "My attempt to understand and relate to the world and to the part that I, as a black man, must play in it, is a question which plagues me more than that of studies alone." A similar statement was made by another young black on the Dean's List at a prestigious southeastern university: "I feel it would be a tragic mistake to try to withdraw into the academic community and hide from the reality of the conditions of the outside world." Another honors student said, "I have decided to study urban economics to discover what I can do personally to improve my community, Watts."

Merit scholars, on the other hand, appear to be strongly theoretically inclined, and they strive hard to be intellectually autonomous. Self-ratings and the ratings of both teachers and peers all agree in characterizing the Merit finalist more frequently than less able students as independent, assertive, idealistic, unconventional, cynical, rebellious, and argumentative (Watley, forthcoming). This is not to suggest that they tend toward emotional instability or that they do not care about the pressing problems of the world. On the contrary, Merit finalists are keenly aware of the times, and there is plenty of evidence that they tend to have strong feelings about the war in Indochina, environmental pollution, and so on. It is very doubtful, nevertheless, that their perspective of racial injustice has the depth of commitment felt by many young blacks today.

THE BRIGHT BLACK FEMALE

Regardless of skin color, the problems and expectations of women are understandably not all the same as those of men—and bright women are no exception. Traditionally, many white women with intellectual promise have gone to college, done well academically, and developed considerable knowledge in a wide variety of areas. But it is not customary, as it is for men, for them to routinely move from college into productive and satisfying careers. Moreover, even those who do manage to establish careers have another set of problems that men typically do not worry about—they also have to manage a home and family.

Although white women are themselves now engaged in spirited and noisy protests over equal work rights, the problems and concerns of the black woman are not all identical with those of bright whites. And her educational motivations and career expectations often differ also from those of black males.

One important aspect of the family organization among blacks, for example, is that, for a variety of complex reasons, the mother more frequently than the white mother has the dominant role as head of the household. The percentage of broken homes among blacks is much higher even among parents of college students (Edwards, 1963; Froe, 1964; Fichter, 1967). About a third of the black college students report that they come from broken homes. Thus, a great deal of pressure is placed on many black mothers to serve as the breadwinner. Even among Achievement scholars and finalists, almost a quarter live with their mothers only, the father being absent because of death, separation, and the like.

Like white females, black females do tend to do better in high school than their male counterparts, and until recently a higher percentage of them graduated (U.S. Bureau of the Census, 1968). In 1960, for example, 39% of the nonwhite males aged 16 to 17 who were enrolled in school were at least one full grade below the mode for their age, while the comparable percentage for the females was only 27%; the difference was in the same direction for whites, but much smaller (U.S. Department of Labor, 1965). Interestingly enough, college attendance is much greater for white males over females, the ratio being on the order of about 3 to 2. Many more black women than men get the bachelor's degree, although the men who do graduate more frequently take postgraduate and professional training (Doddy, 1963). Bayer and Boruch (1969) report that 54% of the entering college black freshmen in 1968 were women. Fichter's (1967) data show that the graduates of predominantly black colleges in 1964 favored the female even more—64% women to 36% men.

That black females tend to do better in high school is reflected in the fact that about 60% of those nominated for the first two years of the Achievement competition were female. And in recent competitions, when academic ability test scores have been used to select the finalists, the ratio has decreased some, but still favors the females about 54 to 46%. Since about 50.5% of the nonwhite high school students 14 to 17 years old are female (U.S. Bureau of the Census, 1965), the females' superior performance does not appear to be due to there being significantly more of them in the schools.

A follow-up of the 1956-1960 women Merit scholarship winners in 1965 revealed that 85% of them definitely wanted a career (another 6% were uncertain) and about 79% planned to combine marriage with a career (Watley and Kaplan, 1970). Thus, although trying to adjust to the marriage-career

form of double life is a traditional problem of women, the current generation of white female "brains" seems more determined than earlier generations to find a workable solution. If educational aspirations are any indication, bright, achieving black women may be following suit—about 50% of the Achievement scholars say that they want a doctoral level degree and most of the rest want a master's degree. In contrast, only about 16% of the black women who entered college as freshmen in 1968 sought a doctoral level degree, and about 43% stated that their goal was a master's degree (Bayer and Boruch, 1969). Like the white Merit scholars, 78% of the Achievement scholars and finalists said they wanted to be married career women with children, apparently having no intention whatever of giving up the added responsibility of motherhood (Blumenfeld, 1966).

EDUCATIONAL PROGRESS

Rapid growth and development characterized American higher education throughout the 1960s. College enrollment nearly doubled from 1960 to 1968, while the population of 18-24-year-olds was increasing about 30%. From 1964 to 1968, the number of blacks enrolled in college increased 85%, and the proportion of blacks aged 18-24 who were attending college increased from 8 to 15% (U.S. Bureau of Census, 1969). Altogether, 6 to 7% of the entrants to college in 1968 were black (Bayer and Boruch, 1969), but just 3% of the college graduates in 1965 were Negroes (Astin and Panos, 1969). Still, the odds are now much higher than they were just ten years ago that a bright, academically achieving black will attend college.

If they had their choice, which colleges would outstanding Negro students want to attend? This question was asked 1,029 Achievement finalists in 1966 (Blumenfeld, 1968). Since they came from every region, one might expect that a wide variety of colleges in different geographical locations would be named. However, this was not the case. Rather, like bright whites (Astin, 1965; Nichols, 1966), they had a very small group of highly prestigious colleges in mind. The great majority—84%—named a college with a predominantly white student body. Among males, the ten most popular colleges were, in order: Harvard, University of Michigan, Yale, Princeton, MIT, Cornell, Dartmouth, Howard, Columbia, and the University of Pennsylvania. Only one of these—Howard—is a predominantly Negro college. The ten most popular colleges named by females were, in order: Radcliffe, Fisk, Mt. Holyoke, Howard, Stanford, University of Michigan, University of Pennsylvania, Hampton, Cornell, and the University of Texas. Three of these—Fisk, Howard, and Hampton—are attended mostly by blacks. Clearly, they had definite opinions about their first-choice colleges, and the most desired ones are the affluent and widely advertised ones where other bright students are known to congregate.

Altogether only 8% of the males and 19% of the females named a predominantly black campus as their first-choice college. Blumenfeld (1968) notes that naming a predominantly Negro college was related to being female, being from the South, having a lower scholastic ability test score, and coming from a relatively lower socioeconomic background. He says (Blumenfeld, 1968: 339):

> Items characterizing students naming Negro colleges suggest a family where college was not given much consideration until recently, a larger family, a home with lower parental education and lower family income, a home with fewer books, a small town or rural community, more TV watching, considering material awards more important than social rewards in choosing a job or career, being from a public school, and more friends who dropped out of school.

But college preferences named on the basis of "if I won a scholarship" do not always indicate which colleges students actually enter. About 11% of all those who received scholarships during the first five years of the Achievement program (1965 to 1969) actually entered Harvard and Yale, with Harvard leading the way. Behind these, the colleges, in order, that have enrolled the most Achievement scholars are: Howard, Michigan State, Radcliffe, Stanford, Cornell, Penn State, MIT, Princeton, and Columbia. In another study, Borgen (1970) found that 29% of the males and 43% of the females who reached the commended stage of the Achievement competition in 1965 attended campuses that were predominantly black, although the majority of each sex were at privately supported colleges. According to Borgen, the public Negro colleges were most likely to enroll students ranking low on socioeconomic factors like parental education, family income, and father's occupation; on the other hand, less than 17% of these students in highly selective white schools had unskilled fathers and only about one-fourth had fathers who were not high school graduates. About a third of the schools attended were classified as predominantly white and highly selective.

Who encourages outstanding black high school students most regarding college attendance? About 60% of the Achievement scholars and finalists say that it is their parents, and another quarter of them trace most encouragement to teachers and school officials. Interestingly, however, males and females differ somewhat on how long it has been understood by the student himself and his parents that he would probably attend college. About 70 to 75% of the females indicate that it has always been understood that they would go, but only 60% of the males say that the idea has been accepted that long. More males than females indicate that college attendance did not become understood until they reached junior high and high school.

Their educational aspirations are high, although the goals of the males tend to be even higher than those expressed by the females. Prior to college entrance, 65 to 75% of the males state that they hope to acquire a doctoral level degree, and almost all the rest want a master's degree (Roberts and

Nichols, 1966; Blumenfeld, 1966). These are very similar to the desires of Merit scholars (Watley, 1969), but much higher than those expressed by the typical black freshman (Bayer and Boruch, 1969). Borgen (1970) observes, however, that the aspirational level of blacks depends to some extent on the type of college they enter; for example, men in Negro colleges have higher aspirations on the average than those in low-selectivity white colleges.

The amount of education sought by the women Achievement scholars and finalists is even higher than the goals of female Merit scholars when they enter college, about half saying that they want a doctoral level degree. But, of course, people's plans can be hindered for various reasons. Thus it remains to be seen just how far they will go. One pessimistic note comes from research conducted by the National Opinion Research Center, Miller (1963: 30) reporting that among the 1961 college graduates "even those Negroes with definite plans to enroll were considerably less likely to do so than whites."

Engineering has consistently been the most popular college major of the male Achievement scholars and finalists. Premedicine and mathematics follow engineering in frequency of choice, but prelaw and political science have become increasingly popular in the last few years. The majors blacks choose are related, however, to the type of college attended (Borgen, 1970). For example, about twice as many men in private Negro colleges chose the physical and natural sciences as those in highly selective white colleges. Nevertheless, the kinds of training that black men choose most frequently have a clear practical application. Women most frequently choose the social sciences, with psychology and education leading the way. Like the men, many black women also choose majors in mathematics and in premedicine.

There is now a great deal of interest in learning how well blacks perform in college. In his study of 1965 Achievement program commended students, Borgen (1970) found that, in general, the freshmen in Negro colleges got higher grades than those on the largely white campuses: one-fourth earned grade averages of B+ or higher on the one hand, but only 10% earned averages that high on the other. The differences in grades between Negro and white schools was the reverse of the difference in scholastic ability scores; that is, students on black campuses earned higher grades despite the fact that their test scores tended to be lower. Altogether, Burgdorf (1969) found that slightly over half the 1965 Achievement scholars and finalists earned a freshman grade average of B or better, and about 95% earned at least C averages. Only a handful failed to finish the freshman year, and about 97% said that they expected to persist with their plans. About 81% of the 1965 scholars had a bachelor's degree by the end of the 1968-1969 school term—four years after entering college (National Merit Scholarship Corporation, 1969).

For the first time, substantial numbers of blacks are being admitted to the highly selective white colleges—environments which are extremely competitive and where academic rewards tend not to be easily obtained by either whites or blacks. How do outstanding black high school graduates do? Borgen (1970) found that 4% of the males reaching the 1965 commended stage of the Achievement competition who entered highly selective white colleges earned B+ or higher freshman grade averages, and 7% of the women obtained averages that high. But about 78% of men and 80% of the women had averages of at least a C. Interestingly, the proportion getting averages of C— or below was no greater in the highly selective white colleges than it was in other white institutions classified as moderate or low selectivity—about 22% of the men and 18% of the women got averages that low in the lower selectivity colleges. Students in the most selective colleges were least satisfied with their grades, probably reflecting the disparity between their expectations and their performance. Nevertheless, those in the highly competitive schools most often expressed satisfaction with their college choices. Moreover, 98% of the men and 91% of the women said that they planned to return to their same colleges for the sophomore year. Studies by Tetlow (1969) at Cornell University, by Nicholson (1970) at Brown University, and by Clark and Plotkin (1963) provide additional data regarding the persistence of blacks at prestigious colleges. The flow of black talent now trickling into these colleges has led some observers (Dyer, 1967; Jencks and Reisman, 1967; Harding, 1968) to suggest that we are currently witnessing a "black brain drain," many of the brightest and the most able students being taken away from the predominantly black campuses.

CAREER OBJECTIVES

If blacks are to substantially better themselves socioeconomically, then Professor Lewis (1969) of Princeton seems to be on target in his assertion that a measure of whether blacks are winning the battle is in how many rise to the middle and to the top occupationally. Clearly, the road toward the top runs through higher education. At present, blacks are underrepresented in college (Bayer and Boruch, 1969), although some gains are now being made. Thus, as one would expect, studies of employment in the 1960s (e.g., Campbell and Belcher, 1966; Sharp, 1970; Blum and Coleman, 1970) indicate that despite some improvements in the relative employment status of blacks, the "employment gap" between blacks and whites is still substantial, particularly at the upper levels. A critical shortage of blacks exists in virtually all the professions; relatively few blacks are gainfully employed as physicians, engineers, psychologists, and so forth.

What do bright, achieving blacks have in mind regarding their future occupations? As we noted earlier in looking at their college majors, the career objectives that are most popular among male Achievement scholars and finalists are engineer, physician, and lawyer. Prior to entering college, however, quite a few—about 15%—say that they are still undecided about what they want to be. Regardless of the type of college attended, relatively few of them expect to find employment in the social sciences (Borgen, 1970). And the goal of working in education is not nearly as strong among the men as it is among the women, although, interestingly enough, "other educational fields" (not elementary or secondary) were found by Fichter (1967) to be the most frequent choices of the 1964 graduates of predominantly black colleges. In contrast, the most often-stated career field objectives of black males who entered college in 1968 were business and secondary education (Bayer and Boruch, 1969).

The single most frequently stated career objective of the female Achievement scholars and finalists is teaching. Many also state that they want to be physicians and psychologists. Although a number select "other" career fields which are more difficult to classify, in general the majority of these women choose careers in education, the health sciences, and the social sciences. Thus, they appear to be rather strongly oriented toward work in the "helping" professions.

It is difficult to say where the services of intelligent, highly educated blacks are most needed, and there are many different opinions. While many young blacks today appear to be attuned to the needs of their own people, it is nevertheless an unknown process concerning how blacks—or whites—somehow decide to enter one career field in preference to another. Seldom are such individual decisions made in accordance with some national manpower balance which somehow determines the number of people needed in this field or that. For blacks, it can only be recorded that serious shortages now exist in virtually every professional field. Narrowing the numerous alternatives down to one tends to be a difficult task for them, although, judging from the proportion of bright whites who change their plans, the job of deciding is not easy for many of them either.

It can be expected that the competition to enroll outstanding black students will not only continue, but that it will substantially increase during the course of this decade. As the recruitment inducements by the various professions increase, one might also expect to see many blacks concern themselves with a difficult dilemma: whether to follow altruistic goals regarding service to the black community or whether to pursue positions that will pay larger dividends for service to the affluent middle and upper classes. Thus it is not at all easy to predict what the career behavior trends will be during the 1970s for the more outstanding black students.

FINAL COMMENT

The history of mankind is replete with examples where nations or various smaller groups have either sought to dominate others or themselves attempted to flee from some sort of repression. The rising tide of expectation among blacks today is another attempt by man to better himself through the elimination of unfair and artificial barriers. In the march to equality, black youth of today seem to feel that they have a special role to play. But one gets the feeling that outstanding, bright blacks such as those who have been named Achievement scholars and finalists see a particularly positive part for themselves. Education is seen as the primary route to betterment.

REFERENCES

ASTIN, A. W. (1965) "College preferences of very able students." College and University 41: 282-297.

——— (1964) "Socioeconomic factors in the achievements and aspirations of the Merit scholar." Personnel and Guidance J. 42: 581-586.

——— and R. J. PANOS (1969) The Educational and Vocational Development of Students. Washington, D.C.: American Council on Education.

BAYER, A. E. and R. F. BORUCH (1969) The Black Student in American Colleges. Washington, D.C.: American Council on Education.

BLUM, Z. D. and J. S. COLEMAN (1970) "Longitudinal effects of education in the incomes and occupational prestige of blacks and whites." Center for Social Organization of Schools Report 70, Johns Hopkins University.

BLUMENFELD, W. S. (1969) "Selecting talented Negro students: nominations vs. test performance." NMSC Research Reports 5, 6.

——— (1968) "College preferences of able Negro students: a comparison of those naming predominantly Negro institutions and those naming predominantly white institutions." College and University (Spring): 330-341.

——— (1966) "Some characteristics of finalists in the 1966 National Achievement Scholarship Program." NMSC Research Reports 2, 4.

BONEY, J. D. (1966) "Predicting the academic achievement of secondary school Negro students." Personnel and Guidance J. 44: 700-703.

BORGEN, F. H. (1970) "Able black Americans in college: entry and freshman experiences." NMSC Research Reports 6, 2.

BURGDORF, K. (1969) "Outstanding Negro high school students: a one-year followup." NMSC Research Reports 5, 4.

CAMPBELL, J. T. and L. H. BELCHER (1966) "Changes in nonwhite employment 1960-1966." Educational Testing Service Research Bulletin 66-53.

CLARK, K. B. and L. PLOTKIN (1963) The Negro Student at Integrated Colleges. New York: National Scholarship Service and Fund for Negro Students.

COLEMAN, J. S. et al. (1966) Equality of Educational Opportunity. Washington, D.C.: Government Printing Office.

DODDY, H. H. (1963) "The progress of the Negro in higher education, 1950-1960." J. of Negro Education Yearbook 32: 485-492.

DREGER, R. M. and K. S. MILLER (1960) "Comparative psychological studies of Negroes and whites in the United States." Psych. Bull. 57: 361-402.

DYER, H. S. (1967) "Toward more effective recruitment and selection of Negroes for college." J. of Negro Education 36, 3.

EDWARDS, G. F. (1963) "Marriage and family life among Negroes." J. of Negro Education Yearbook 32: 451-464.

FICHTER, J. H. (1967) "Graduates of predominantly Negro colleges." U.S. Department of Health, Education and Welfare PHS Publication 1571.

FLANAGAN, J. C. et al. (1964) The American High School Student. Pittsburgh: University of Pittsburgh Project Talent Office.

FROE, O. D. (1964) "Educational planning for disadvantaged youth." J. of Negro Education 33: 290-303.

GARDNER, J. W. (1961) Excellence. New York: Harper & Row.

GRAY, S. W. (1964) "Some implications of research on young culturally deprived children," in J. M. Hunt (chm.) Implications of Research in Cultural Disadvantage for Counseling Psychology, Symposium at APA, September.

HARDING, V. (1968) "Black brain drain." Columbia Forum 11, 38.

HILLS, J. R., J. C. KLOCK, and S. LEWIS (1963) Freshman Norms of the University System of Georgia, 1960-1962. Atlanta: University of Georgia Office of Testing and Guidance.

HOLLAND, J. H. (1969) Black Opportunity. New York: Weybright & Talley.
HUMPHREYS, L. G. (1969) "Racial differences: dilemma of college admissions." Science 166, 167.
JENCKS, C. and D. REISMAN (1967) "The American Negro college." Harvard Educational Rev. 37: 3-60.
JENSEN, A. R. (1969) "How much can we boost IQ and scholastic achievement?" Harvard Educational Rev. 39: 1-123.
KENDRICK, S. A. and C. L. THOMAS (1970) "Transition from school to college." Rev. of Educational Research 40: 151-179.
LEWIS, A. W. (1969) Black Power and the American University. Princeton, N.J.: Princeton Univ. Press.
McGRATH, E. J. (1966) Universal Higher Education. New York: McGraw-Hill.
––– (1965) The Predominantly Negro Colleges and Universities in Transition. New York: Columbia Teachers College Press.
MILLER, N. (1963) "One year after commencement." National Opinion Research Center Report 93: 27-30.
National Merit Scholarship Corporation (1969) Annual Report. Evanston, Illinois.
NICHOLS, R. C. (1966) "College preferences of eleventh grade students." NMSC Research Reports 2, 9.
––– (1965) "The financial status of National Merit finalists." Science 149: 1071-1074.
––– and A. W. ASTIN (1966) "Progress of the Merit scholars: an eight-year followup." Personnel and Guidance J. 44: 673-686.
NICHOLS, R. C. and J. A. DAVIS (1964) "Some characteristics of students of high academic aptitude." Personnel and Guidance J. 42: 794-800.
NICHOLSON, E. (1970) Success and Admission Criteria for Potentially Successful Risks. Providence, R.I.: Brown University.
PETTIGREW, T. F. (1964) "Negro American intelligence: a new look at an old controversy." J. of Negro Education 33: 6-25.
ROBERTS, R. J. and R. C. NICHOLS (1966) "Participants in the National Achievement Scholarship Program for Negroes." NMSC Research Reports 2, 2.
SHARP, L. M. (1970) Education and Employment: The Early Careers of College Graduates. Baltimore: Johns Hopkins Press.
SHUEY, A. M. (1966) The Testing of Negro Intelligence. New York: Social Science Press.
STALNAKER, J. M. (1965) "Scholarship selection and cultural disadvantage." Bull. of National Assn. of Secondary School Principals 49: 142-150.
STANLEY, J. C. (1970) "Predicting college success of educationally disadvantaged students." Center for Social Organization of Schools Report 79, Johns Hopkins University.
––– and A. C. PORTER (1967) "Correlation of scholastic aptitude test scores with college grades for Negroes versus whites." J. of Educational Measurement 4: 199-218.
TETLOW, W. L., Jr. (1969) "Academic standards of COSEP." Cornell Chronicle 1: 6-7.
U.S. Bureau of the Census (1969) "School enrollment: October 1967 and 1968." Current Population Reports, Series P-20, 190.

––– (1968) "Social and economic conditions of Negroes in the United States." Current Population Reports, Series P-23, 26.

––– (1965) Statistical Abstract of the United States: 1965. Washington, D.C.: Government Printing Office.

U.S. Department of Labor, Office of Policy Planning and Research (1965) The Negro Family: The Case for National Action. Washington, D.C.: Government Printing Office.

WATLEY, D. J. (forthcoming) "Bright achievers: their characteristics and some expected behavior patterns." Youth and Society.

––– (1969) "Career progress: a longitudinal study of gifted students." J. of Counseling Psychology 16: 100-108.

––– and R. KAPLAN (1971) "Career or marriage?: aspirations and achievements of able young women." J. of Vocational Behavior 1: 29-43.

––– (1970) "Progress of Merit scholars: does religious background matter?" NMSC Research Reports 6,5.

2

BRIGHT ACHIEVERS
Their Characteristics and Some
Expected Behavior Patterns

DONIVAN J. WATLEY

As the title suggests, this paper has two main objectives: (a) to describe some of the characteristics of bright academic achievers and (b) to predict some of their important behavior patterns during this decade. Although much remains to be known about them, describing their characteristics is still far easier than forecasting their behavior with any degree of certainty for the years just ahead.

Even in calmer circumstances one might do well to heed Sir Thomas Browne's advice:

> Amuse not thyself about the Riddles of future things. Study Prophecies when they are become Histories and past hovering in their causes. Eye well things past and present, and let conjectural sagacity suffice for things to come.

But these are not ordinary times. College students are more upset than usual, and the end is nowhere in view. Charles Palmer (1970), president of the U.S. National Student Association, told President Nixon's Commission on Campus Unrest:

As long as the war in Indochina continues with no end in sight; as long as there is repression of black, brown, and red people; as long as women are denied equal opportunity; as long as the desires and problems of working men are bypassed; as long as there is poverty in this country; as long as the United States continues its collision path with its environment, students and young people will continue to make noise.

Until these things are changed, we will continue to make life uncomfortable and at times unlivable for the men in positions of power and influence in this country. That I can promise you.

Since it is a virtual certainty that all these problems will not be resolved during this decade, the prediction that the 1970s will be noisy is probably a sound one. Being more specific is difficult. For this reason, the predictions made here will be limited to those which seem reasonable in terms of available data. Wild speculation would serve no useful purpose anyway. The data discussed come largely from the research program of the National Merit Scholarship Corporation, which has studied bright achievers since 1957. An attempt will be made to tie these results with the general findings for high-ability students.

Who are being referred to here as "bright achievers"? Both "bright" and "achievers" are important—students who obtain scholastic aptitude test scores in the top two or three percent on national norms *and* who attain top marks in high school. In terms of social usefulness, just being bright is not enough; what one does also matters. There are many test-bright individuals who never seem to accomplish much of anything.

Philosophers, psychologists, and educators have puzzled for a long time with the problem of defining and measuring intelligence, aptitude, ability, creativity, or some other label that is attached to qualities that enable certain individuals to perform particular tasks more accurately or skillfully than others. Whatever these mental qualities may be, one seems so certain of their presence, yet at the same time they never quite materialize themselves distinctly enough to permit full agreement on what they really are. "Talent," says Hersey (1956) "is elusive, fragile, manifold, fast-moving, luminous, tantalizing, and incredibly beautiful, like aurora borealis on a cool September night." Yet "Who would give a weatherman a bag of money and tell him to go out and catch some northern lights?"

Capturing "intelligence" or "ability" is indeed a difficult assignment. While the debate continues over the relative roles of genes and environment in the origin and development of human ability, one must conclude that we really do not know what *pure* ability is. Ability is pinned down at all only in terms of defining it functionally—the ways that it seems to manifest itself.

RECENT HISTORY

Historically, the emphasis on high intelligence has seen both ups and downs. In general, the rise and development of a nation of strength and prosperity hinges partly on the cultivation and use of its talent. In *The Republic,* Plato proposed the idea that the leadership responsibilities of the ideal state be placed in the hands of philosopher-kings, who were assumed to possess greater intelligence than those of lesser standing. At least the idea of identifying and hand-picking youth of high ability and educating them for the good of one's broader society has been copied in many lands, although a great many problems are involved in getting the idea to work in practice. This practice also tends to preserve the concept of the "elite"—the idea that some members of a society perform functions that are of greater importance than those performed by others. Concerning the value of trained intelligence, Alfred North Whitehead (1929: 22-23) offered the following prophecy:

> In the conditions of modern life, the rule is absolute: the race which does not value trained intelligence is doomed. Not all your

heroism, not all your social charm, not all your wit, not all your victories on land or sea, can move back the finger of fate. Today we maintain ourselves. Tomorrow science will have moved forward yet one more step, and there will be no appeal from the judgment which will be pronounced on the uneducated.

In America, the idea that individuals differ in their native talents seems to have sometimes come into conflict with the idea of "equality of everyman." While "talent development" emphasizes differences among people and seeks the "best" for given positions, ideal democracy at work offers every man equal opportunity for self-development. The latter carries the implication that every man has the right to be educated to the extent of his ability and desire, a belief which began to gain momentum in the nineteenth century and has snowballed in the course of the present century, especially since the 1950s.

On the surface, this seems to bring into play a collision of interests—what is best for *society* and what is best for the *individual.* Although in principle this is not so, making the idea work in real life is not simple. In fact, Americans seem to have difficulty deciding whether to capitalize on human differences or stress "equality," emphasizing first one and then the other depending upon the particular problems of the day. Crisis states in America seem to affect what is stressed at a given time, not only during war but also, for example, when the nation's honor is at stake.

Consider the life of the serious, able youngster who devotes himself to scholarly activity. Prior to the mid-1950s, such an individual—white or black—received very little public acclaim. Stalnaker (1961: 514) notes that "His classmates regarded him as a 'brain'—a term of opprobrium at the time—and ignored him." Moreover, common stereotyping had him pegged as strange, puny, introverted, sickly, and bespectacled. Stalnaker (1961) writes that following World War II the schools were permissive, relatively noncompetitive, and paid little attention to standards of performance.

Intellectual excellence was neither particularly respected nor encouraged. Catharine Cox Miles pointed out (1954: 1028) that "the gifted, the potential leaders, discoverers, and creators . . . are usually left to develop their own skills, in their own way, and in terms of personal initiative alone." The Sputnik launchings changed this attitude. The image of the United States as the leader in science was threatened, the result being that the nation's human resources again needed to be rallied together. This time it was the services of bright achievers that were required; technological advances require a great deal of brainpower rather than just raw, physical brawnpower. The impact of this awakening to the need for brainpower was not only highly influential in bringing about a reevaluation of the nature and quality of the American educational system, but the "brain" was then valued in a quite different light.

THE IDENTIFICATION OF "BRAINS"

Three commonly used ways of identifying bright academic achievers are standardized tests, scholastic performance, and teacher recommendations. In a nationwide search for "brains," an efficient first step involves the administration of a scholastic aptitude test. The "brains" discussed in this paper were identified from the approximately 750,000 students attending about 17,500 high schools who each year take the National Merit Scholarship Qualifying Test (NMSQT). In an annual nationwide talent search, the NMSQT is taken voluntarily by juniors in high schools that enroll approximately 95% of all eleventh-grade students in the United States. It is estimated (Nichols, 1969) that about 28% of all eleventh graders participate, but a very high proportion of the most scholastically able students take the NMSQT.

The highest scorers in each state are selected as Merit

semifinalists. The number of semifinalists named in each state is less than 1% of the graduating high school seniors in that state. The semifinalists who are endorsed by their high schools and whose scores are verified by a second test—the Scholastic Aptitude Test (SAT) of the College Entrance Examination Board—become Merit finalists. A selection committee and scholarship sponsors use high school records, recommendations, and test scores to select the Merit scholars for each state. Merit finalists and scholars have been studied during and after college and have been compared with groups representative of college students in general (e.g., Holland and Stalnaker, 1958; Nichols and Davis, 1964; Astin, 1964b; Nichols and Astin, 1966; Watley, 1969b; Watley and Kaplan, 1970a, 1970b).

In addition to getting high test scores and good grades, what else can we say about "brains"? In many respects the male and female brains are quite similar, but in some important ways they are very different. Let us, therefore, look at the sexes separately.

MALE BRAINS

THEIR CHARACTERISTICS

Does the brain deserve the reputation of being introverted, puny, sickly, and bespectacled? The work of Terman et al. (1925), Cox (1926), Hollingworth (1926), and others began to show that this picture is rather badly distorted. What is he really like?

One striking feature of the bright academic achiever is that in contrast to the average college student he typically comes from a family of higher socioeconomic status—his parents have more education, the family income is higher, and his father is more likely employed in the professions. These factors even differentiate between scholars who have made most educational progress from those who have made least (Watley, 1969b). But, of course, not all fathers are highly educated, nor do they all draw big salaries or have big incomes. Some are firemen and some are mail carriers. High-ability students can be found in virtually every walk of life (Witty, 1951; Miles, 1954).

Since being a brain is related to one's socioeconomic status, it is important to determine whether many of the differences observed between the more and the less able are really attributable to social status rather than to differences in high or low test performance. One experimental way of doing this is by attempting to cancel out the effects of socioeconomic status by matching more and less able students on socioeconomic characteristics. When socioeconomic status is controlled in this way, there seems to be little effect on the variables that show up as correlates of measured ability (Nichols and Davis, 1964; Astin, 1964b). Thus, despite the advantages which are surely embedded in a favorable home environment, many variables hold their relationship to ability regardless of whether attempts are made to control socioeconomic status statistically.

As one might expect, then, tested high scholastic aptitude is more frequently found in ethnic groups with high social, economic, educational, and professional attainments. Parents from Jewish, English, and Scandinavian stock, for example, produce more than their share of test-bright children, while Negroes, Mexicans, and American Indians produce less.

Youth of high academic aptitude differ from the average students in many other respects. The wide range of differences is illustrated by one study (Nichols and Davis, 1964) in which college seniors who had been Merit finalists were compared with a group representative of college seniors in general. The two groups differed significantly on every item of information obtained on a twelve-page questionnaire administered by the National Opinion Research Center (see Rossi et al., 1961). Merit finalists came more frequently from the suburbs of large cities than the average senior, and less frequently from farm areas. The finalists were almost entirely white and only 6% of the sample of seniors were of nonwhite races. Finalists were more likely the first-born in their families, and a larger percentage came from small families. If a male scholar has any siblings at all, it is seldom more than one or two.

Contrary to some popular opinion, brains are physically neither puny nor sickly. Health records show that they are uniformly slightly above average on nearly every physical characteristic studied such as height, weight, and age of pubescence (see Hildreth, 1938; Parkyn, 1948; Terman, 1947).

About two-thirds of the 1956 and 1957 male scholars reported that they were raised in Protestant homes, a figure which agrees fairly closely to 1957 census data for men (fourteen years of age or older and white) and with the percentages reported by Greeley (1963) for a sample of college graduates. On the other hand, Catholics appear to be underrepresented among male scholars, while Jews are overrepresented (Watley and Kaplan, 1970b).

Do they maintain their religious affiliations? Brains appear generally less likely to claim their background faiths than do typical college graduates. Among about 1,000 male scholars queried seven to eight years after entering college, 62% of the Protestants, 75% of the Catholics, and 72% of the Jews still claimed their reared religions. Greeley reported that corresponding percentages among college graduates were 85, 91, and 84. Almost all the scholar changers said they accepted no religious doctrine.

An important—indeed, a crucial—feature which sets the bright achiever of either sex apart from both the average college student and the less motivated high test scorer is the burning desire to achieve and to excel. Not only is he bright, but he is also highly industrious and persevering. He tends to be very involved in many aspects of his life, although he does

seem to keep his career foremost. While desiring an interesting life, he typically says that he also wants it to be
worthwhile. Indeed, this appears to be a major consideration
in planning his life and his career. Not only do brains set their
sights high, but they are able to state their plans and future
objectives clearly (Watley and Kaplan, 1970b). They are
willing to sacrifice if they see that their goals are brought
nearer, but they do not like distractions.

What more can we say about the personalities of male
brains? One way of describing them is that they tend to be
intellectually autonomous, audacious, and aggressive. About
this there seems to be little doubt. Holland and Stalnaker
(1958: 20) said of the typical male scholar that his goals tend
to be "directed at self-development and directed at securing
new experience rather than an interest in people *per se.*"
Later, Nichols (1967) noted that self-ratings and ratings by
teachers and peers all agree in characterizing Merit finalists
more frequently than less able students as independent,
assertive, idealistic, unconventional, cynical, rebellious, and
argumentative. These descriptions also agree that the finalist
tends to be less friendly, sociable, easy-going, obliging,
cooperative, and submissive. In contrast to the self-
descriptions of the average college student, the brain sees
himself as more intellectual, dominant, forceful, impetuous,
high-strung, moody, and reserved. Interestingly enough,
ratings agree that the finalist is more mature, dependable,
well-adjusted, and honest than the average student. There is
some evidence that scholars who have made the most
educational progress over a seven- to eight-year span are more
domineering than those making less progress. Nevertheless,
those who progress fastest generally seem to be emotionally
stable. In thinking about bright achievers, Nichols (1967:
494) sized them up like this:

> we have come to think that talented students of college age are
> more like cannon balls than like tender plants. They maintain

their momentum with great inertia, they tend to knock over obstacles in their way, and they are not easily deflected from their path. They will not wither and die if they are neglected, and they do not need a hothouse environment in which to develop.

Goodenough (1956) said that gifted young people are more apt to be autonomous than suggestible, and Drews (1960) said of them they they are more apt to be brash than brainwashed. But the weight of the evidence strongly indicates that the bright achiever is not strange, as the popular stereotype suggests. The work of Terman and Oden (1959), Hollingworth (1942), Witty (1940), and Parkyn (1948) lends support to this conclusion. Lewis (1943) remarked that "abnormality and queerness" is clearly not typical of the very bright student.

One area where personalities have played a big part in recent years is in student protests. Assuming that brains of this decade will be similar in temperament to those of the past fifteen years, what can we expect from them on college campuses? Politically speaking, they are much more inclined to be liberals and independents than conservatives. In fact, although college students in general report their political positions as liberal more frequently than as conservative, this liberal leaning is even more pronounced among Merit finalists.

From all indications, the bright achieving male is more likely to be engaged in campus political activity than the average student. He is more apt to attain leadership positions, and he is more likely to be actively involved in the discussion of political and social issues on the campus scene. He is unlikely to be altogether satisfied with the status quo. Not only is his voice more likely to be heard than that of the average student, but he is more apt to be argumentative and less respectful of traditional rules and regulations. Thus, there is little doubt that he is prone to involvement in student protest movements.

Despite these tendencies, it is interesting that he seldom

goes so far in his behavior or demands that he is singled out for punitive action. Or if he does go "that" far, he is seldom caught. Of the 14,392 males receiving Merit scholarships between 1956 and 1969, only a handful have received campus punishment, as far as is known, in the form of being suspended, expelled, put on probation, and the like for their activist conduct. If a scholar did, in fact, receive some sort of formal censure, this should be known from the regular progress reports that are filed in order to continue to receive aid through the Merit program.

The relative absence of punitive action against Merit scholars suggests that, although they definitely do become involved in protests and may often be key leaders, they seldom go so far as to jeopardize their careers. Because of the weighty social problems now facing the world and because many colleges themselves are now in the midst of transition, the best guess is that the brain will continue to play some part in the current challenge for change. Many young people feel that they have no choice. To do otherwise would mean that they themselves are good examples of living hypocrisy. In a report prepared by Muscatine (1966) on the Berkeley disturbance, the following account was given on how the intelligent but nonconforming student views our society:

> As these students see it, while the dominant group claims to champion freedom, religion, patriotism, and morality, it produces and condones slums, racial segregation, migrant farm laborers, false advertising, American economic imperialism, and the bomb. In private life, moreover, the students find as much immorality and injustice as in public life. They commonly explain it as the product of an all-pervasive hypocrisy.

Many intelligent youth today seem to harbor some appreciation of these views. But if his past record is any guide, the top-flight academic brain probably will steer clear of serious trouble that endangers development and progress toward his personal objectives. To him, that goal has top priority. Perhaps he feels that he cannot work effectively toward his goals if he comes under severe bondage from the law. Since the bright achiever is himself a respecter of reason in attempting to resolve problems, college officials today may do well to invite more open and free exchange with him. The brain of today is unlikely to be very sympathetic with an aloof, authoritarian approach on the part of jittery college officials. Perhaps he has learned too well how to question and to challenge. Perhaps events of the day have encouraged him to be more assertive and tenacious in the expression of his convictions.

EDUCATIONAL PROGRESS

Which colleges do the top test-bright students most want to attend? For a number of years, the approximately 50,000 students scoring highest in the National Merit talent search were asked to name their top two college choices (Astin, 1965; Nichols, 1966). Since these students came from every state in the union, one might expect that they would desire to spread themselves widely among many colleges. This is not the case. In this popularity contest involving only the very brightest students, a relatively small number of colleges are named. Stanford, Caltech, University of California, Yale, Princeton, Cornell, Columbia, and the University of Michigan. When the number of able students naming a particular college is expressed as a percentage of the number of students that institution admits, a different rank ordering is found. Caltech ranks first by this method, being named as the first or second choice by over five times as many boys as are admitted into its freshman class. Next in order were: MIT, Rice, Harvard, Swarthmore, Stanford, Reed, Amherst, University of Chicago, and Harvey Mudd.

The consistency of these results indicates that the brightest students do indeed have a definite opinion about the colleges they most want to attend. Basically, the most desired ones are affluent and well known campuses where other bright students are concentrated. One institution alone—Harvard University—has attracted 1,291 Merit scholars or about 9% of all awards given to males. The ten most popular colleges have enrolled about 38% of all male and female Merit award winners.

Now there is talk about open admission policies regarding the selection of new students. It is difficult at this time to predict the trends of action, but it appears that the administrations of many colleges are now in the mood to try out various admission strategies. The fact remains, however, that the most successful students desire to attend the most prestigious colleges. But this fact has caused some investigators to question whether the success of graduates of prestigious colleges is really due to the superior environments which these campuses supposedly provide or to the characteristics of the students who are admitted.

Although bright males choose a wide variety of college majors, they most frequently select the physical sciences, mathematics, and engineering. Data collected for Merit finalists since 1958 show that engineering is consistently the most frequent choice, while mathematics and physics have been selected by 25 to 30% each year. Discounting those undecided about their majors, the stability of choices is illustrated by the fact that in both 1968 and 1969 about 18% of the finalists selected engineering, 37% chose the physical and natural sciences, 33% picked the humanities and social sciences, and 7% wanted to enter the health sciences. In contrast, Terman and Oden (1959) reported that the five leading major fields chosen by their sample of test-bright males were: social sciences, 42%; physical sciences, 17%; engineering, 15%; biological sciences, 10%; and letters, 9%. It should be remembered, however, that the average person in Terman's sample is now in his early 60s.

Scholastically, brains do very well in college. About 95% of the Merit scholars earn at least a bachelor's degree, and a high proportion graduate with distinction. For example, 80% of the 1956 male and female scholars graduated with some academic honor, a fifth of them being in the top 1% of their classes. Close to 100% of the Merit finalists enter college, and of those who eventually graduate, about 25% get A or A— averages despite the stiff competition they face. About 70% make the Dean's List, 10 to 15% become Phi Beta Kappa members, and about half have membership in other honor societies. It is interesting that of Terman's California sample of gifted children with IQ's of 140 or higher, 15% did not even enter college, and 30% did not graduate.

Some Merit scholars take longer than four years to complete their undergraduate programs. A good estimate is that about 20 to 25% drop out of college, the majority for only a brief period.

As we observed previously, brains tend to set their sights high. They have high educational aspirations, about 75% of the men aiming for a doctoral level degree. In fact, during the first four years of college, more raise than lower their educational goals. The lowering of sights is apparently done only with great difficulty.

Granting that most top-flight, test-bright achievers are intellectually autonomous, audacious, and aggressive but highly ambitious, industrious, and persevering, in what types of educational atmosphere do they thrive best? Any talk about "best" depends on personal biases. Moreover, there really is no such thing as *the* best atmosphere for another important reason: what may influence one person to blossom and be fruitful may cause another to rot on the vine; the perfect hothouse setting for one may be considered stifling by others. Nevertheless, the real world of teaching does require guidelines, and there now appears to be a general consensus that the traditional system of higher education is no longer satisfactory in a rapidly changing society.

Basically, the traditional form of education has consisted of the indoctrination of students with the "facts"—a fixed and limited body of knowledge that was assumed by both teacher and student alike to represent final truths. As late as about 1700, it was possible for a highly motivated scholar to learn most of what there was to know in the Western world. Since then, a host of developments has brought about tremendous changes in what were formerly held to be ultimate and final answers regarding truth and morality. Arnold Toynbee (1968) has identified some of the reasons that education became more dynamic in the West:

(1) the seventeenth-century revolt against accepting the Christian and Aristotelian dogmas on faith and the subsequent launching of experimental science;

(2) the eighteenth- and nineteenth-century application of experimental science to technology;

(3) the nineteenth- and twentieth-century progressive acceleration in the advance of science and technology;

(4) the nineteenth- and twentieth-century start and spread of universal primary education.

Even today, basic changes are still attempting to be incorporated into the American higher educational system. One is that "truth" is not known in any final sense; men have either already created or will create in the future many answers to virtually every question that can be raised concerning "truth" and morality. Today's "truth" in the empirical sciences may no longer be "truth" tomorrow since all empirical laws are subject to revision or perhaps to complete withdrawal. Thus, the idea of building up a solid body of knowledge, block upon block, is itself subject to revision because in time much of the foundation may become obsolete and have to be replaced. Dogmatic answers to difficult questions no longer suffice when it is obvious that we do not know the final answers. How do you teach people to live in harmony with mutual respect for each other? It is clear enough that the final answer, if indeed there is such a thing, is not known. What do we know about the inner workings of man's mind? Not much. What, in fact, is the purpose of life itself?

A second change concerns the now-spreading belief that every desiring person should have access to some form of higher education—to develop himself to his fullest capacity. Traditionally, higher education was reserved for the elite—the privileged few who were hand-picked to serve in certain professions such as law, theology, and medicine. But today colleges are springing up rapidly to provide classrooms for those who formerly would have had no chance to enter institutions of higher learning.

These two types of changes have strong implications for how teaching should be done and who should be taught. Since everyone agrees that the brain should be educated, the remaining question is how to do it.

There is reason to believe that many bright achievers find their higher educational programs, particularly at the undergraduate level, dull and unstimulating. While the image of the brain brightened considerably in the post-Sputnik era, the reshaped conditions also contributed to a tightening up of standards of academic performance and to an increased demand upon quantity of work by students. Katz and Sanford (1965) note that the resulting pressure has been felt by good students as well as the poor ones. Still other factors have led to mounting student rebellion and resentment:

faculty efforts to raise standards, arousing in students a sense of being forever tested and evaluated and generating competitiveness that inhibits friendship and results in a lack of community; the growing involvement of the university in our technology, with a resulting depersonalization of campus life; a decline in the nurturing function of the college-as-parent while the control and punishment functions remained intact; the tendency of graduate students to find their situations increasingly frustrating and to side with the undergraduates; and finally—on the positive side—increased sophistication and knowledge of the world on the part of entering students [Sanford, 1968: 188-189].

Merit finalists of both sexes more frequently cut classes, argue with teachers, and sleep or daydream in class than the average college student. With a heavy proportion of the teaching load being carried by graduate teaching assistants who themselves lack experience and maturity, one can see why the brightest students may become bored. But having only tenured professors carry the teaching load is not the simple solution either. Many of the best-known leaders in their fields have little time for students, having attained their reputations through dedicated efforts to professional organizations or to research. If there is little *truth* in areas like the humanities and social sciences, it seems legitimate to ask why the brightest students should be required to occupy their time with information that happens to interest a particular professor. Then, in graduate school, there are the traditional research and foreign language requirements, in addition to the numerous other assignments which consume much time but seemingly serve no genuinely worthwhile purpose. There may be little relationship between these activities and what the student does after they are completed. Importantly, most of the material is quickly forgotten anyway. Instead of shortening the time to complete requirements, the trend toward greater specialization only tends to lengthen it.

Nor in general has there been much interest among educators to learn from the experience of conducting honors programs. According to Ralph Tyler (1964: 18), this is not surprising: "Commonly, college educational programs are judged by the faculty involved on the basis of their personal impressions, and the achievements of college students are judged by those who teach them on the basis of their performance in class or on teacher-made examinations using personal standards." He points out further that the correlations between the judgments of participating teachers regarding the success of innovative teaching programs and students' performances on comprehensive examinations and later success in advanced courses are often approximately zero!

A number of signs suggest that brains profit considerably from their own independent study. The long and fixed educational requirements seem not to take sufficiently into account the fact that the bright achiever is already highly motivated to excel and that many are capable of self-direction at an early age. For the brain, intellectual independence at the earliest possible age would appear to be a desirable objective.

Interestingly, almost no one contests the point that extremely bright and motivated achievers blossom best under flexible and accelerated programs of study. Yet brains in colleges today are frequently required to follow the same intellectual paths of other students, although there may be little relationship between what a student knows and the number of years he spends in college (Learned and Wood, 1938). According to Terman (1954: 226), "The sensible thing to do, it seems, would be to quit crediting the individual high school or the individual college and begin crediting the individual student."

CAREER DECISIONS

Although there would undoubtedly be wide disagreement among manpower authorities concerning the optimum distribution of talent among career fields, the recent campaign to attract bright students into science, engineering, and teaching programs represents some consensus regarding the need for talent in these fields. Are the most academically able students anticipating careers in fields where their skills are most needed?

The career decisions of Merit finalists have been logged since 1957, and the physical sciences, engineering, teaching, law, and medicine have consistently been the most popular choices among boys when they entered college. Thus, the most rapidly developing intellectual fields over the past 10 to 15 years and the ones with the most widely publicized needs for talent drew the major portion of the nation's best intellectual talent. Top students were undoubtedly attracted by the intellectual challenge offered by these fields, as well as by the favorable employment opportunities. Changes can be observed in the popularity of various occupational choices since 1957. For example, the physical sciences–the most frequent choice–showed a sharp increase in 1958, but has since leveled off to being the precollege career choice of about a quarter of the boys. The sharp increase in 1958 was partly at the expense of engineering, which dropped from 34% in 1957 to 25% in 1958. From its high water mark in 1957, engineering was chosen by a smaller percentage each year until a low of 18% was reached in 1962. Roughly 20% have selected that field since then. Interest in the social sciences has been almost the mirror image of the physical sciences: declining in 1958 and 1959 but increasing gradually since then. The preference for teaching rose from 8% in 1957 to 15% in 1962 and has remained at about that level since then. Most prefer teaching at the college level. Business and other practical fields have shown gradual but steady declines over the past decade, which is the reverse of the trend of interest in the humanities.

Precollege versus later decisions. Thus far, reference has been made to finalists' precollege career choices. But precollege selections are often not a good indicator of what students wind up doing. Let us look at some recent trends as to career changes made by test-bright achievers in the course of completing their college work. Among Merit scholars, engineering suffers the greatest loss of talent to other career fields. The results suggest that the effort to recruit exceptionally talented male freshmen into engineering has indeed been successful, but brains often become dissatisfied after entering college and transfer into other more appealing programs. Viewed in this light, the critical problem facing engineering leaders does not appear to be one of initially attracting top talent but rather one of retaining their precollege recruits. The physical sciences also suffered a net loss of talent to the other fields. However, since the physical sciences and engineering initially drew the majority of the scholars, it is not surprising that changes occurred and that the other fields, which attracted fewer men initially, stood to gain most. The heaviest flow of transfer is almost always away from science-oriented programs with extensive prerequisites and toward programs that are more flexible in their background requirements. The humanities profit most from the turnover that occurs. Although initially drawing proportionally fewer scholars, medicine, law, and the biological sciences have in recent years been the only fields able to keep at least 50% of their initial recruits. The education field has the most difficulty holding its young recruits.

Future decisions? What can we expect from brains in the 1970s regarding career decisions? It is one thing to trace trends in career decision-making, but it is quite another to identify the factors which directly affect career choice behavior.

Considering the national importance of the career decisions of test-bright achievers, it is paradoxical that the fields they enter are not selected by manpower experts aware of the nation's employment needs, but by the bright but inexperienced youngsters themselves. This is because the choice of a career is a personal decision. It may be based on an assessment of one's interests and abilities; it may be the result of drifting in the direction of least resistance; it may be influenced by factors such as family expectations, persuasive advisers, and the example of peers. Whatever the reasons may be, researchers have found the problem of career decision-making extremely complex and difficult to unravel. Nevertheless, the real world requires that long-term decisions be made by youth who are still some years removed from entering their professions and whose perceptions of the work involved and the rewards offered may be quite unrealistic. However made, few would contest a young person's right to decide for himself.

But if one cannot be sure which factors affect the career decisions of able youth, it is obviously hazardous to predict which fields they will choose in the 1970s. The external means used by leaders in the various fields to attract top talent are largely haphazard and uncertain. Although the competitive market uses wage scales, status symbols, employment opportunities, and other special inducements to affect the attractiveness of a particular occupation, these methods frequently operate too late to significantly affect the entrance into occupations that require long periods of education and training.

The prediction picture is further clouded by the occurrence of particularly exciting events such as those connected with recent space triumphs or with exploration of the ocean depths. And one thing seems certain: Brains are very much aware of the current scene. In this rapidly changing world, it can be expected that there will be many new excitements not only in old fields but perhaps in entirely new ones as well. Moreover, it is difficult to say at this point what effect the current causes (e.g., brotherhood, pollution, racial discrimination, the war) will have on the career decisions of the brains of this decade. One might only expect, however, since highly intelligent youth are now in no mood to ignore the pressing problems of the day, that many will become increasingly motivated toward taking steps which they believe will help resolve them. For example, we probably will witness the emergence of new roles within traditional professions, such as "Nader's Raiders" within the legal profession.

Judging from past trends, it appears likely that engineering and the physical and natural sciences will continue to attract at least half the top-flight, test-bright achievers at the time they enter college. The rate of transfer out of these fields is alarming, however, to those who desire that they remain. Perhaps better high school counseling could alter some of the massive attrition, but this alone does not appear to be the whole answer. One aspect of the problem is that many bright achievers find such programs dull and confining. In their view, there is too much regimentation, and the complaint is frequently heard that courses are too abstract for students to attach any practical meaning to them. Others complain that professors care little about the progress of individual students. Whatever the reasons may be, it is in the hands of college administrators to decide what courses of action to take to stem the tide of departure from their programs. Not only do students often find the lack of confinement in the humanities and social sciences more appealing, but topics found in these areas are currently "in" on many campuses. In short, initially attracting top students to the hard sciences is now only half the job; keeping them there appears to be just about as difficult.

FEMALE BRAINS

THEIR CHARACTERISTICS

Let us now turn our attention to test-bright achieving women. What is the typical female brain like? She is a great deal like the male brain in many respects, but she is different, too.

Like the bright, achieving male, she more frequently comes from a family of higher socioeconomic standing than the average college student (i.e., more education, higher incomes, fathers more frequently employed in the professions, and so on). Most come from homes which seemingly provide a superior climate for the pursuit of scholastic and intellectual excellence. A follow-up study of women Merit scholars showed that the two-thirds who advanced most quickly into their graduate programs are particularly blessed with such surroundings; about 60% of both parents are college graduates, many of whom are still actively involved in scholarly activities, and their homes are well stocked with educational and learning materials (Watley, 1969). Like the men, high scholastic ability among women is where you find it; not all their fathers draw big salaries or work in the professions.

The woman of exceptionally high test ability differs considerably from the average student: she typically comes more frequently from the suburbs, she tends to be first-born in her family, she seldom has more than one or two siblings, the color of her skin is almost always white, and she tends to be healthy.

About 70% of the women scholars indicate that they were raised as Protestants, which is a slightly larger percentage than the census data indicates for Protestants in the general population and larger than the figure found by Greeley (1963) for college graduates. Jews are also overrepresented, but Catholics are underrepresented relative to the census data and to Greeley's findings. Regarding the permanence of religious affiliations, able women are just as likely as are men to relinquish their background faiths, many claiming after college that they no longer accept a religious doctrine. In a study of scholars' religious preferences (Watley and Kaplan, 1970b), only 66% of those raised as Protestants, 74% with Catholic backgrounds, and 65% reared as Jews still claimed allegiance to their respective faiths. Altogether, 22% said they never attended church, but about a third reported going more than 40 times a year.

Much of what was said earlier about the personalities of male brains also applies for women. They are clearly ambitious, industrious, persevering, and motivated toward academic excellence. Others find them to be independent, idealistic, somewhat unconventional, and so forth. Still, there is evidence to support the view that women brains are reluctant to adopt the more masculine, often uncamouflaged aggressiveness of their male counterparts. In contrast to the men, they appear a bit more passive, cooperative, and methodical. Like the men, they do get involved in campus political activities, often attaining organizational and leadership positions, and they are more apt than the average student to discuss religious, social, and political issues with teachers and fellow students. Tending toward liberal political views, most have strong feelings about the important political and social issues of the day. But most, like the bright male achiever, have clear and overriding personal objectives which apparently they will not sacrifice for the sake of over-involvement in other interesting but potentially goal-shattering activities. About 85% express the desire for a vocational career.

Although their desire to be intellectually autonomous may incline them toward less than total respect of traditional campus routine, women brains almost never go far enough in their activism to be singled out for discipline. At present, there is no strong reason to believe that they will reverse form and go "too far" in the 1970s. While many are highly vocal, there is reason to believe that many exceptionally bright achievers have some sensitivity regarding the testing of limits, and perhaps their ability to assess potentially harmful situations with some accuracy prevents them from taking their rebelliousness to the point of getting into serious trouble.

It should be noted that while bright achievers lean toward liberal and untraditional views, the full range of attitudes, values, beliefs, and behaviors can be found among them.

CAREER OR MARRIAGE?

Women brains have many of the same kinds of problems that men do in establishing careers, but they also have some very different ones. Unlike men, women interested in a career often also have to worry about managing a home and family. A follow-up of the 1956-1960 women scholars in 1965 indicated that 85% of them definitely wanted a career (another 6% were uncertain) and 79% planned to combine marriage with a career (Watley and Kaplan, 1970a). Trying to adjust to this form of double life is a traditional problem of women, but the current generation of brains may be more determined than earlier generations to find a workable solution. Perhaps this rekindled fighting spirit should be expected in accordance with the nature of the times, when the testing of traditions and past expectations is now more apt to be tolerated.

Most young women in the United States traditionally have placed top priority on marriage and full-time motherhood. Apparently, it has been assumed that most women do not have the physiological make-up or the emotional drive necessary to do a creditable juggling act of combining both home and career. Those who have entered career fields in other than a desultory manner have often been labeled "overly ambitious," "masculine," or worse. Women themselves have put a limit on the education they aspire to, so that only a trickle has reached graduate school beyond the master's level, and a scarce few are found in high-level professional and corporate positions. According to the 1960 census, 4% of the lawyers and 7% of the physicians are women and only 11% of the doctorates are awarded to women.

Most women, even those at the highest levels of measured intelligence, do not pursue careers. Terman's well-known longitudinal study, started in the early 1920s, included 671 women with an average IQ of 150. When the women were in their mid-forties, Terman and Oden (1959) reported that fewer than half were employed outside the home, and, for most, a career was not of primary importance. They went on to say:

The accomplishments of the gifted women do not compare with those of the men. This is not surprising since it follows the cultural pattern to which most of the gifted women as well as women in general have succumbed. Not only may job success interfere with marriage success, but women who do seek a career outside the home have to break through many more barriers and overcome many more obstacles than do men on the road to success. Although the gifted women equalled or excelled the men in school achievement from the first grade through college, after school days were over the great majority ceased to compete with men in the world's work. This characteristic appears to be due to lack of motivation and opportunity rather than to lack of ability [Terman and Oden, 1959: 106].

From interviews with college girls about their vocational plans, Ginzberg et al. (1951) found that for most there was a real element of uncertainty about their futures. While many indicated that they had done some career planning, this frequently was done only halfheartedly, knowing that they really preferred not to work after college or that they would defer their plans to the wishes of their future husbands (see also Wolfe, 1954).

In reviewing research on gifted women reported by Ginzberg et al. (1966) and Mattfield and Van Aken (1967), McCormack (1967) reached conclusions similar to those of Terman and Oden. Commenting on the general life patterns found among talented women, she stated (1967: 188) that "the overall impression is of a group of women who are intelligent, rarely intellectual; competent, rarely creative; performing necessary and useful services, rarely critical. They are in every sense of the word—socially, intellectually, and economically—underemployed." In short, it has not been customary for women brains to move from college into productive and satisfying career roles. Horner (1969) says that a bright woman is caught in a double bind in achievement-oriented situations: she worries not only about failure but also about being too successful. "Some of our brightest women students," says Schmidt (1960: 177), "make every attempt to conceal their intellectual ability because they fear intellectual achievement will frighten away prospective husbands."

Although a man expects to have a marriage and a productive career, a bright woman is typically faced with more difficulty in establishing a successful dual role for herself. A young woman, much more so than a man, seems to have to make important decisions as she goes along regarding the prospects of marriage and a career. For example: What will her future husband, whom she might not have met yet, think about a wife who works? How can she be sure that she can even find the type of satisfying job she thinks she wants? Can she be both a successful wife and a career woman? Can she work and raise her children properly at the same time? Her prospective employers also have some inkling of her internal conflicts, and they also know that the attrition rates for women are different from those for men. Moreover, a women's attitude toward her work sometimes changes after marriage, and it is still the woman's job to have babies. Such uncertainties color both her own and her employer's attitudes about her place in the labor force.

Nevertheless, while women scholars of today are strongly career-minded, they also are very marriage-oriented: 88% say that they definitely plan to marry, and another 6% express uncertainty about whether to marry or not. There is little indication, except from a scattered few, that the prospect of motherhood is perceived as carrying with it an undue burden or imposition that they wish to avoid. They want *both!* A successful marriage and a satisfying career is clearly the aim of most. Moreover, longitudinal studies show that the marriage and career plans of many married women scholars are apparently not strongly affected by the presence or absence of children. About 50% of those who plan a combination marriage/deferred career reported having no children, while about one-third of the marriage/immediate career group already had children in their homes.

No doubt the decade of the 1970s will be a crucial time for the female brain in determining what inroads she can make in man's world of work. There certainly seems to be a rising tide of expectation at present. One sign of this is that the girl of high ability is now just as likely to attend college as is the boy of high ability (Werts, 1968), although the total enrollment figures in institutions of all types still favor the boys by about 3 to 2.

EDUCATIONAL ASPIRATIONS AND PROGRESS

Which colleges do they choose? In order, the ten institutions that female finalists in the Merit program most frequently name as their first or second choices are: Stanford, Radcliffe, Cornell, University of California, University of Michigan, Wellesley, Duke, Northwestern, Barnard, and Smith. When the number of students naming a particular college is expressed as a percentage of the number of students that institution admits, a different ordering is obtained. First is Radcliffe, being named by over two and one-half times as many girls as are admitted to the freshman class. Next are Swarthmore, Rice, Reed, Middlebury, Stanford, Carleton, Pomona, William and Mary, and Brandeis. As is the case with bright men, able women have definite and consistent opinions about which colleges they prefer to attend.

Each year since 1958, women Merit finalists have most frequently selected majors in the fields of mathematics and English. Languages made rapid gains during the late 1950s, and since 1960 it has joined mathematics and English as one of the three most frequently chosen fields. In a broader sense, the consistency of women's selections can be seen in the fact that during both 1968 and 1969 about 56% of them chose the humanities and social sciences, 29% each year selected the physical and natural sciences, and about 9% each year picked the health sciences.

As undergraduates, women scholars do about as well as the

men. About 95% finish their baccalaureate programs successfully, and many graduate with distinction. A number lead their classes—like the young woman who entered a college of mining and ranked first in her class, composed largely of men, each of her four undergraduate years. She graduated with high honors and, incidently, gained a husband in the process.

The decision a bright woman makes regarding her marriage/career plans has a direct connection with the amount of education she desires. In general, those who want careers seek a great deal more education than those who do not, and those who plan to begin their careers immediately seek more education than those planning to delay entering them. Of the women test-bright achievers who want to be full-time wives and mothers, less than 5% aspire to a doctoral degree. On the other hand, well over half those planning a career but no marriage want a Ph.D.

At the time of entering college, the amount of education planned by exceptionally bright women is not as high as that planned by bright men. But as time goes along, bright women adjust their aspirations upward, although proportionally fewer of them either plan or reach the educational goals attained by bright, achieving men. The 1970s probably will see the wide gap between the formal educational attainments of men and women brains narrowing somewhat.

Some interesting differences have been found among women scholars who express satisfaction, dissatisfaction, or mixed feelings about their educational and career progress. Factors such as grades or degree aspirations do not differentiate satisfaction from dissatisfaction, but whether one's education has been interrupted is very relevant. Dissatisfied women, much more than the satisfied ones, also tend to express strong and uncomplimentary feelings about their particular schools or major departments. Such expressions are much more common among dissatisfied women than among dissatisfied men.

CAREER PROGRESS

Each year since 1957, teaching has been by far the most frequent career choice of women Merit finalists at the time they first entered college; the proportion choosing this field each year runs from 35 to 40%. Careers in the physical sciences and medical sciences consistently have been the second and third most popular choices. The amount of change in plans occurring during college, however, is tremendous. Education and "other" fields (those careers which cannot otherwise be classified in the usual categories) are consistently the biggest losers of talent. Although about 10% decide that they want to be housewives only, the humanities and fine arts careers typically wind up as the biggest gainers of talent from the others.

Which career field a bright woman chooses depends upon her thoughts about marriage. Of those who plan a career but no marriage, about half wind up in the humanities, fine arts, and "other" fields. Almost none chooses the social sciences, medicine, law, business, or education. Of those wanting marriage with an immediate career, about one-quarter choose the humanities and fine arts. Another quarter choose careers in education, medicine, law, and business, tending more toward the traditional fields of employment. Education is the most frequent selection of brains who plan marriage with a delayed career.

In general, women who are dissatisfied with their career progress have changed their career goals more frequently than the satisfied ones, and more of them would choose a different career if they had to make the same decision over again. As one might expect, more of them are still confused and uncertain about what they want to do. A woman dissatisfied with her progress is also more likely to be employed outside her preferred field, but if she does work in her chosen field she more often finds the work less enjoyable than she thought she would when she began.

One gets the impression that many able women who

express mixed feelings about their long-term progress are happy with one phase of their lives—work or home—but unhappy with the other. In a recent study (Watley and Kaplan, 1970a), about one-quarter of the women scholars with mixed feelings reported that they were, in fact, homemakers, although not nearly that many wanted to be housewives only. This seems to connect with the fact that they tended to have larger families, since dissatisfaction or mixed feelings about one's progress was not related to whether a woman was married.

In short, dissatisfaction or mixed feelings among women Merit scholars appears to be, in part, an expression of having failed to find a satisfactory compromise in establishing a dual life. At least 90% of the scholars are highly motivated toward educational and occupational attainment, and the majority —about three-quarters of them—say they are satisfied with their career progress. But some are blocked in one way or another by situations in their lives which force interruptions, postponements, and changed plans altogether. Others seem to be bogged down more generally by personal problems which show up in the form of career indecision, general unhappiness, frustration, and the like. In neither case could the dissatisfaction have been accurately predicted. We simply do not know enough to determine in advance whether a brain at some later point in life will look upon his or her progress with satisfaction. The very thing which seems to hold one person back may be a decisive force in driving another person to even greater accomplishment.

Few women scholars mention having encountered major problems in making and carrying out their career plans. Those with clear-cut "marriage only" or "career only" decisions seldom speak of major problems of this type. Interestingly, the most frequently mentioned problem by women with marriage-deferred career plans is that of frustration over being pulled in too many directions.

Many women do feel that they have encountered problems

pursuing their intellectual goals because of their sex. Although discrimination against women is the problem mentioned most frequently, internal conflict over the feminine-masculine role and insufficient time are other problems frequently expressed. Jewish women in particular report these problems more frequently than do Protestants or Catholics.

A number of bright women are keenly upset because of problems they trace directly to their gender. One described her sex-role conflict this way:

> I think intelligent women have a hell of a time, because they read great books and aspire to imitate great deeds of the past. The trouble is, the great books were written by men and the great deeds done by men. This is probably one of the main reasons why women never write great books or do great deeds; we're much too frustrated trying to decide whether to act like men or like women, never succeeding in doing either properly.

On the other hand, a few scholars see *advantages* to being a woman in pursuing their intellectual objectives, although this view is not shared by many colleagues. For example, as an afterthought, one noted sarcastically: "Oh yes, the *advantage*—the ladies room is seldom crowded in the math building."

Although traditionally women, even the brightest ones, seldom pursue professional careers, most brains of today give many indications they have no intention of maintaining this custom. It should be remembered, however, that we are referring here not only to women who are very bright but to those who are also highly motivated to excel. Nevertheless, they are very marriage-oriented. While some of them express sentiments of intense feeling about injustices they have themselves personally either experienced or witnessed, there is no suggestion of rebellion among them; that is, rebellion to an extreme degree. There is every reason to believe, for example, that many will continue, and perhaps even increase, their efforts in women's liberation movements. But most have multiple expectations and plans for themselves as wife-mother and as active contributors in their chosen fields. Although the scene in America today is one of not only challenge but change, there is the impression that most of their demands, at present, for gratification in untraditional areas are made not on society but on themselves. Whether these demands become more externalized in the 1970s likely depends on the extent to which man's world of work is willing to compromise.

REFERENCES

ASTIN, A. W. (1965) "College preferences of very able students." College and University 41: 282-297.

――― (1966a) "Personal and environmental factors associated with college dropouts among high aptitude students." J. of Educational Psychology 55: 219-227.

――― (1966b) "Socioeconomic factors in the achievements and aspirations of the Merit scholar." Personnel and Guidance J. 42: 581-586.

COX, C. M. (1926) Genetic Studies of Genius. Stanford, Calif.: Stanford Univ. Press.

DREWS, E. M (1960) "Intelligence, social class, and life adjustment," in B. Shertzer (ed.) Working with Superior Students: Theories and Practices. Chicago: Science Research Associates.

GINZBERG, E. et al. (1966) Life Styles of Educated Women. New York and London: Columbia Univ. Press.

――― (1951) Occupational Choice. New York: Columbia Univ. Press.

GOODENOUGH, F. (1956) Exceptional Children. New York: Appleton-Century-Crofts.

GREELEY, A. M. (1963) Religion and Career: A Study of College Graduates. New York: Sheed & Ward.

HERSEY, J. (1956) "Connecticut's committee for the gifted." Educational Leadership 13: 230-231.

HILDRETH, G. (1938) "Characteristics of young gifted children." J. of Genetic Psychology 53: 287-311.

HOLLAND, J. L. and R. C. STALNAKER (1958) "A descriptive study of talented high school seniors: National Merit scholars." Bull of National Assn. of Secondary School Principals 42: 9-12.

HOLLINGSWORTH, L. S. (1942) Children Above 180 IQ. New York: World Book.

——— (1926) Gifted Children: Their Nature and Nurture. New York: Macmillan.

HORNER, M. S. (1969) "Fail: bright women." Psychology Today 6.

KATZ, J. and N. SANFORD (1965) "Causes of the student revolution." Saturday Rev. (December 18): 64-67.

LEARNED, W. S. and B. D. WOOD (1938) "The student and his knowledge." Carnegie Foundation Advanced Training Bull. 29.

LEWIS, W. D. (1943) "Some characteristics of very superior children." J. of Genetic Psychology 62: 301-309.

McCORMACK, T. (1967) "Styles in educated females." Nation 204 (January 23): 117-118.

MATTFIELD, J. A. and C. G. VAN AKEN [eds.] (1967) Women and the Scientific Professions. Cambridge, Mass.: MIT Press.

MILES, C. C. (1954) "Gifted children," in L. Carmichael (ed.) Manual of Child Psychology. New York: John Wiley.

MUSCATINE, C. (1966) Education at Berkeley: Report of the Select Committee on Education. Berkeley, California.

NICHOLS, R. C. (1969) "Where the brains are." NMSC Research Reports 5, 5.

——— (1967) "The origin and development of talent." Phi Delta Kappan 48: 492-496.

——— (1966) "College preferences of eleventh grade students." NMSC Research Reports 2, 9.

——— and A. W. ASTIN (1966) "Progress of the Merit scholars: an eight-year followup." Personnel and Guidance J. 44: 673-686.

NICHOLS, R. C. and J. A. DAVIS (1964) "Some characteristics of students of high academic aptitude." Personnel and Guidance J. 42: 794-800.

PALMER, C. (1970) Quote in Chronicle of Higher Education (August 3).

PARKLYN, G. W. (1948) Children of High Intelligence: A New Zealand Study. London: Oxford Univ. Press.

ROSSI, P. H. et al. (1961) Great Aspirations, Career Plans of America's June 1961 College Graduates. Chicago: University of Chicago National Opinion Research Center.

SANFORD, N. (1968) "The college student of 1980," in A. C. Eurich (ed.) Campus 1980. New York: Delacorte.

SCHMIDT, L. G. (1960) "Problems of superior and talented students," in B. Shertzer (ed.) Working with Superior Students: Theories and Practices. Chicago: Science Research Associates.

STALNAKER, J. M. (1961) "Recognizing and encouraging talent." Amer. Psychologist 16: 513-522.

TERMAN, L. M. (1954) "The discovery and encouragement of exceptional talent." Amer. Psychologist 9: 221-230.

——— (1947) Mental and Physical Traits of One Thousand Gifted Children. Stanford, Calif.: Stanford Univ. Press.

——— and M. H. ODEN (1959) The Gifted Group at Mid-Life. Stanford, Calif.: Stanford Univ. Press.

——— et al. (1925) Genetic Studies of Genius. Stanford, Calif.: Stanford Univ. Press.

TOYNBEE, A. (1968) "Higher education in a time of accelerating change," in A. C. Eurich (ed.) Campus 1980. New York: Delacorte.

TYLER, R. W. (1964) "A commentary on evaluating honors programs." Superior Student 6: 17-19.

WATLEY, D. J. (1969a) "Career or marriage?: a longitudinal study of able young women." NMSC Research Reports 5, 7.

––– (1969b) "Career progress: a longitudinal study of gifted students." J. of Counselling Psychology 16: 100-108.

––– and R. KAPLAN (1970a) "Merit scholars and the fullfillment of promise." NMSC Research Reports 6, 3.

––– (1970b) "Progress of Merit scholars: does religious background matter?" NMSC Research Reports 6, 5.

WERTS, C. E. (1968) "A comparison of male vs. female college attendance probabilities." Sociology of Education 41: 103-110.

WHITEHEAD, A. N. (1929) The Aims of Education and Other Essays. New York: Macmillan.

WITTY, P. A. (1951) The Gifted Child. Boston: D. C. Heath.

––– (1940) "A genetic study of gifted children," in G. M. Whipple (ed.) Intelligence, Its Nature and Nurture. Chicago: Univ. of Chicago Press.

WOLFE, D. (1954) America's Resources of Specialized Talent. New York: Harper.

3

COMING OF AGE IN A RACIST SOCIETY
The Whitening of America

DORIS Y. WILKINSON

"**Youth is a universal phenomenon** and through the ages a major task faced by every society is the socialization of its young" (Gottlieb and Ramsey, 1964). Socialization has traditionally been defined as that process by which the young child develops a human personality. This developmental and dynamic method of transmitting the culture of a people results in the acquisition of mannerisms, habits, values, attitudes, roles, and expectations which are congruent with those of the existing social order. It is a learning process wherein the infant is both consciously and unconsciously trained in status-role identification and concomitant performance. It involves not simply the learning of one's culture but the acquisition of a self-conception. In addition, it is viewed as a continual process.

While it is agreed that socialization is a most significant sociological phenomenon wherein the infant, the young child, the adolescent, and the adult continue to acquire role

AUTHOR'S NOTE: *I am grateful to James A. Tillman, Jr. for permission to include selected items from the test in* What Is Your Racism Quotient?; *and to The Ronald Press Company for permission to quote brief excerpts from James W. Vander Zanden,* Sociology, *copyright © 1965 by The Ronald Press Company, New York.*

expectations, values, and self-conceptions, the implication that the process involves totally positive dimensions is erroneous. In addition, the assumption that man is not human until socialized is also questionable. What sociologists have neglected here is the fact that man can be socialized to behave inhumanly: to despise, to be aggressive toward, to hate, to perpetuate injurious values, role expectations, and derogatory images of self and others. Thus the fundamental example of the negative character of socialization is involved in the process of "whitening." This process of conditioning to America's racial ideology begins early in the lives of Black and white children. Basically, it represents a process by which Black and white neophytes learn their society's racial history and culture, become fitted into its racial structure, and learn to behave in relatively predictable ways on the basis of color. Via this sociocultural transmission procedure, the young child, Black or white, acquires a cognitive map of racial connotations, concomitant attitudinal, role, and color-caste positional orientations.

> Learning that one is a "white" or a "Negro" is part of the process of acquiring the behavior associated with one's racial position. In the process of answering the question, "Who am I?" the child needs to answer its corollary "And who are all those?" The answers to these questions are already contained in the culture of the child's society and are commonly transmitted to him by his family members [Vander Zanden, 1965b].

In learning to classify and identify himself and "outsiders," he acquires a set of meanings relative to pursuing an appropriate and culturally prescribed course of action based on skin color—acceptance or rejection, inclusion, or exclusion.

Research studies have shown that racial awareness and, hence, racial bigotry develop early in a child's life. Renninger and Williams (1966), for example, found that white children's awareness of the meaning of color designations develops between the ages of three and five. They also found that children demonstrate prejudice not only against Black color but against Black playmates. They expressed a consistent preference for the color white and white playmates. In a more recent investigation, coinciding with earlier work of Clark and Clark (1947), Williams and Roberson (1967) point out that awareness of racial differences develops simultaneously with color connotations. They suggest that the meaning of color differences probably reinforces racial awareness.

Color meanings are *directly* associated with racial identification and awareness. For the child internalizes the value and ideological components of his society—a sense that Black is taboo, white is right, along with related feelings of guilt, shame, or hatred if racial meanings are disturbed in later years or racial norms are violated. He is reinforced in his earlier socialization within the family by all of the major institutional sectors of his society, which are founded on the same historical base and cultural definitions of race: the school, the church, the courts, the economic order, the political arena, the mass media, the health and welfare systems, and the sciences. And insofar as the socializee accepts the racial beliefs which have been transmitted to him, and performs throughout his lifetime in accordance with the objectives of the process, he has been adequately or thoroughly socialized—i.e., "whitened."

The Black child is also whitened—i.e., socialized to America's racial belief structure.

For the black youth in white American society, the generalized other whose attitudes he assumes and the looking-glass into which he gazes both reflect the same judgment: he is inferior because he is black. His self-image, developed in the lowest stratum of a color caste system, is shaped, defined, and evaluated by a generalized other which is racist or warped by racists. His self-concept naturally becomes a negatively esteemed one, nurtured through contact with such institutionalized symbols of caste inferiority as segregated schools, neighborhoods, and jobs and more indirect negative indicators such as the reactions of his own family who have been socialized to believe that they are sub-standard human beings. Gradually becoming aware of the meaning of his black skin, the Negro child comes to see himself as an object of scorn and disparagement, unworthy of love and affection [Poussaint and Atkinson, 1970: 44].

Baldwin (1962) states that Blacks in America "are taught to despise themselves from the moment their eyes open on the world. The world is white and they're black." The central ingredient of the "whitening" process is indoctrination, consciously and unconsciously, into the ideology of racism. Neither Black nor white has an immunity to the process. As an ideology to which the newcomer is conditioned racism embodies explicit premises about Black-white role relationships, and expected interactional patterns. It represents a culturally legitimated body of racial doctrine and myths to which the young child is socialized, embodying as its most fundamental premise that of biological and intellectual superiority and purity of whites over Blacks. As such, racism functions as a pervasive gestalt underlying *and* transcending the entire value and institutional fabric of American social structure.

Racism posits the assumption that the white race is superior to Black races. It denotes a doctrine of purity of one race over the other and involves a design for racial domination (Snyder, 1962: 10).

The ideology of racism consists of the following elements:
1. The various races were offshoots of the evolutionary tree at different stages of development, so that the Negro race is lowest, not far above the apes, while the white race is highest.
2. Culture is a product solely of biological capacity, so that each race produces the artifacts and institutions of which it is capable and a lower race is not capable of carrying on the cultural life of a higher race.
3. The offspring of a mixed racial union would at best be midway, in biological capacity, between his two parents, and sometimes an anomaly would be created so that he might even be inferior in certain respects to his lower parents.
4. Amalgamation of two races would therefore result in the rapid deterioration of the culture of the higher race [Rose and Rose, 1966: 313-317].

Thus racism is any clustering of beliefs which holds that "genetically transmitted" differences between the races are related to psychological, social, and cultural factors. It legitimizes differentiation, discrimination, and segregation between racial categories. "Only when group differences in physical traits are considered a determinant of social and moral or intellectual qualities, can we properly speak of racism" (Van den Berghe, 1967: 11, 23).

These basic components of the ideology of racism are shared, transmitted, and internalized in order to keep America "whitened." The "whitening" process continues throughout the life cycle of both Blacks and whites, transcending psychological variables such as the authoritarian personality and sociological ones such as social class. With respect to psychological interpretations, Fanon (1967a) states that the "habit of considering racism as a mental quirk, as a psychological flaw, must be abandoned." One of the basic traits of racism as an ideology is its omnipotent character. Anti-Black beliefs in American society loom above all other out-group belief orientations. But perhaps white America's first real confrontation with its pervasiveness, consequences, as well as its *existence,* resulted from the insurrections of the sixties, culminating in the following pronouncement:

White racism is essentially responsible for the explosive mixture which has been accumulating in our cities since the end of World War II. At the base of this mixture are . . . the most bitter fruits of white racial attitudes:

 (1) *Pervasive discrimination and segregation*
   a. continuing exclusion of great numbers of Blacks from the benefits of economic progress
   b. their enforced confinement in segregated housing and schools
 (2) *Black migration and white exodus*
   a. growing concentration of impoverished Blacks in our major cities
   b. a growing crisis of deteriorating facilities and services and unmet human needs

(3) *Black ghettos*
   a. rampant poverty
   b. families without men
   c. men and women without jobs
   d. schools where children are processed instead of educated
   e. crime
(4) *Frustrated hopes*
(5) *Legitimation of violence*
   a. white terrorism directed against nonviolent protest
   b. open defiance of law and federal authority by state and local officials resisting desegregation
(6) *Powerlessness*
(7) *Police encounters and brutality*
   "Symbols of White power, White racism, White repression"
   [National Advisory Commission on Civil Disorders, 1968]

With regard to the "whitening" phenomenon, there has not been enough meaningful research on the white adults of tomorrow and the kinds of belief structures they will bring to the future institutions and value systems of our society. There is a need to analyze systematically white self-conceptions and resulting behavioral manifestations of these conceptions, as these have their foundation in a gradually changing historical heritage. There is a need to understand the specific nature of the perpetuation of racial beliefs via socialization (Goldschmid, 1970).

The beliefs of a society tell people about their history: their friends and their enemies, their gods and devils, their heroes and villains. They tell people about the structure and processes of society, about such things as internal differentiation—for instance, of social classes, how they came into being, how they differ, how people "get ahead" or "fall behind." . . . Beliefs provide a tension-management function for a society—that is, they provide a framework for appraising, understanding, and dealing with occurrences that might otherwise pose a severe threat and constitute a source of considerable anxiety . . . beliefs may coalesce to constitute a set of ideas—an ideology [Vander Zanden, 1965a].

The ideology of racism represents a configuration of beliefs:

1. Segregation is part of a natural order and is instinctive in nature. Segregation is a natural order—created by God . . . who made black men black and white men white. Each man should be proud of his race and should constantly strive to preserve its purity.
2. Segregation is natural and best.
3. The Negro is a different kind of human being. . . . The Negro is inferior to whites.
4. Negroes are different from whites. . . . There are great social and emotional differences that quickly come to the surface when aroused. Their mental processes are different.
5. The Negro is irresponsible.
6. Racial amalgamation or intermarriage is bad and dangerous. Racial intermarriage will result in racial suicide [Vander Zanden, 1965b].

Although the broader and primary concern of this paper is with the sociocultural process of socializing the newcomer to white America and hence to its racial ideology, a secondary emphasis is on the network of beliefs which comprise racism for adolescents. The specific problem under exploration represents an attempt to discover selected racial beliefs of a sampling of white adolescents involving a focus upon the following:

(1) Given that the urban ghetto school system represents the consequences of racism in America, what do white adolescents feel can be done to alter this condition? Do they feel that there should be a racial balance in the school system? How do they feel this can best be achieved? What concessions, relative to the national issue of busing, are white adolescents willing to make to achieve racial integration and thus better quality education for Black youth in the schools? (a) Bus Blacks in or (b) bus whites out?

(2) Juxtaposed with the notion that Blacks are intellectually and biologically inferior is the belief that Blacks are morally and culturally different. Embodied in this notion is the myth that the culture of a people is a product of mental and biological capacities. Given these closely interwoven tenets of the racial ideology, do white youth believe Blacks have a different life

style even though the Black child is socialized through the same "whitening" process?

(3) If white adolescents believe that Blacks are culturally different and if they are oriented to cultural assimilation rather than pluralism, what do they feel should be done to assimilate Blacks into the fabric of white society? Should the process of "whitening" Blacks be perpetuated via having Blacks go to school with whites or living in white neighborhoods, rather than have the ghetto school upgraded and the Black community rebuilt? Should they date Blacks in order to continue the training process in "whiteness?" Do they believe that marriage between the races should be promoted in order to eliminate biological differences and hence racial prejudice? Or should exogamy be perpetuated in order to maintain the purity of the races?

These are the more general questions to which this research is oriented.

The research instrument consisted of the usual demographic and personal data items, a series of questions from the Campbell and Schuman (1968) study, a revised social distance scale, and items from the Tillman and Tillman (1968) racism quotient test. Only five of the items from a total of 38 are reported on in this presentation. Thus the findings presented are only a portion of a larger project. It should also be added that the results do not attempt to reflect on the specific nature of the socialization process nor the major facets of a racist ideology. What is involved is the assumption that the white youth studied have been socialized into America's racial ideology, and the research is simply oriented to ascertain some of the racial beliefs these adolescents hold in the selected areas heretofore mentioned: busing, cultural differences, dating, and intermarriage.

The procedure involved administering a structured questionnaire en masse to selected classrooms in the two schools evaluated here. Prior to administering the instrument, a brief discussion of the project was held and a need for each student's participation was stressed. After completing the questionnaire, students raised questions about the items and expressed their reactions to them.[1] One of the items discussed by a number of students in the other schools not analyzed, and by a few in the two groups under study was: "Do you think Negroes are just born that way and can't be changed, or that changes in the Negro are possible?"

Results of this analysis are based on a relatively small number of white high school students (n=379) between the ages of 14 and 18, with 211 males and 168 females. Most of the youth come from families where the father has at least a high school education. A total of 376 of the respondents are from Catholic families. There was a relatively equal distribution of the ranks freshman to senior for both groups. A considerable degree of homogeneity was achieved on the variables of education, occupation, age, and religion.

In a recent study of Ohio high school students (Bryant, 1970), it was found that only 29% were in favor of busing as a solution to racism. In this investigation, the two items on busing were aimed at uncovering which alternative white students would prefer in order to achieve racial integration in the school system. Table 1 shows that a much greater percentage of the males and females objected to busing whites to Black schools than to busing Blacks from the city to their school. Yet, on both items, a greater percentage of males than females objected to busing Blacks and whites. While only 30% of the females expressed an objection to busing whites from their school into the city in order to integrate an all-Black school, 56% of the males expressed such an objection. These findings are corroborated by those of a 1971 Harris poll of youth between the ages of 15 and 21 which showed 66% opposed to busing (Life, 1971a).

In Table 2, the differences between the sexes are negligible. But what is striking are the percentages of these adolescents who believe Blacks have a different way of life than white Americans. Whether this is a significant component of America's racial ideology accepted only by whites may be questioned. But in evaluating the original item appearing in the racism quotient test: "The American Negro's culture is different from the American white's culture," Tillman and Tillman (1968: 15) state that the "correct" response is no. If a white checks yes, this indicates, in the two authors' interpretation, that the respondent does not "view the Negro as an American . . . but as a foreigner possessing a culture different" from that of white Americans.

The finding of an overwhelming majority of both the males and females believing that Blacks have a different life style coincides with data in Table 3. Data in this table show that a considerable number of these students feel that only by going to school with whites or living in their neighborhoods can Blacks be socialized to the white culture. However, a slightly greater percentage of females than males holds this position. More males, 7%, were unwilling to make a commitment on this item in contrast to females and in contrast to the males who responded to the previous one. Tillman and Tillman's interpretation of these responses states that if a white respondent agrees, he holds the belief that whites are "intrinsically superior and, therefore, should always be placed in the role of teacher for Negroes. Again, this erroneously assumes that there are two cultures in the U.S.: black and white" (Tillman and Tillman, 1968: 17).

It may appear ironic that white youth who believe Blacks are different would, in spite of this, express a willingness to date them. There is, interestingly enough, no significant percentage difference between males and females on the dating item. But an expression of a willingness to date is no indicator or predictor of behavior in this area. In fact, a recent Harris poll showed that 51% of those interviewed agreed with the statement that: "Any white girl who goes out with a black man is going to ruin her reputation" (Life, 1971b: 66).

Some of the comments to the dating item written in by females are as follows:

"My parents wouldn't hear of it."

"Don't know because I have had few Black acquaintances."

TABLE 1
Percentage Distribution by Sex and Objections to Busing of Black and White Students

| | Busing Blacks[a] | | | | Busing Whites[b] | | | |
| | Male | | Female | | Male | | Female | |
Would Object	%	n	%	n	%	n	%	n
Yes	23	(49)	9	(16)	56	(117)	30	(51)
No	74	(155)	90	(151)	38	(81)	68	(114)
No response	3	(7)	1	(1)	6	(13)	2	(3)
Total	100	(211)	100	(168)	100	(211)	100	(168)

a. Item 11: Would you object if Black students from the city were bused out to your school?
b. Item 12: Would you object if white students from your school were bused into the city in order to integrate an all-Black school?

TABLE 2
Percentage Distribution by Sex and Belief that Blacks Have a Different Life Style[a]

| | Males | | Females | |
Acceptance of Belief	%	n	%	n
Yes	78	(165)	71	(120)
No	19	(40)	26	(43)
No response	3	(6)	3	(5)
Total	100	(211)	100	(168)

a. Item 27: The American Negro has a different way of life than the American white.

TABLE 3
Percentage Distribution by Sex and Belief Blacks Should Learn Behavior of Whites[a]

| | Males | | Females | |
Acceptance of Belief	%	n	%	n
Yes	44	(93)	51	(85)
No	49	(104)	47	(79)
No response	7	(14)	2	(4)
Total	100	(211)	100	(168)

a. Item 34: Only by going to school with or living in otherwise white neighborhoods can Blacks learn the ways of life and action of white Americans.

TABLE 4
Percentage Distribution by Sex and Willingness to
Date a Black

Willingness to Date a Black	Males[a]		Females[b]	
	%	n	%	n
Yes	68	(143)	66	(111)
No	29	(61)	32	(53)
Don't know	1	(2)	2	(4)
No response	2	(5)	0	(0)
Total	100	(211)	100	(168)

a. Item 14: If you knew a Black girl well as a friend and liked her, would you ever consider taking her out?
b. Item 13: If a Black guy from your high school, church group, or some situation asked you out and seemed like a nice person to you, would you go out with him?

"My mother would oppose."

"But I'd have problems at home."

"I don't know; never known any Black people."

A male student commented: "Hell no, I wouldn't touch her." These comments on interracial dating are understandable in view of the fact that:

Dating status, whatever its nature and intensity, brings with it a number of emotional and structural changes in the middle class family and the various interactional sub-systems comprising the family complex [Wilkinson, 1970a: 305].

Thus, interracial dating would certainly increase emotional trauma within the white family. To what extent this would hold true for Black families as it reflects their socialization to white values might be worthy of study.

Moreover, the content of the dating questions may be a factor in the numbers expressing a willingness to date a Black. Descriptive labels such as "nice" or wording such as "If you knew a Black girl *well* as a *friend* and *liked* her" could contribute to the frequency of "yes" responses. For as shown in Table 5, most of the males and females, 63 and 68% respectively, do not believe in marriage between the races.

Here again the structure of the item may be a factor in the distribution of responses. But despite the somewhat double implications involved, comments written in and discussions after the administration of the questionnaire brought out two things: (1) an anti-interracial marriage belief, and (2) a rejection of the notion that marriage between the races would reduce prejudice. A few students wrote in that this is not a good way to reduce prejudice.

However, it was difficult to ascertain their views on the maintenance of the purity of the races, but it was clear that they were against racial exogamy for various reasons. Tillman and Tillman (1968: 15) state that the appropriate or nonracist response on the intermarriage item is no. In their explanation of the meaning of this item, they state that if one responds yes this "indicates that the individual does not believe it is possible to have peace, order, tranquility and justice in a multiracial society but only in a uniracial society" (Tillman and Tillman, 1968). But their interpretation of this as well as their other explanations of components of the racism quotient test may be questioned, since the item has a dual meaning. It asks on one hand whether there should be marriage between the races and on the other whether intermarriage will reduce racial prejudice. A number of the respondents stressed the latter, expressing the view that marriage between Blacks and whites should not be a means for the reduction of prejudice. Data tabulated for the females

TABLE 5
Percentage Distribution by Sex and Belief that Intermarriage
Can Eliminate Prejudice[a]

Acceptance of Belief	Males		Females	
	%	n	%	n
Yes	28	(59)	26	(43)
No	63	(133)	68	(114)
No response	9	(19)	6	(11)
Total	100	(211)	100	(168)

a. Item 28: Marriage between the races is good because everybody will be alike and there will be no race prejudice.

(n=168) only, show a continued emphasis on genetic differences and concur with the foregoing:

"On the average, Negroes in America have worse jobs, education, and housing than white people. Do you think this is due mainly to Negroes having been discriminated against, or mainly due to something about Negroes themselves?"

	n	%
mainly due to discrimination	80	47
mainly due to Negroes themselves	6	4
a mixture of both	81	48
no information	1	1
	168	100%

"Do you think Negroes are just born that way and can't be changed, or that changes in the Negro are possible?"

	n	%
Negroes are born that way	12	7
changes are possible	141	84
no information	15	9
	168	100%

This second item from the Campbell and Schuman (1968) study has similar shortcomings to many of those in the racism quotient test. The mere structuring of this item and either choice is indicative of a racist response. What is striking about tabulations for this second item are the numbers of female adolescents who feel Black Americans can be "changed," with the subtle implication that they should be changed. In connection with this, responses to the question on employment opportunity, education, and housing reveal that these white adolescents feel it is not simply discrimination which results in Blacks having "the worse" jobs, housing, or education, but that there is something about being Black which has certain consequences that Blacks are assumed to be the cause of. In fact, most of the female respondents believe that Blacks themselves cause prejudice. Percentages for the following item reflect this belief:

"Negroes are as much responsible for prejudice as whites."

	n	%
1. yes	115	68
2. no	45	27
no information	8	5
	168	100%

One of the myths embodied in America's racial ideology is that Blacks are responsible for prejudice and discrimination, and thus white racism, either by their Blackness or in reacting to discrimination and segregation. One of the basic axioms of the racist belief structure is that: "Racism exists only because of the actual presence of oppressed races. . . . By the same token, racism ceases whenever a black has accumulated enough Caucasian genes to 'pass' in the white world" (Kovel, 1970: 179). These are the hidden dimensions or latent aspects of racism which are blatantly obvious to Blacks and which demand continuous scrutiny by social and behavioral scientists.

Findings from this investigation reveal the following beliefs of this selected group of white Catholic adolescents:

(1) An acceptance of the busing of Black students to integrate schools.

(2) A rejection of the busing of white students to integrate schools.

(3) A tendency for males to object more often than females to busing either group.

(4) Belief that Blacks are culturally different.

(5) An expressed willingness to date Blacks.

(6) An objection to interracial marriages per se.

(7) An objection to interracial marriages as a means of reducing prejudice.

(8) A belief that being Black plays a role in their being discriminated against.

(9) A belief that Blacks are genetically different but that changes are possible.

(10) A belief that Blackness causes prejudice.

More systematic inquiry into racist beliefs and the socialization to America's racial ideology is required to lend credence to the above tentative generalizations in order to plan a program of attack and resocialization for white Americans.

But specifically where should we go from here? Perhaps a brief listing of what could and should be done will illustrate the present author's thinking on the subject of racism:

(1) Studies on Black youth's self-conceptions, racial identity, and the like need to cease. A new mood has emerged among considerable numbers of Blacks in America which indicates a conscious and deliberate attempt to redefine their self-images and restructure the process of socialization in their families and in the schools (Saunders, 1970). We know enough about the derogatory images white culture has presented Blacks, but we might learn something about socialization as it is observed in the expression "Black is beautiful" or in demands for Black history, Black studies, and the wearing of Afros. Here is a bold attempt to redefine the content of the "whitening" process. How might it be employed to restructure the thinking of white Americans?

(2) No more studies are needed which emphasize the prejudiced personality or authoritarianism among children and youth. But research aimed at policy formation is needed, research into authoritarianism as an aspect of American culture and social structure. One of the erroneous assumptions of our time is the labeling of certain selected personality types as racist. This has given rise to the avoidance of racism as the central ingredient of the history and social structure of American society. No white has an in-built immunity to racism.

(3) We need to know how white youth feel about themselves, what it is like to feel biologically superior and to believe one is intellectually superior. We need more research on their racial beliefs, their limits of interaction with Blacks, and techniques of disengagement from a racist society. Is there a connection between the "cop-out," drug, and psychedelic phenomena and feelings of powerlessness to change America's color-caste system that the only escape is a "trip?" What has white America's history done to its own youth?

(4) We already know about racial awareness in young Black and white children; we need to know the depth of hatred among white children, adolescents, and adults. Hatred is a sociological phenomenon. It needs to be studied intensively. We need to know the consequences of hatred. Whites need to know, to feel its impact as Blacks know and feel its meaning. What types of terrorism result from hatred and white racism (Wilkinson, 1970b)? What can local, state, and federal governments do to resocialize white American youth?

(5) Social scientists must stop concentrating on the white lower class and the working classes who have become scapegoats for middle-class scientists who deny the pervasiveness of institutional racism and the fact that we need to study its pervasiveness and impact with the aim of at least attempting to "unwhiten" America.

(6) No more theories are needed on the etiology of prejudice, the frustration-aggression complex, scapegoating, contact-prejudice reduction, and so on. Social and behavioral scientists need to look directly at the historical roots and sociocultural dimensions of racism and its perpetuation through the process of socialization and survival in all of America's institutions.

(7) We need to know what it is like for young white children to come of age in a racist society, to grow up in Klan

communities; what they feel, what they learn, and the paths they might pursue as they enter the future.

In summary, what social and behavioral science requires is an honesty about the problem of white racism in our country and how it is affecting Black and white youth. Both disciplines need a perceptive innovator and a creative man of integrity to revolutionize the consciousness of their fields of study, political and economic systems, and key figures who control them. Social research must make an impact on the wider society through exposing racism for what it is, what it does to Black and white children, and to design programs of action to deal with it. Social science can no longer remain worthy of study or public consumption and respect if it continues to remove itself from the serious problems of American culture (King, 1968). For the history of the "whitening" process to America's racial ideology requires the creation of a plan for the reorganization of that process and hence the total structure of the society.

NOTE

1. Questionnaires were administered after advance notice was given to principals and teachers; discussions were led by Kathleen Sullivan, research assistant on the project.

REFERENCES

BALDWIN, J. (1962) "Letter from a region in my mind." New Yorker 38: 65.
BRYANT, B. E. (1970) High School Students Look at their World. Columbus, Ohio: R. H. Goettler.
CAMPBELL, A. and H. SCHUMAN (1968) Racial Attitudes in Fifteen American Cities. Ann Arbor, Mich.: Survey Research Center, Institute for Social Research.
CLARK, K. B. and M. K. CLARK (1947) "Racial identification and preference in Negro children," in T. M. Newcomb and E. L. Hartley (eds.) Readings in Social Psychology. New York: Holt, Rinehart & Winston.
FANON, F. (1967a) Black Skins, White Masks. New York: Grove.
--- (1967b) Toward the African Revolution. New York: Grove.

GOLDSCHMID, M. L. [ed.] (1970) Black Americans and White Racism. New York: Holt, Rinehart & Winston.

GOTTLIEB, D. and C. E. RAMSEY (1964) The American Adolescent. Homewood, Ill.: Dorsey.

KING, M. L. (1968) "The role of the behavioral scientist in the civil rights movement." Amer. Psychologist 23: 180-186.

KOVEL, J. (1970) White Racism: A Psycho-History. New York: Pantheon.

Life (1971a) "A new youth poll: change, yes–upheaval, no." 70 (January 8): 22-30.

––– (1971b) "Black/white dating." 70 (May 28): 56-67.

National Advisory Commission on Civil Disorders (1968) U.S. Riot Commission Report. New York: Bantam Books.

POUSSAINT, A. and C. ATKINSON (1970) "Black youth and motivation." Black Scholar 1 (March): 43-51.

QUINN, O. W. (1954) "The transmission of racial attitudes among white Southerners." Social Forces 33 (October): 41-47.

RENNINGER, C. A. and J. E. WILLIAMS (1966) "Black-white color connotations and racial awareness in preschool children." Perceptual and Motor Skills 22: 771-785.

ROSE, S. and C. B. ROSE [eds.] (1966) Minority Problems. New York: Harper & Row.

SAUNDERS, C. R. (1970) "Assessing race relations research." Black Scholar 1 (March): 17-25.

SNYDER, L. L. (1962) The Idea of Racialism. Princeton, N.J.: D. Van Nostrand.

TILLMAN, J. A. and M. N. TILLMAN (1968) "Racism quotient test," pp. 9, 15-17 in What Is Your Racism Quotient? New York: Tillman Associates.

TOFFLER, A. (1970) Future Shock. New York: Random House.

TOMLINSON, T. M. (1968) "White racism and the common man: an extension of the Kerner Commission's report on American racism." Washington, D.C.: Office of Economic Opportunity.

VAN DEN BERGHE, P. (1967) Race and Racism. New York: John Wiley.

VANDER ZANDEN, J. W. (1965a) "Functions of beliefs," pp. 70-71 in Sociology: A Systematic Approach. New York: Ronald Press.

––– (1965b) "The ideology of white supremacy," pp. 71-73 in Sociology: A Systematic Approach. New York: Ronald Press.

WILKINSON, D. Y. (1970a) "Dating status of American college women as a predictor of interactional patterns with parents." International J. of Comparative Sociology 20 (December): 300-306.

––– (1970b) "Political assassins and status incongruence: a sociological interpretation." British J. of Sociology 21 (December): 400-412.

WILLIAMS, J. E. and K. A. ROBERSON (1967) "A method for assessing racial attitudes in preschool children." Educational and Psych. Measurement 27: 671-689.

4

YOUTH DISCONTENT AND THE NATURE OF WORK

HAROLD L. SHEPPARD

The nature of the job world and its problems for American youth is perhaps a reflection of certain other general features of American society as a whole. For example, we do little planning for the economy or the community as a whole (corporations and the Defense Department being the major exceptions). Career-planning is, at best, a concept in textbooks for counselors. It certainly does not exist, in any widespread or meaningful sense, among and for individuals —especially young people about to enter the labor force or already in the labor force for only a few years. This failure also manifests itself among many middle-aged and older workers (of all levels) in the form of "mid-career malaise" and the need for job counseling in this phase of life. The basic pattern, in my opinion, has not changed much over the past few decades. This pattern involves—at least for working-class youth—haphazard choices of early jobs based on limited knowledge of the full range of types of occupations and kinds of employers, often motivated by a desire for inde-pendence from the family or a desire for money, even at low wages, in order to keep up with one's peers (which includes the ability to attract "dates").

There are, thus, too many stories of young men taking dissatisfying jobs (in terms of the intrinsic content of the tasks involved) in the belief that they will escape them in time but find themselves, after the years ebb by, more or less "trapped" in such jobs.

In the current epoch, however, a new dimension has been added. The young workers of today are of a different generation; by this I mean they have a different social character than the youth of thirty or forty years ago. In those years, a young man felt himself lucky if he had a job and today, having reached middle or old age, still bears the anxieties of job insecurity that have their roots in the Depression. But the young of today, in comparison to the young of the past, have not lived through serious and long-term unemployment experiences. This is true despite the impression that may be conveyed by the high rates of joblessness among younger job seekers. Unemployment rates are not the same as duration of unemployment. By comparison, the under-thirty labor force, when unemployed, does not remain unemployed as long as (1) the older worker group (especially those fifty and older) and (2) the young jobseekers of the decade before World War II.

To repeat, a new dimension has been added to the portrait of the young worker. He has grown up in years of relative prosperity (despite our preoccupation with poverty—a preoccupation which may be a by-product of the development of an "affluent" society). He spends more years in a school, and education, regardless of the current attacks on its quality, does bear a striking correlation to a number of sociologically significant phenomena. These include, above all, increased expectations out of life and a greater anti-authority orientation. Without recognition of these types of differences that differentiate the young workers of today from those of the past (or from the older workers of today), one is bound to be perplexed and misled by all the other events and behavior associated with the young workers of the modern scene.

Let me try to back up some of these generalized observations with the empirical results of interviews held with nearly 400 workers (of all ages) in five urban areas of Pennsylvania and Michigan, conducted in the summers of 1970 and 1971. It is, first of all, important to note that all these workers are white males and members of trade unions. We are not in a position to argue beyond any doubt that our conclusions, based on interviews with such a group, are applicable, say, to nonwhites, women, or nonunion members (especially those in occupations typically not organized by the labor movement in the United States). We believe, however, that our sample does reflect the "mainstream" of the American male working class. At the very least, our finding might provide some insights and possible leads for other segments of our labor force.

I have said that the young worker of today is characterized by a greater degree of anti-authoritarianism, compared to the older worker. In our study (sponsored by the Upjohn Institute with partial support from the Ford Foundation and in cooperation with the unions involved), we classified the workers according to four degrees of authoritarianism, from those with extreme nonauthoritarianism to those with extreme authoritarianism. Three questions from the familiar battery of authoritarian personality items were used in our survey, all of them containing an obedience/discipline/strong leadership theme: the most important thing to teach children is absolute obedience to their parents; any good leader should be strict with people under him in order to gain their respect; and a few strong leaders could do more for this country than all the laws and talk.

The workers in our interviews were asked to indicate their degree of agreement or disagreement with each of these statements. The results indicate that more than one-half of the young workers (under 30) but only one-seventh of the oldest workers (55 and older) fall into the lowest quartile —i.e., are extremely nonauthoritarian. When we take the two lowest levels of authoritarianism, the young workers are still less authoritarian than the oldest by a 2 to 1 ratio (75% are in the low authoritarian range, compared to 37% of the 55+ workers).

To borrow a concept from Erich Fromm, my basic theme is that authoritarianism is part of one's social character. The implication here is that, even as they grow older, these men, now under 30, will continue to be non- or anti-authoritarian. Authoritarianism, in other words, is not "situational." It is not subject to very much change over the life-span as the individual undergoes changes in socioeconomic experiences. In this sense, the society in general will be different in the future because of the shift in the social character of its population (after all, the old will die, and the young will become middle-aged and then old).

But what does all this have to do with the topic of work in modern-day urban America? Why should the issue of a man's extent of authoritarianism be of interest to industrial social scientists? The answer is all very simple when one begins to think about the variety and autonomy in the nature of job tasks and work environments. If a worker with an anti-authoritarian personality is in a job or work environment characterized, for example, by little autonomy and a minimum of challenge to his potential or desire for some degree of responsibility, he is likely to be turned off and demoralized by such a job or work environment.

This is true regardless of that worker's age. It just so happens that a higher proportion of the young than of the old are anti-authoritarian.

Our research has suggested to me that, contrary to some theories and viewpoints widely accepted in some intellectual and academic circles, work and work satisfaction do not serve as critical molders of a man's degree of authoritarianism. This is one of the implications of Fromm's writings, by the way, that social character (degree of authoritarianism being one dimension of social character) is the result of the individual's work life. This conclusion is based on our findings that workers reporting little or no (a) variety, (b) freedom, or (c) responsibility in the kinds of jobs they perform turn out to be more tolerant of jobs that entail few of these intrinsic task attributes, and, to repeat, authoritarians are found more among the oldest workers than among the youngest.

Another important point: it is possible for a worker to report that his job has all or many of these negative features, but that does not necessarily mean that he is bothered by such features. In the case of the younger workers in our sample, if they did refer to their jobs as having little variety, freedom, and responsibility, they were more likely to be bothered by this lack than older workers. While each of the two extreme age groups (those under 30 and those 55 or older) constituted 21% of our total sample, 28% of the workers with a "high severity" evaluation of (bothered frequently by) negative tasks were the very young, but only 16% of the "high severity" workers were the very old. For example, among workers reporting they had almost no opportunities to learn more about their work and to increase their knowledge of the process and skills involved, one-third of the under 30 workers but only one-sixth of the 55+ workers were bothered by this nearly all the time or often.

Contrary to many popular images about the new, young workers, our interviews draw a portrait of them as feeling their jobs offer them little chance to exert a sense of responsibility. Our measures of such concepts as job responsibility, autonomy, and variety were adapted from Turner and Lawrence (1965). It is not surprising, therefore, to find that a large majority of these young workers rate their jobs as having little importance (as indicated in their replies that almost anyone or a good many people can do their type of work) in contrast to less than half of the oldest workers.

Nor should it be surprising, in light of this discussion, that only a third of the under-30 workers, in contrast to nearly two-thirds of the oldest ones, say they are satisfied with their jobs most of the time. About one-fourth of the young workers report infrequent satisfaction as compared to less than one-tenth of the 55+ generation. And, once again, it is primarily young workers in tasks with little variety, autonomy, and responsibility who are least satisfied.

Thus, the young workers of today are and will become increasingly dissatisfied with jobs that have little intrinsic content value. One of the controversial facets of this remark has to do with the question of "adaptation." Will, in other words, such workers come to resign themselves to performing undesirable tasks, or will they continue to be dissatisfied if forced, for one reason or another, to remain in such jobs if industry (as well as unions and government) does little or nothing to restructure the organization of work tasks or rotate workers among different tasks or create greater mobility opportunities to enable young people to move out of low-level tasks?

This issue should not be confused with the economic issue of job security and decent wages. Workers in our study with no unemployment (in the 20 months prior to being interviewed) and with high wages (compared to the rest of the sample) were dissatisfied more frequently if they were employed at jobs with negative task attributes.

My prediction of their greater refusal to "adapt" is based, once again, on the fact that they are anti-authoritarian and have higher expectations. Their greater expectations do have some economic implications as well, despite the fact that their wage levels are roughly equivalent to those of the older workers. The under-30 group in our sample is less satisfied with the adequacy of their take-home pay—even of their total family income. They also expect a steady rise in their income in the years ahead, more than do the oldest workers. If anti-authoritarianism can also be considered a rough correlate to feelings of equalitarianism, we might more readily understand their desires and expectations concerning higher income, and we should, therefore, also anticipate the consequences, especially in the political and collective bargaining spheres, of any failure on their part to achieve such economic goals.

There are other aspects of their jobs and job attitudes that are worth reporting here. For example, nearly two-fifths of the young workers (and more if we concentrate only on those in jobs with negative, low-level tasks) have thought very often about making a change to an occupation radically different from the ones they now have; compare this with the mere 10% among the 55+ group. Few of them are so attached to their current jobs that they would not change jobs for more money, as compared to nearly one-half of the oldest workers who have a high job attachment.

Of course, seniority benefits and the possibility that older workers have already gone through some degree of occupational change play a role here. But we cannot ignore the contention that young workers of today play it "loose," and, in the job world, this means a lower identity of self with a particular occupation. At the same time, it may be asked, how have our societal institutions (the schools, our vocational training sources, unions, and employers included) themselves deviated from the notion that a person should be guided toward or trained for one occupation or profession as a lifelong goal? Very little, indeed, has been achieved in the direction of structuring opportunities for "second [or third and fourth] careers."

To return to one of the themes discussed at the beginning of this chapter concerning early job choices, our young workers are less likely to consider their current jobs as very much like the kind they wanted when they first took them. The answers to many other questions inquiring into their jobs reinforce the conclusion that many of them will try to leave their current jobs. What the high unemployment rate of 1971 does to their opportunities to do so is, of course, a critical question. If these opportunities are reduced, we might expect an aggravation of the existing level of discontent in this group. I want to return to their current political viewpoints and voting behavior in this connection.

But the basic point here is that it is still true, as in the past, that these kinds of job attitudes, especially among young workers in negative task jobs, are partially an outcome of "lack of guidance in choosing work, haphazard ways of finding employment, and the indifferent attitudes of employers, children, and parents alike" (Carter, 1966: 158). The new dimension, to repeat, is that the social-psychological and political consequences of such poor occupational choice-planning may become more serious than in the past, if my reading of the social character of young workers today is correct. This social character leads to a greater emphasis among young workers on opportunities to do interesting and enjoyable work. More of them give importance to improving the quality of their work than to improving their pay. For example, 51% stress quality of work, but only 38% cite more pay. Their overall rating of the need to make work more interesting is much greater than in the case of the oldest workers, and they are also least satisfied with their current opportunities to engage in interesting work.

We have not referred yet to the traditionally posed question concerning how workers feel about promotion opportunities and their chances to "get ahead" in their current jobs. In keeping with their higher expectations, the under-30 workers are much more optimistic in this respect than the oldest (45% of the youngest but only 26% of the oldest feel that their chances for getting ahead are above average or excellent). But, if a young worker does claim he has little or no chances, he is bothered more frequently by this lack of mobility opportunity than the average old worker. In this connection, they are much more responsive to any educational or training opportunities that might be offered which would get them a better job. Furthermore, among all the workers saying they would take advantage of such opportunities (with enough financial support for themselves and their families), more of the young workers would choose those opportunities in order to leave their current employer, by a ratio of 2 to 1, when compared to the 55+ group.

How do these young workers feel about their current employers? The previous finding is one answer to that question. They also give a lower rating to their employers' interest in the workers doing quality work on their jobs. Perhaps more important, the younger workers apparently feel left out or neglected by the unions to which they belong. Fewer than two-fifths of them, but almost seven-tenths of the oldest workers, say their union is very helpful to its members. This lower rating of their unions is especially prevalent among the young workers in jobs paying higher wages (an unexpected finding), but with fewer fringe benefits. The young workers giving low ratings to their union are also more likely to be employed in their current jobs only a short period of time (less than a year), which suggests that if they do stay where they are now employed, their understanding of the usefulness of their union might increase. They are also less educated. But, more important (and related to our major theme concerning job attitudes), they are more likely to express, through their answers to a number of questions, less satisfaction with the intrinsic contents of their jobs. Finally, these young workers, with less-favorable attitudes toward their unions, are also characterized by a high discrepancy between their aspirations and their actual achievements.

The intangible aspects of the job, much more than wage levels, thus help explain many of the differences between those young workers with pro-union evaluations and those with less-favorable union ratings. Their expectations of the kind of job they wanted when they first took their current one, how they now rate it, and how frequently they are satisfied with that job provide us with greater insights into why they rate their unions as poorly as they do.

We have already emphasized the critical part played by authoritarianism among these young workers. We found that if nonauthoritarian young workers were in jobs with negative task attributes, they were also much more likely to be highly alienated. Our measure used to tap this dimension was based on three items in the familiar Srole scale: "These days a person doesn't really know who he can count on; in spite of what some people say, the lot of the average man is getting better, not worse; it's hardly fair to bring children into the world with the way things look for the future." To put this another way, the only group of young workers who were in the least alienated category are the nonauthoritarians in jobs that have a high degree of variety, autonomy, and responsibility. Our basic formulation is that alienation is "situational" and that the nature of job tasks (as mediated by the worker's degree of authoritarianism) constitutes one of these situations. This means to me that alienation can be changed to the degree that we can change the nature of job tasks; this becomes an imperative for the new generation of workers who are typically anti-authoritarian. If such changes are not to be made, all of us may suffer the consequences.

Let me spell this out in political terms. The young worker (any worker for that matter) who is not only alienated but who also feels politically impotent (as measured by such questions as "People like me don't have any say about what the government does") is less likely to vote at all or, if he does, is more likely than other workers to have voted for George Wallace in 1968. Alienation is also associated with a tendency to identify oneself as a "conservative." Analysis of the workers calling themselves "conservative" versus those calling themselves "liberal" reveals that such self-designations are not a matter of chance or caprice. "Liberals" and "conservatives" are different (for example, with respect to their racial attitudes, feelings of political effectiveness and authoritarianism, choice of political parties, and their respect of the rights of both unions and employers to engage in politics).

While all our workers cited the Vietnam War, above all, as among the three most important issues they want political candidates to talk about during election campaigns, younger workers cite this issue more frequently than older workers (80 versus 60%). But one new, emerging issue—pollution and environmental quality—reveals how different the new generation of workers is. For the under-30 workers, it is apparent that they will be judging political leaders on the basis of this issue of the new era much more than their older friends, parents, and relatives. The ratio of youngest to oldest workers citing this topic as one which they want to hear about from political candidates is more than 3 to 1. Nearly one-half (48%) of the young workers but only 15% of the 55+ group referred to pollution, the environmental problem, and ecology.

There are some political commentators who pooh-pooh pollution as an elitist concern and who feel that the working class could not care less about such a problem—that "bread-and-butter" issues, as in the past, are and will be the preoccupations that make this class tick (with a dash of Agnew's "social issues" thrown in). In part, such a view itself is elitist. It implies that workers (regardless of other characteristics) cannot rise above their own immediate, personal concerns and cannot grasp intellectually the import of such matters as the consequences of disruption of the ecological balance.

Persistence in acceptance of this distorted image of the working class is based on a failure to recognize that there is a generation gap *within* the working class, at least among the kinds of white male union members we interviewed. The gap between generations, of course, is not something invented yesterday, but the significance of this phenomenon today is that the new group of workers are not carbon copies of their older coworkers (partly due to the differences in the socioeconomic conditions in which the separate generations grew up). I expect also that the kinds of social-political concerns of these younger men will remain a part of them as the years pass by, as they move into their adult, middle-aged, and older years.

The older workers of today are, in part, the product of the Depression, the New Deal, and a major world war. The younger workers of today are, in part, the products of the nuclear age, the industrial megamachine, the "affluent" society, and U.S. involvement in Southeast Asia. Each generation, to add another dimension, entered the labor force with different levels of schooling, resulting in different levels of knowledge and life expectations.

Given these widely contrasting "socialization contexts," we should not be surprised to find that young workers have little confidence in the two major parties. Precisely half of them, when asked which party represents their point of view best, said instead that the parties are all the same, that none of them represents their point of view, or cited a minor political party. In contrast, only one-fourth of the oldest workers rejected the two major parties.

My argument here is that for the young workers of today, their unions and the two major parties are part of the Establishment, which they feel is not responsive enough to their interests and orientation. Only one-fourth of the under-30 men in our sample are both pro-union and pro-Democratic (compared to two-fifths of all other workers). The disjuncture between the young workers and this Establishment may also be reflected in the fact that more young than old workers call themselves "liberal." Older workers tend to be more pro-union and pro-Democratic.

Our interviews with these workers confirm the analysis of a much larger sample by Irving Crespi (1971) who has shown the demographic sources of the preference for Wallace to be heavily loaded in the direction of the young manual workers regardless of region. If the young worker in our sample voted at all (and less than 60% compared to nearly 90% of the 55+ workers did vote), he was much more likely than his old peers to have voted in 1968 for George Wallace. By a ratio of nearly 6 to 1 (23% versus only 4%), young workers compared to the oldest workers, chose the one prominent candidate that year who seemed to challenge the Establishment.

This portrait points to the possibility that the decreasing power of the Democrats and Republicans to attract the young electorate (especially in the white working class) will be a basis of strength for any number of new political party offshoots whose candidates capture the imagination and give vent to the frustrations and aspirations of a significant minority of the new, young, white worker. The added millions of voters under 21 (and the other millions of slightly older ones too young to have voted in 1968) make a new ball game for the political arena of 1972 and thereafter.

We need to know much more about the socioeconomic and the social-psychological characteristics of the young Wallace voter from the working class, but precious little is being done to find out what those traits are. Our limited evidence suggests that, compared to other young workers, they are typically from smaller urban areas; are more likely to feel that they are further behind in the things they wanted out of life as compared to ten years ago and compared to what they had hoped for when they finished school; earn lower wages than the non-Wallace young workers; feel less politically effective; and consider themselves "liberal" just as much as the other voters (and reject the two major parties, naturally). Few of them feel their union is helpful; they are much less concerned with problems of pollution as an important political issue. They enjoy much lower family incomes (even though their education levels are higher). Finally, they are dissatisfied with their jobs more frequently than the young workers voting for other political candidates than Wallace.

This brings us full circle to jobs. The young workers in general, but the Wallace voters in particular, are more difficult to mollify when it comes to employment in what we might consider "demeaning" tasks. The young Wallace voters also, incidentally, suffer from more unemployment than other workers. Employment in such jobs, with high unemployment risks and with dissatisfying work tasks, does not contribute very much to the development of the now resurrected virtues of a "work ethic." Such an ethic cannot be created through presidential sermons about there being no such thing as a demeaning job. They can only be created through national economic policies that lead to full employment, intelligent occupational planning (by society and by individuals), and a greater priority on the importance of structuring the world of work so that jobs containing little in the way of providing dignity and meaningfulness are reduced to a bare minimum.

REFERENCES

CARTER, M. (1966) Into Work. Baltimore: Penguin.

CRESPI, I. (1971) "Structural sources of the George Wallace constituency." Social Sci. Q. (June).

TURNER, A. and P. LAWRENCE (1965) Industrial Jobs and the Worker: An Investigation of Response to Task Attributes. Boston: Harvard School of Business.

5

WHAT DO YOUNG WOMEN WANT?

ELIZABETH BRALY SANDERS

Women represent approximately 53% of the population of the United States. To ask the question "What do women want?" cuts across all human divisions, except those reserved for dividing men exclusively. Sex qualifying rules (sometimes called sex roles) are attached to almost every position in society. This, in itself, is significant in considering what women want, for when this "group"—which permeates more completely than any other (except men), all parts of society—becomes self-conscious, publicly organizes itself, and begins to ask for change, the pervasiveness of changes needed to accommodate the dissatisfactions becomes evident.

What dissatisfied women want cannot be easily summarized. Women's needs often differ according to which of various segments of the population they identify themselves

AUTHOR'S NOTE: *The author has gathered the impressions included here through four sources: direct association as a member over a period of one year with young women who are active members in Women's Liberation; discussions with groups of high school and college students* with. Various differences which have divided women in the women's movement (for example: age, race, class, work value systems, educational level, life styles, and child-rearing attitudes—each of which is considered below) clearly indicate that women's needs are not monolithic.

Despite these divisions, women have not given up the attempt to organize around areas of common interest. In the process, we are gaining a tolerance for differences among us that has been sadly lacking in the past, and that may well be a sign that the future we hope for is not so impossible. Many of us feel we are coming to a new understanding and appreciation of our differences along with our similarities. We hope to spread this understanding through the whole society—to create a new tolerance and appreciation for the rights and dignity of human individuality, and in turn to create a society with goals consonant with this attitude. The awareness of conflicts among women who are beginning to value each other because they are women leads us to examine possible social changes which would reduce these conflicts. Thus through examination of women's dissatisfactions may arise a social consciousness more unified then any previously experienced. This is one potential of the women's movement.

There are desires which are common to many dissatisfied women *because they are women*. Many women are dimly aware of, some more conscious of, and others raging about the sex-imposed discrepancy between the state of their lives and their personal goals. The focus differs from person to person: some are concerned about the state of the world and connect this to the fact that persons with masculine styles have usually controlled intergroup relations in the past; some are concerned with the blatant sex discrimination of our legal

---

in which I acted as a representative of Women's Liberation; specific inquiry of individual young women informants in the context of preparing this paper; and exposure to the literature of the women's movement. Although much of the information comes from my involvement in Women's Liberation, this paper does not represent all the views of women in the women's movement.

codes; some are concerned with what seem arbitrary definitions according to sex of appropriate and inappropriate
involvements in the home, at work, in political organizations,
in religious institutions, or in other organizations; some are
concerned about pressure to conform to sex-typed cognitive
and personality styles; some are concerned about the
interference with the quality of human relationships caused
by sexual and sex role definitions of persons; some are
concerned about how reproduction and child-rearing relates
to sex roles; some are concerned about their economic
insecurity and consequent state of dependence on men; some
are concerned with their inability to get work relevant to
their training, or training commensurate with their abilities;
some are concerned with the lack of available information
organized around such questions as "How are the sexes
different, and why?" and "Given that I am a woman, what
can I expect my life to be like, and why?"

In short: Dissatisfied women are concerned that we can, or
want to do things we are not allowed to do because of our
sex; and that we cannot, or do not want to, do things we are
expected to do because of our sex. Many of us extend this
concern to include similar discrimination against males who
are troubled by their sex roles. Women are coming to
understand that we can contribute much more than the
society has appreciated, and to see how both men and
women have been brainwashed to accept definitions of
ourselves as incomplete human beings due to our sex.

If women have been denied due to their sex the privilege
and responsibility of economic independence, intellectual
development, full public life, and leadership roles in the past,
it is no less true that men, due to their sex, have been denied
the privileges and responsibilities of child-rearing, personal
self-sufficiency, full emotional lives, and justification for
certain esthetic and leisurely activities. Together, some men
and women have begun to question whether these imbalances
imposed by our past understanding of sex roles are not

detrimental to us all. Women are saying not only that they have been deprived in comparison to their male counterparts, but that males, too, have had limited options available in life due to their sex.

Having summarized the general areas on which women's dissatisfactions focus, we turn to a consideration of how the needs of some of the segments of the population of women in the United States fit together and possible changes to meet these dissatisfactions. We will then consider how policy-making relates to these changes. Since we are primarily concerned with women among our youth, we will start with a consideration of age.

AGE

For purposes of preparing this paper, informants from two age groups—17-19 and 22-24—were consulted.

Age as a variable is meaningful as an ordered series of developmental states or transitions which everyone passes through at the same chronological periods in a lifespan. As such, its earlier stages, being more consistent across individuals, and across social groups, are more meaningfully categorized chronologically than are its later stages. As age increases, there is less monthly or yearly consistency in changes which can be expected by individuals in a cohort due to their age. As age increases, the use of a chronological index as a meaningful developmental variable becomes more and more fraught with other differentiations within age categories that obscure the influence of purely chronological categories of age.

Developmental stages occur in combination, not singly. For instance, women in the first age bracket with which we are concerned (17-19) are in various stages with regard to a number of developmental strands in their life; such as dating, marriage, schooling, development of individual self-concept, group identifications, future orientation and planning, occupational status, breadth of social experience, available family structure, independence desired, independence experienced, and others. There is even more variation among women in our second group, the 22- to 24-year-old bracket, with regard to the combined stages of development within these strands. This diversification of individuals in age cohorts will continue as life unfolds.

The first age group (17-19) with which we are concerned holds in common the transition accompanying completion of the years when being a high school student is the expected occupation with which a good portion of each weekday is filled. The second age group (22-24) is not nearly so homogeneously defined by our society as the first. Of those who continued uninterrupted in the educational process, it is an age of similar termination of classification as a student, this time with a bachelor's degree. But for a large portion of young women, college is not a part of experience in early adulthood. For all, these are years of transition to less adolescent, more adult self-concepts, and social expectations.

More and more we hear young women raising questions about this very transition, concerned about the meaning of assuming an adult role in this culture. Many of these women are alienated from the only available social forms they find. They take themselves, their lives, and their role in society seriously.

Where does such a young woman go when privacy is at a minimum; yet in her public isolation, she is constantly pressed to keep her voice sweet, her face smiling, her manner pliant, her hair groomed, and her diet-rite body adorned in layer after layer of currently stylish make-up, scent, and clothing in correct combination; when she is bombarded with ads reflecting an ideal image of the American woman with an outdated preoccupation with housework, superficial sexuality, cigarettes, and soda pop (or beer)? Often she pays the price of human companionship. She conforms to the latest fads, to greater or lesser degrees. She lives her life as best she can, making whatever compromises with the stereotypes of the past she feels she must to avoid ostracism. Given this state of affairs, young women sometimes have a short-range focus on life; what many young women say they want is confused by present preoccupations with getting a husband, a particular boyfriend, a date, or just having fun before the responsibilities of adulthood descend on them.

Yet, for many, thought processes have begun to lead to questions which pose conflicts within these very activities. Beyond the immediacy of the dating and marrying world, young women across the nation are beginning to look ahead, to question what promise life holds for an American woman in the next fifty years or so. That such thought is growing in importance is evidenced by the increasing numbers of women's organizations operating under such rubrics as Fem Lib, Women's Liberation, and so forth, on high school and college campuses across the nation, by the flood of feminist literature on the market these days, and by the new pressure for women's studies programs and response to that pressure by a gradual opening of this new field as one of legitimate professional and policy-making interest.

What are the issues these women are raising? What do these women want?

The most common response of my informants to the question "What do young women want," has been to mention the feeling that being thought of as "young" and therefore less important than other adults is objectionable to them. This status classification has been noted in the literature of social science, and aptly dubbed "age-ism" — taking its place beside sexism and racism. "Age-ism is prejudice by members of one age group against another group (or groups); it implies stereotyping, interpersonal distance, and often, conflict of interest"(Bengston, 1970). A respect for the young as equals would represent an attitudinal change of great depth in a society so deeply authoritarian as is ours. The response of youth to the adult authoritarian coalition has been to form its own coalition, rejecting adults as equal human beings. Some young people are aware of the similarity of the positions of youth and adults in this process, each being a form of age-ism. They see one answer to this problem in the search for nonauthoritarian structures considered below in the discussion of social class.

Since the educational system and the family have dominated their lives at the ages under consideration, many see their strongest objectives in terms of changing these particular institutions. Some see these socializing units as basically sound, with a need for change in the information passed through them to the individual. Others see the institutions themselves as obsolete and irrelevant. Along with these concerns about the immediate impact of the educational and familial institutions is a concern about the lack of continuity provided by those institutions for participation in the adult world of work and the family. This problem has been noted in the literature of social science as well (Komaravsky, 1952).

Some of the thought of women on problems which affect youth in education and in the family is considered below. However, before taking up the issues of the family, work, and education, we will consider other divisions that cut across our age groups, and the implications of these divisions for women's goals as a group.

RACE

Martha—how old you—eighteen? What you want to do in life? What you want to be?

I don't want to have to ask nobody for nothing. I want to be able to take care of my own self.

Then what are you doing on Welfare?

What else I gon do? Go out and scrub somebody else's toilets like my mamma did so Larry can run wild like I did? No. I stay on Welfare awhile, thank you [Williams, 1970].

The concept of race in American culture is confused with the concept of status or class. The culture associated with the dominant white race is often thought of as the American culture, and other cultures are called subcultures. The most vocal of these other cultures is the black culture, and we cite below some of the problems black women see differently from white women within the context of the women's movement. What black women say is often applicable to other nonwhite cultural groups in America as well.

Black women in the movement often tell us they consider their oppression to come from three value systems: first, from racial prejudice; second, from social class stigma; and third, from male chauvinism—that they are in triple jeopardy. They also tell us that they know the operations of race and class to keep the black woman "in her place" are closely related. Because of the multiple sources of oppression for black women, the removal of any one of them by achievement of equality still leaves much to be desired: if black women become equal to white women, they are still not going to be equal to men. Black women see their problem as more complex than that of white women. They have often learned economic self-sufficiency, but they suffer the pain of seeing their men unable to get work. They recognize that they themselves suffer indignity through the male chauvinism of the black man, but they understand his pain, and how it has intensified his lack of respect for the humanity of the black woman, as well as for himself.

Given that equality is often thought of in terms of individual economic status, it is limited in a competitive economic system by the number and status of jobs available. The implication of giving more jobs to women from a limited job market is that fewer men will have jobs. Black women understand that the likely effect of such a change without extensive changes in racial relations would be to leave even more black men jobless than is already the case. Black women are not eager to see the black man further degraded by such a state of affairs. For this reason, black women are concerned first about job discrimination based on race and class before job discrimination based on sex.

Some white women see this issue as important also. Our goal is not to gain equality by further suppression of the black people, but to create equality for all.

SOCIAL CLASS

The two major differentiating components of social class will here be considered economic controlling power and class value systems. Both are divisive forces among women.

Economic control: A major source of the stigma attached to joblessness, considered above in the discussion of race, is the accompanying economic powerlessness. Many women are unwilling to accept the assumption that a person's status should be measured by the money or wealth the person controls; however, aside from the status attached to higher-paying jobs, a higher-paying job means a chance to exert more control over one's life, by choosing how to spend one's pay. And no job at all means practically no control.

Women understand where the following reasoning leaves them in terms of self-sufficiency: A married woman has an income through her husband, therefore she does not need a job; if a married woman is hired, her income along with her husband's will put her in an income bracket above that of the families of the men she works with on the same job, and the men would not feel right about that, so it is best not to hire her and stir up problems with those already employed in male-dominated fields; a single woman will probably get married and quit; a recently married woman will probably get pregnant and quit; a woman who has taken a maternity leave will need retraining, whereas a man does not need these extended leaves—hire a man, if possible; women do not succeed so well as men, therefore give men priority in training and hiring.

Women do not get hired at all in many fields. In others, they get hired, but they get paid less than men for doing the same jobs. The jobs available to women in general carry lower pay and lower status than those available to men. The kind of work available to women, as well as to men, is also tied to the individual's social status. The competition among women for jobs adds to the effect of differential status attached to the social class value systems discussed below, as a divisive force among women.

The result of all these attitudes combined is that women are left in positions of economic dependence and lowered job status which has nothing to do with them as individuals, but which contributes to feelings of inadequacy and inferiority and interferes with performance, producing a self-fulfilling prophecy: women do not succeed as well as men. Possible solutions to this problem are developed in the discussion of work ideologies below.

Value systems: The value systems which are associated with differing socioeconomic classes are densely interwined with sex roles. To attack the sex roles is to attack a part of the structure of the value systems themselves. Much in common is also found across classes in the sex roles. In attempting to develop new structures to take the place of the sex roles, much is learned about how society is put together. Learning to value women as individuals transfers to learning to value social class members as individuals. An attempt is being made in the women's movement to reach the point where value systems may be viewed as simply different rather than evaluated as better and worse or higher and lower. The part of the value systems of the classes which makes power or authority or status cumulative is objectionable to women: Why should a person who has authority and therefore control in one institutional situation be assumed the appropriate person to control in other situations, especially outside that institution or organization? Why should men always hold the superior decision-making positions? Why should decision-making power in one area lead to control in others? Why should more wealth control mean more power? Why should a person who likes rock music and dresses in work clothes be considered less knowledgeable and responsible than one who likes Mozart and spends money on formal clothing? If one removes the status differential from social class, the concept of class as we know it is drastically changed.

Women do not accept past social processes and structures as necessarily resulting from "the nature of man," except in a historical sense. We believe change is possible. We are interested in evolving nonauthoritarian structures. The small groups of the women's movement could be viewed as workshops for the future. We have found how exciting equality can be. Through conscious attempts to create situations in which no one person can be identified as the leader, we seem to find everyone contributing more and feeling good about it. There is much to learn about the human potential for functioning in nonauthoritarian structures. We would like to think that the division of labor which grows out of such structures can escape the status connotations of the past—that a nonauthoritarian society is possible. We are certain that a *less* authoritarian society is possible.

Experience and knowledge in specialized areas may be recognized as making an individual valuable in cooperating to reach certain goals without an overemphasis on status differentials. Everyone's contribution is important in cooperation. Such an argument, however, has often been misused to convince women to accept more than our share of work which no one wants to do.

WORK IDEOLOGY

Some women want to work outside the home. Others do not. The system which supports those who do not is based on a very old family form. It allows women to be used as a marginal labor force when there are not enough men around to fill the jobs available. This adds to the discontinuity of women's careers, which is used as one argument against hiring them when men are available.

Some women and some men like to work with children and do domestic work. Others do not. Many women are dissatisfied because they feel little control over their life involvements. Since there are not, as the economy is presently organized, sufficient jobs for everyone, some economic reorganization will be necessary for women (and men) to be satisfied. Factors other than women's dissatisfaction in the economy are already pointing to reorganization: the presence of worker alienation is one; the technological lag created by the demand that as many jobs as possible be retained, although they are obsolete, is another. A woman may find herself, along with many men, doing jobs which she is well aware could be done by machines much more efficiently, but she does the job if she can get it in order to have the money that will allow her some control over other areas of her life.

Given the level of technological advancement which this society has reached, no person should have to spend time doing many of the more boring, repetitious tasks which are low-paid and traditionally low-status and which may contribute to one's sense of powerlessness and meaninglessness. Dissatisfied women want everyone to feel the benefits of the level of technological achievement which humanity has now reached, rather than a few (mainly men) now in control, who seem to be using much technology in destructive rather than in creative ways.

In order that everyone is integrated into the technology of the age, training and retraining programs must be open to all who do not have the skills to do what they want and what it is agreed needs to be done. If everyone has training to do desirable work, undesirable jobs could be distributed in such a way that everyone had some undesirable work to do along with the desirable, rather than some people having none and others having all undesirable work.

Given a limited number of jobs and a surplus of prospective employees, equal job distribution will require a reorganization of the ideology concerning work. Full equal employment would either require that we create "part-time" jobs for everyone or stagger employment for everyone. Such a reorganization of the economy would require a redefinition of the meaning of work, which is now confused with the meaning of money and with the value of the individual human being—people who work full-time or for more money being considered more important than those who work part-time or for less, and both being considered more important than those who cannot get work at all. In a full employment economy, the right of every individual not to work as well as the right to work will probably be important.

Adding every healthy adult woman to the work force would also create jobs which have not been paid for in the past—those of child care and domestic work, which women have traditionally performed for no pay at all. Included in training available should be training in child care skills.

CHILD CARE VALUES

The pregnant woman is doing a service to society. She is using her physical self for nine months in the job of supporting a new member of the human race. As she is doing a job that must be done for humanity as a whole (as well as for particular societies) to survive, she should be recognized and honored for her work. It is the opinion of many women that she should be paid, financially, as well, by the society which will socialize her offspring into membership. Instead she is, even in contemporary America, shunned and usually deprived of financial benefit (through employment) *because* she is pregnant, or even because she might get pregnant or married.

After she is delivered of the child, it is assumed to be her responsibility to provide for it, or, if she is married, her husband helps her with the financial responsibility. With the instability of marriage as an institution, more and more women find themselves faced through divorce or separation with the full responsibility for society's children. This responsibility in combination with the second-class status of women in the job market is not what socialization has prepared most women for. And it is no longer the kind of life women are prepared to accept without complaint and concerted remedial action.

In order that women shall be considered equal to men in the work force, child care for working parents must become a part of the economic planning of the nation. Industries are seriously considering day care institutions in response to women's demands (see Urban Research Corporation, 1970). Given the necessity for new child care institutions, two major questions arise; one is the quality of care available, and the other is, who is going to pay for this care?

Many women are determined not to allow industry to provide inferior baby-sitting services in order to keep their women workers docile. Instead, they point out that child care is a very special kind of work – that all our children deserve the highest-quality care and training possible. We must provide adequate funds to pay dedicated personnel for child care.

In trying to plan acceptable child care services, many questions arise concerning the meaning of parenthood and how children fit into the family and world of tomorrow. These questions seem to come down to a single summary question: "Whose are our children?" Many women, especially young women who were not so long ago children, would like to answer, "Our children belong to themselves," but in reality we recognize that our own socialization makes it very difficult to operate in such a way that our actions represent that position.

In turning children over to child care institutions, a parent relinquishes a part of the traditional socializing function of the family. This raises the whole issue of the meaning of parenthood. The issues of tolerance and authoritarian relationships are more strongly related to the family than any other institution in the society. A part of the meaning of parenthood in the past has been the control over what values children are exposed to. The age at which complete control is exercised by the family has been gradually diminishing, with the advent of public schools and kindergartens. Many of the values that women are working so hard to create in themselves—especially the appreciation of social differences—could have been learned in earlier life, had we been exposed to these differences in positive interchanges with other children, and had an effort been made to eliminate actions and statements based on prejudiced assumptions in our presence. Most parents are not ready to relinquish all control over what experiences their own children are exposed to, and many are concerned about what experiences children in general are to have in day care institutions.

Among those interested in day care, it is generally assumed that parents need to have some choice available as to which kind of centers their children will have, and, indeed, whether they choose to send their children into these centers; that parents who choose to provide their own child care should be paid for so doing, since child care is a part of society's work; that objectives of child care centers must be clear and public; that parents should be allowed some time to observe their children in the centers; and that parents should have some influence over the policies of the centers.

The question of who will pay for day care is related to the question of to whom the responsibility for children belongs. Our children represent humanity's future. Placing the total responsibility for children on the nuclear family unit or on the individual mother who bears them is a haphazard way of providing for the future. Some broader planning should be undertaken to see that every child is provided for to the fullest of the society's ability. The term "society," used this way, however, represents a dodge; for it can mean a local group with a single institutional network, a city, a state, a nation, the world, or perhaps someday a universe. Our humanity may be as broad or as narrow as we choose to define it.

Related to the question of child care and responsibility for children is the question of child-bearing and who makes the decision as to when and whether particular adults procreate. Some women see this question in terms of controlling their own bodies; some see it in terms of population control; some see it in terms of genocide; and some see it in combinations of these three. The questions of birth control (including abortion) and sterilization are very much related to the issues of child responsibility, economic systems, racism, and nationalism. What women want in this area varies a great deal, but in general we want information about our bodies and the right to make our own individual decisions about bearing children. We also want men and the broader society to assume their share of the concern and responsibility for providing a good life for our children as well. Many women agree that different individuals should be able to take different parts of this responsibility without sex-typing the specializations of the task. Others remain traditional in the sex role division of labor in child-rearing.

Young women see these problems as relevant to their own lives in the future. They base their ideas on the experiences they themselves have had as children in the family and as partners to men in the dating world. Some see one potential for change in women's studies programs, which is further developed in the discussion of education below.

LIFE STYLES

Some women grow more and more uncomfortable with the life styles available to them in the present American culture as they become conscious of the prejudice and discrimination against them embedded in their surroundings. Women want to work on changing their own lives to be consistent with what they believe about the nature of women. They recognize that to a large extent women are what we believe they are. Many women are now ready to work on creating for themselves lives more consistent with what they believe.

Most women do not want to become "like men." We do not reject all traits that have in the past been labelled "feminine," nor do we reject the masculine either, except where we find masculine styles are destructive to other human beings. Certain styles are emerging as possibly more comfortable and productive than some of those traditionally associated with males. These could perhaps be labelled cooperative (as opposed to competitive) or nonauthoritarian.

Because few men are willing to work on living nonauthoritarian lives, some women are trying to withdraw from interdependence with males, in order to share this experience with each other. Of course, males control so much of the technology, the money, the jobs, and the means of production in the broader society, it is presently impossible for women totally to withdraw from interaction with males, and maintain the technological base necessary to have the freedom to innovate in other areas. Some women are ready to withdraw to women's communes, lesbian life styles, or living alone to escape the interference of male and sex role definitions in their lives. They are often bitter and exhausted from dealing with a society that denies them human dignity. The alternatives available are perhaps as difficult as the original source of frustration. Financial support remains a crucial issue. Women who are willing to do without males in their personal lives are not considered normal. In the work world, this is an additional strike against them in gaining and holding employment, and women do often find it difficult to be self-sufficient in areas traditionally thought of as masculine. All their lives they have been socialized to believe that they are deficient in areas which they need to develop in order to survive alone.

Some women have withdrawn with men from the broader culture as much as possible to create alternative life styles. One of the changes among them is often a conscious attempt to avoid sex role and family role influence in the assignment of living tasks and responsibilities. There are both women and men who want to learn to be more self-sufficient in the skills of everyday living, and to specialize in chosen activities because they like them rather than because they are male or female. These new cultural forms, often called communes, are not broadly accepted in society. Pressure is often applied to individuals participating in them to give them up.

Some women believe that sexism can only be eliminated by withdrawing from the existing culture and creating a new culture. Many believe that the present culture will not allow such withdrawal. Others desire changes within the present culture which will create opportunities for women to be more thoroughly integrated into the world of work and be economically self-sufficient. All over the country, small groups of adults, with children sometimes involved, are experimenting with new cultural forms which allow everyone more flexibility in work and in how they spend their time. Often included in the plans or activities of these cultural reform groups are innovative educational and child care institutions.

EDUCATION

The schools and colleges function in American culture as a major socializing institution. They channel young people into their adult roles; they also function as training agencies; and they provide a framework for independent learning experiences.

As socializing agencies, the schools are subject to the same scrutiny of dissatisfied women as are the family and potential new child care institutions.

As channeling agencies, the schools function most overtly through counseling activities. Counselors are aware, however, that teachers also impart attitudes about life planning (see a book entitled *New Approaches to Counseling Girls in the 1960's*). Women are often channelled into courses in home economics, and secretarial and clerical skills, while men are encouraged to go into the sciences or more technical areas, and to learn to do woodworking and shop. Women are encouraged to choose less ambitious courses and colleges. Awareness of the meaning of the educational process in the context of an individual's life seems to occur largely in retrospect. My informants in the 22- to 24-year-old age group who had not finished college were often into a period of discontinuity in their work lives, when their children were small. Those who wanted to return to school saw school as training for work. Others who had begun to work felt that their schooling was not very relevant to the work they were doing. Those in school mentioned problems with dating. If they liked their schoolwork, it was usually because they found it intrinsically interesting, rather than because they felt it was preparing them for future work; but if they did not like it, they usually mentioned its irrelevance to living their lives.

Much of the socializing in the schools takes place among the students as peers, rather than between authority figures and students. Most of the women informants felt much was lacking in male-female relationships among their peers. They felt the need of realistic sex education, with an emphasis on training in human relations. Such training would probably lead to the elimination of popularity contests which treat women as ornaments and sex objects rather than as complete human beings.

Jennie Bull (1970) points out that "schools view women's education as training for subservience rather than as equipping her to choose her own potential by exploring a wide range of possibilities." She also notes that teachers often degrade women in ways similar to those in which blacks have been degraded in the classroom, and proposes these teachers should be fired.

Women are often uncomfortable with the pressure for competition, status consciousness, conformity, and authoritarian obedience which is present in the educational system. In the article cited above, Ms. Bull observes

The aggressiveness and competitiveness with which men [are taught to] relate to each other and to intellectual things is a long way from the human ideal of respect for people, as equals. . . . The woman who does not accept the inferiority assigned to her must also reject the competitive male role and learn how to relate to her mind in a *human* way, allowing her to share ideas with people, rather than using her mind as a weapon or status symbol.

Some feel strongly that the school does not provide a favorable atmosphere for learning. They often question the compulsory attendance laws, feeling that a better learning situation might be created outside the existing schools.

Again, the withdrawal from existing institutions in an attempt to create a more satisfying social system is often proposed as a solution to the problem. Corrections to the exisiting institutions are also proposed, but it is pointed out that much of the problem is at the personal and interpersonal level and cannot be changed through formal means.

The introduction of women's studies programs in all institutions of learning would create more possibility for correcting the situation at the personal level, by exposing both women and men to information about women which is left out of the traditional curriculum. However, as was pointed out at the Women's Conference on Education for Liberation sponsored by the Committee to Defend the Right to Learn, in New York City, May 1970, the value of allowing traditional institutions which have never treated women fairly to control such programs is questionable. Women know that they could probably do the job better outside the institutions, and yet there is hesitation to withdraw.

POLICY IMPLICATIONS

While it is not the business of policy makers to change attitudes, it is their business to interfere with suffering caused by intolerance. It is their business to create situations for the groups of our citizens who have values inconsistent with the majority, but consistent with human rights, so that these future-oriented individuals can make their contributions with as little suffering as possible for differences with the past.

There is no level of policy-making that does not have implications for women, yet many policies are made only with men in mind. If we are concerned about women's rights, we must consciously make an effort to examine every policy for its probable effect on women until we have learned to include women automatically in our policy-making decisions. For this purpose, women should be consulted, not men.

Focusing on particular areas of policy-making, we will now suggest some specific changes that seem consistent with women's rights. The following areas in which policy-making relates to young women's lives will be considered: educational policy; economic policy (including employment policy and job-training policy); and population policy. These recommendations are based on arguments developed earlier in this paper:

A. Educational Policy

(1) Teach women and men the skills they have not learned in the past due to sexist assumptions, including home management and creative home crafts (the old home economics and shop), and sports.

(2) Encourage a representative proportion of males to females enrolled in all classes and courses of study.

(3) Provide high-quality sex education programs in schools, colleges, and community programs, sex education which includes a strong human relations element.

(4) Rewrite textbooks and children's books, removing sexist statements and pictures.

(5) Introduce women's studies programs into all educational institutions.

(6) Distribute the same information concerning career planning to both men and women.

B. Economic Policy

(1) Remove sex and personal details as criteria for filling work positions and retaining personnel. In general, treat persons as individuals, not as unequal parts of a family unit in making job distribution decisions.

(2) Remove sex as a relevant factor in determining who receives financial support for training.

(3) In job distribution, stop assuming women are weak, and men are strong. Some people are more muscular than others. Those who choose to use their muscles should be encouraged to do so. If their bodies are not strong, they should not be forced to do heavy physical work, such as scrubbing floors, shovelling snow, lifting children, and digging ditches.

(4) Redistribute economic remuneration to reflect the recognition that child care and housekeeping are work which benefits society and as legitimate a kind of involvement for anyone of either sex as sitting at a desk pushing papers or digging ditches.

(5) Pay women for the work they do bearing children.

(6) Remove the stigma, temporary assumption, and low pay associated with part-time and odd-hours work for both men and women.

(7) Create reeducation programs for women (and men) who want to reenter the job market but have no job-relevant skills.

C. Population Policy

(1) Fund living experiments for cultural change and study the implications for future population distribution. Innovation in family and living styles is obviously here. Why not deal with the change creatively and publicly rather than treating it as a scandal?

(2) Create community study programs to disseminate the latest information concerning birth control and population control, in order to allow individuals to make more controlled and informed decisions concerning reproduction.

YOUNG WOMEN AND THE FUTURE

Women want many things. The most summarizing principle of the present women's liberation movement would seem to be humanistic revolution. This means that women in the movement entertain the possibility of creating a humanistic society; that is, society which is organized around the principle that producing the greatest possible human dignity for every member from birth to death is the primary goal of society.

Human dignity rests on the assumption of partial self-determination, limited by the interference with or destructiveness of other human lives, and human products. What young women seem to be saying they want is a right, or at least a hope, for more self-determination in their lives than has in the past been possible. Since human society is a cooperative endeavor which imposes control from outside the individual, the only way to maintain dignity in society is to create a society in which each human being participates voluntarily because the advantages of cooperation to reach common goals are recognized.

Many young women want to help create a society in which they feel it is to their positive advantage to cooperate; in which women—and men—have more options available as to how we will live our lives; in which we are not told what we should or should not do or feel or want because we are women, rather than because we are human and have decided together to cooperate with other human beings; in which we cooperate to create things we want rather than to avoid punishment; and in which all human life is supported in equal state of dignity—dignity which will allow human beings better to fulfill our creative potential together.

Young people are asking the chance to try to live their lives consistently with their values. To do this, some are withdrawing from large parts of the culture they have been presented by their forefathers and investing their very lives in cultural experimentation. Many are continuing to push for change more within the present institutional structures. The policy makers of the nation cannot create many of the changes required, for much of the work of women's liberation, or human liberation, must be done at the personal level. Policy makers can, however, create situations more favorable to personal change.

Without some drastic changes at both the policy and personal levels, young women will continue to find themselves caught up in a life cycle they have not been led to anticipate. Those who do question the culture will continue to feel helpless and alienated, accompanied by various degrees of frustration. Emotional acting out against their subhuman definition will continue. Women will continue to evidence a high degree of neurotic behavior based on pent-up rage. The degree to which women's rage against injustice can be organized into effective cultural change, political action, violent action, or passive resistance will become more apparent. It is my opinion that very effective organization can be accomplished and that, for women, new progress is in sight within the decade. I do not think that young women will be content to remain silent and suffer through these years.

REFERENCES

ALLEN, P. (1970) Free Space: A Perspective in Women's Liberation. Albany, Calif.: Women's Liberation Basement Press.

DE BEAUVOIR, S. (1952) The Second Sex. New York: Alfred A. Knopf.

BENGSTON, V. (1970) "The generation gap: a review and typology of social psychological perspectives." Youth and Society 2, 1: 7-32.

BULL, J. (1970) "High school women: oppression and liberation," pp. 95-195 in Women's Liberation: Blueprint for the Future. New York: Ace.

FOOTE, N. (1969) "Changing concepts of masculinity," pp. 141-153 in C. Broderick and J. Bernard (eds.) The Individual, Sex, and Society. Baltimore: Johns Hopkins Press.

HOWE, J. (1971) Female Studies: No. 2. Pittsburgh: Know, Inc.

KOMARAVSKY, M. (1952) "Cultural contradictions and sex roles," in E. Schuler et al., Outside Readings in Sociology. New York: Thomas Y. Crowell.

KONOPKA, G. (1966) The Adolescent Girl in Conflict. Englewood Cliffs, N.J.: Prentice-Hall.

KRADITOR, A. [ed.] (1970) Up From the Pedestal: Selected Writings in the History of American Feminism. Chicago: Quadrangle.

MORGAN, R. (1970) Sisterhood is Powerful: An Anthology of Writings from the Women's Liberation Movement. New York: Vintage.

ROSSI, A. [ed.] (1970) John Stuart Mill and Harriet Taylor Mill: Essays on Sex Equality. Chicago: Univ. of Chicago Press.

TANNER, L. [ed.] (1970) Voices from Women's Liberation. New York: New American Library.

TOBIAS, S. (1970) Female Studies: No. 1. A Collection of College Syllabi and Reading Lists. Pittsburgh: Know, Inc.

Urban Research Corporation (1970) Proceedings of the Conference on Industry and Day Care. Chicago.

WILLIAMS, S. (1970) "Tell Martha not to moan," pp. 42-55 in T. Cade (ed.) The Black Woman, An Anthology. New York: Signet.

Women, a Journal of Liberation (1971) How We Live and With Whom (Special issue) 2, 2.

6

DIONYSUS–CHILD OF TOMORROW
Notes on Postindustrial Youth

LAUREN LANGMAN

> Young people sometimes get rebellious ideas, but as
> they get older they ought to get over them and settle
> down.
>
> Agree_____Disagree
>
> —California F-Scale

The **"conflict of generations"** is deeply rooted in the human condition. Almost every society in history has been shocked by its offspring and has bemoaned the future. This tradition may be as persistent as reproduction, for it has continued to this very day. Critics of the left note that 1984 is only thirteen years away. They see today's youth as quixotic heroes battling the computerized, faceless, all-powerful, totalitarian state presaged by Orwell, C. W. Mills, Marcuse, Fromm, and others. The voices from the right take note of Ortega y Gassett and Eric Hoffer and fear for the imminent downfall of a society that allows the emergence of mobs of unwashed, oversexed, drug-crazed rabble who flaunt (established) authority and proselytize debauchery and rebellion on the mass media.

Judeo-Christian religion was predicted by prophecy in which divine revelation was made known. In our modern, secular society, the prophetic tradition has been carried on by sociology which plies this ancient trade under such names as social forecasting, futurology, extrapolation of current trends, social indicators, and the like. While clergymen, politicians, and newscasters make predictions, sociologists attempt to separate opinions from facts (*wertfrie,* in Weber's term) and employ scientific methods. The nature of the modern industrial state makes planning mandatory (Galbraith, 1967) and, therefore, prediction becomes necessary. Questions of urban design, education, social services, and occupational structure all require anticipation of population growth and life styles. Accordingly, a central question in the current study of youth concerns the future, what will become of today's youth, what tomorrow's will be like.

To answer such questions, we must begin with an understanding of the contemporary youth scene, a complete explanation of which is beyond the scope of this discussion. For purposes of exposition, certain problems cannot be dealt with. While intergenerational conflict has been present in many societies (Feuer, 1969), today's generation is a *new* phenomenon arising from unprecedented affluence, technology, and a consumption-oriented economy. As we shall demonstrate, this does not mean there is no continuity between the old dominant culture and the new counterculture. The "youth culture" or "counterculture" is actually a *subculture,* since it depends on the larger, dominant culture for its existence. The parental generation provides financial support, as well as providing offspring for membership. Many of the values of the counterculture are, in fact, values held by the dominant culture, though perhaps unconsciously. The counterculture is emergent in the highly industrial countries of the world. Though Vietnam may have acted as a catalyst for the emergence of the counterculture in the United States, similar factors have produced similar groups in Western Europe. These groups are not to be confused with traditional student movements or radical student movements in underdeveloped countries. Such groups seek a redistribution of political and economic power.

The counterculture seeks a fundamental transvaluation of ethics, alternate life styles, and transformations of consciousness.[1] The "youth culture," as we call it, is more of an ideology, theme, or style than a clearly designated group. Given the intrinsic pluralism of industrial society, adherents of the counterculture may well be a minority of youth when we consider all the squares, greasers, surfers, hot-rodders, bike-freaks, and such. Nevertheless, the "counterculture" is the trend-setting group of today's youth. Therefore, we must be especially cautious in the use of external designations of "membership." Length of hair, style of clothes, drug use, or sexual behavior cannot be used to differentiate the various patterns found. The final consideration of which we must be cognizant concerns the nature of explanation. Structural theories (Davis, Parsons) are as inadequate as psychological theories (Feuer, Bettelheim) for explaining student or youth movements; any single-factor theory is necessarily inadequate (Douglas, 1970).

Therefore, several problems will not be considered, though these conclusions may be subject to scrutiny. The contemporary youth culture or counterculture is:

(1) a new phenomenon, differing from traditional student political movements;

(2) a subculture rather than an independent culture;

(3) emergent in the advanced industrial nations;

(4) a minority of youth, albeit a trend-setting faction;

(5) a style or ideology rather than an external appearance;

(6) inexplicable on the basis of any single structural or psychological factor.

With the above observations in mind, we shall begin with a preliminary definition of "youth culture." Any culture is an integrated configuration of socially transmitted symbols, artifacts, values, and behaviors typical of a group, which differentiate that group from others. Every culture has a technological base (Steward, 1955), normative patterns of interaction, and forms of artistic expression. However, the counterculture is not a genuine culture, since it lacks its own historic tradition[2] and its own economic base. Since this "counterculture" cannot be defined in terms of external appearance, we should try to isolate its distinctive values and life styles which, however, must be considered in relation to the values of the dominant culture. Since both the dominant and countercultures are integral configurations, it may be convenient to use a typology that might clarify these two groups. An adequate typology not only exists, but has a lo tradition in sociology. The dominant culture can be seen Apollonian, while the counterculture might be Dionysian (Benedict, 1934; Gouldner and Peterson, 1962). Before it seems as if we have made a diversion to the philosophical speculations of Nietzsche or Spengler, let us examine these models in comparison with those of social science. Gouldner and Peterson (1962: 33) indicate nine factors that differentiate these polar types according to Nietzsche's *Birth of Tragedy and Genealogy of Morals.*

The Apollonian Model

(1) freedom from all extravagant urges, no excess, "nothing too much"

(2) rejection of all license

(3) stresses "cognitive modes of experience," reason, knowledge, and science

(4) hopeful, melioristic view of world

(5) activistic

(6) "the *principium individuationis,*" "know thyself"

(7) emphasizes the plastic arts

(8) maintains a compensatory belief in gods that lived (e.g., the Olympians)

(9) "It was not unbecoming for even the greatest hero to yearn for an afterlife "

The Dionysian Model

(1) a sense of "glorious transport," "rapture," "intoxication," "demoniac"

(2) "sexual promiscuity overriding . . . established tribal law"

(3) surrenders to "intuition" or "instinct"

(4) tragic view of world

(5) "loath to act"

(6) "the bond between man and man comes to be forged once more," "the vision of mystical oneness," surrender thyself

(7) emphasizes the "non-visual art of music"

(8) (?) acceptance of the "terrors and horrors of existence" without illusion

(9) acceptance of the dissolution of the self

Now let us examine the dominant values of the Western industrial man according to empirical sociological research from Weber's *Protestant Ethic* to Kluckhohn's work on value orientations (see also Kluckhohn and Strodtbeck, 1961; Langman, 1969). These designations are arbitrary and not necessarily mutually exclusive or otherwise independent. These categories have analytic utility and enable comparative analysis. They stand as ideal types (Weber).

Industrial Man

(1) *Rationality:* Suppression of primary process thought, deferred gratification pattern, avoidance of emotional (impulsive) expression. (See, that is, view, Grant Wood's *American Gothic.*) Basis of all technology and bureaucracy.

(2) *Self-reliance, independence, and individualism:* God helps those who help themselves, never depend on other people. Do it yourself. Highly individuated ego structure, internalized "guilt" controls. Personal responsibility.

(3) *Hard work as a moral calling, a beruf* (doing rather than being): Reliability, punctuality, utilitarian emphasis, goal-oriented activity as a prime virtue. Material accumulation as symbol of success.

(4) *Domination over nature:* The world is there to exploit and pollute, man can change the course of rivers, conquer space, diseases, and even destroy the world.

(5) *Future orientation:* Present has meaning only for realization of future goals, immediate experience subjugated to long-term utility, e.g., school → work → raise family → retire → wait to die → enter heaven. Based on economic model of saving → investment → growth. Past unimportant, "History is bunk" said Henry Ford.

It does not take a careful examination to notice the similarities between Nietzsche's Apollonian type and the empirical profile of the dominant American (industrial) values. Gouldner and Peterson (1962) found two dimensions of Apollonianism strongly associated with advanced technology, the individuated self, the Renaissance "heightening of the sense of self and a new spirit of individuality" (Gouldner and Peterson, 1962: 39), and a normative system of impulse control.

In our interpretation, the Apollonian factor entails a complex of norm-emitting, legitimating, surveying, and sanctioning arrangements, emerging as an adaptive response to the intensified social conflicts and growing problems of impulse management which were then occasioned by the growth of Neolithic technology, increasing stratification, and heightened individuality. There is in Apollonianism a development of norm-sending institutions such as ceremonial or ritual and of codified laws, as well as of groups and roles such as a powerful chieftainship, authoritative judges, a restricted council, and an organized priesthood bulwarked by beliefs in the attractiveness of the afterlife [Gouldner and Peterson, 1962: 51].

While there are substantial agreements between the Apollonian formulations of Nietzsche and the findings of Kluckhohn and Strodtbeck (1961) and Langman (1969), the almost identical concerns with impulse control and individuated selfhood must be noted.

In attempting to define the counterculture in terms of its dominant value orientations, it turns out that the counterculture's values are the polar *opposites* of those of the dominant industrial society.

Counterculture

(1) *Anti-rationality:* Impersonal bureaucracy (rational hierarchy) as one of the prime evils, impulse expression as good. These two are often combined in the form of messages inviting the reader or listener to "Fuck the establishment" or "1, 2, 3, 4, we don't want your fucking war." The latter is as much a protest against the advanced technology and impersonal, military bureaucracy as against the moral injustice of that involvement. This anti-rationality is seen in the new popularity of astrology, witchcraft, oriental philosophy.

(2) *Community, engagement, dependence:* Cooperation, involvement, sharing responsibility. These terms used by Slater (1970: 5) are preferable to "Collateral" used by Kluckhohn and Strodtbeck (1961). These terms suggest a diminution of the individualized, competitive, exploitive nature of interpersonal relationships in the urban industrial complex. Rather, the counterculture espouses *shared* assets and liabilities, communal living, living to help others rather than gain extrinsic reward (compare Rosenberg, 1957). A diminution of the extreme individualized ego or the *isolated* nuclear family structure is to be valued. Involvement in *shared* life experiences is seen as good. Note, for instance, that pot smoking is almost always a shared activity. Love is the most important feeling—toward all.

(3) *Hedonic self-expression preferable to goal-oriented activity* (being over doing): Do your own thing, emphasis on tactics—not goals. It doesn't matter what you do—only "Do It" (Jerry Rubin). A Mardi Gras atmosphere of festivity is extended to all life. Freaky clothes are in—no clothes even better. Material things—a drag.

(4) *Harmony with or subjugation to nature:* Back to the simple life—pre-technology, better a worm-bitten apple than one sprayed with paraffin and DDT. Enjoy nature, don't ruin it with an interstate highway, Howard Johnson's, and Holiday Inn. The belief in man's domination over nature now threatens thermonuclear Armageddon. Identification with traditional societies

such as American Indians, Pioneers, or Eastern Societies with pre-technological orientation such as Zen, Yoga, and Hinduism (not only pre-technological but communal). The goal of Satori is annihilation of the individual ego and unity with the cosmos.

(5) *Present orientation:* Immediate experience and sensation in *all* forms good for its own sake. Anti-utilitarian. Drugs and sex provide *good* experiences—therefore they need *no* justifications. There may not even be a tomorrow. Openness to all experience is valued. De-emphasis on cognition and verbal explanations like this paper. There is an emerging concern with the past, a nostalgia for pre-technological days of harmony with nature and community with one's fellows.

If we now go back to the values of the Dionysian model, we note the close parallel of these two approaches. This description of the counterculture is by no means exhaustive; in fact, these five values might warrant fuller discussion. There is nothing sacrosanct about the designation of Dionysian. I use it simply because it has not been used in this context and, therefore, should not evoke emotional responses. If one prefers to use Consciousness III (Reich, 1970), or any other such designation, one may use it.

The values of the counterculture have been found to a limited degree in every culture. In fact, those few societies with advanced technology may be unique in the relative absence of these values as a dominant orientation. What factors have led to the transition from these variant, if not deviant, orientations to a position of dominance among a sizable number of today's youth?

To answer this question, we must analyze values in general. Values are shared conceptions of desirable modes of conduct. Values are the standards by which objects, persons, or actions are judged. Values define the nature of reality (compare Parsons and Shils, 1951; Kluckhohn and Strodtbeck, 1961). Values then serve as regulatory mechanisms which enable societies to adapt to the environment and maintain those types of interpersonal relations conducive to the particular type of adaptation. Finally, values mediate the relation of the individual to society and, therefore, there are strong emotional attachments (cathexes) to the values of the group. The primary function of every society is adaptation (Malinowski, 1944; Aberle et al., 1950; Parsons and Smelser, 1956). Therefore values must be seen in terms of fostering maximal adaptation. The value orientations we described as Apollonian or Industrial are those most conducive to a capitalistic economic system. The "Protestant Ethic" values (Weber, 1905) not only fostered capitalism but science and technology (Merton, 1957). The fusion of business and technology led to the rapid proliferation of a production-oriented, capitalistic economy (Galbraith, 1958). The values that legitimated this system were then even more solidly entrenched—even by opponents of capitalism. The socialists and communists questioned ownership and distribution— never rationality, productivity, hard work, and the like. But capitalism was doomed to destruction, not by its failure but its success (Schumpeter, 1942). The growth of industry led to a separation of ownership and management which then occasioned the growth of bureaucratic administration. The transition from enterpreneurial to corporate capitalism also marked the emergence of consumerism, albeit retarded by the Depression and World War II. Since the war, a heretofore unprecedented economic system emerged.

Since World War II, the industrial nations have witnessed the growth of an *affluent,* consumer-oriented welfare state in which advanced technology not only creates abundant new products and services, but through mass media, instills needs for those products and services. The values that created this system could *not* maintain it. Yet, since values are internalized at early ages, they may be espoused long after they are inappropriate. Ogburn termed this the culture lag. The Industrial-Apollonian values conflict with the demands of the consumer economy.

Rationality is antithetical to the manipulation of consumer tastes—even when the manipulation is done rationally, and the products are created by use of the most advanced technology. Reason would warn against "buy now–pay later." The subversion of rationality began with concentration camps and the atomic bomb. The process was completed with the genocide in Vietnam. The widespread feelings of malaise, alienation, and anomie demonstrate that, while rational technology has provided unheard-of goods and services, most people feel the quality of life has deteriorated.[3]

Individualism cannot be maintained in a society in which mass production provides the majority of goods and even most of the services. Mass media transmit predigested experiences and interpretations to large numbers. Self-reliance is patent nonsense when 85% of the population are employees (Hsu, 1961).

Hard work ensured success in an economy of scarcity; in an affluent economy, the vast majority possess the symbols of success. This is especially true for today's young, who have enjoyed unprecedented affluence without *ever* having worked for it. It is no accident that most participants of the counterculture have enjoyed suburban homes, cars, travel, and so on.

The belief that man can infinitely exploit the natural resources is now being challenged. Air, water, space, and unspoiled natural areas have become scarce resources. To continue to believe that man can dominate nature without retaliation is suicidal.

In an economy based on "instant credit," saving for the future makes little sense.[4] The technology that produced the consumer's utopia also created the weapons that can destroy us all. Though we use the mechanism of "denial," we all agree that the future is problematic. The future promises neither stability nor realization of goals but "shock" (Toffler, 1970). We look to the past for a nostalgic glimpse of preconsumer society, which was peaceful and tranquil; murders happened on the radio or in movies, *never* nearby. Life was slower; entertainment was escapist. Human relationships provided some security and stability.

The growth of the affluent consumer welfare technocracy has not only challenged the Appollonian-Industrial values but the very ways in which the young are raised. While Freud and Spock are generally given the credit for "permissive" child-rearing, the transition from restrictive to permissive child-rearing is more likely due to the changes in the economic system (Wolfenstein, 1951; Miller and Swanson, 1958; Bronfenbrenner, 1961; Clausen, 1968). Just as the Appollonian-Industrial values conflict with affluent corporate capitalism, the achievement-oriented, independent captain of industry could no longer direct managerial teams of faceless bureaucrats. The dominant personality style of the consumer economy was more likely to be a cooperative, nonassertive, yet reliable organization man (Whyte, 1956). Upward mobility in the middle classes is more likely to be associated with the need for affiliation than achievement (Crockett, 1962).

Children born since World War II were more likely to be fed on demand than by schedule. Toilet training was relaxed, ego structure tended to be flexible, rather than rigid. These children were encouraged to express themselves rather than inhibit their "natural" tendencies. They were raised on a steady diet of television; this was the first generation in history raised in the affluent, consumer welfare state we have described.

The emergence of the counterculture was then based on two factors:

(1) the social consequences of an affluent, consumer-oriented technological economy and

(2) the changes in child-rearing practices (compare Roszak, 1969; Douglas, 1970; Scott and Lyman, 1970).

But one more factor must be considered: the counterculture seems to have sprung up overnight! The social and psychological changes were long-term, gradual increments.

To explain the rapidity of the transition, let us recall that the Apollonian-Industrial values were becoming less and less appropriate for the affluent consumer economy. But values learned early in life are recalcitrant to extinction (Bruner, 1956). Values can be cathected as strongly as persons;[5] more men have died in pursuit of ideological causes than in the pursuit of love. Since we have unconscious attachments to values, we must recall perhaps a most important insight of Freud—ambivalence. Love and hate, attraction-rejection are delicate balances and easily upset. Whenever we have a conscious desire, we are repressing an unconscious desire for the opposite. The strength of attraction to that which is forbidden is directly proportional to the strength to which the desire is denied. Thus, in every Apollonian, there is a repressed Dionysian and vice versa. The economic and psychological basis of Apollonianism began to deteriorate in the thirties. Young people, searching for and creating their identities, are generally more open to change than their parents. As Erikson has taught us, the identity of every generation shows a continuity with the past as well as an adaptation to current reality. At some time between the time of the Dionysian frenzy of Elvis Presley's pelvic gyrations and the occupation of Sproul Hall by the FSM, for many of the post-World War II generation, the delicate balance of opposing desires suddenly shifted. Apollo was dead; long live Dionysis.[6]

While this shift may have initially been limited to the children of the liberal, professional, upper-middle classes, sadly we must recall that there are many more followers than there are leaders. Due to many factors, including their intellectual capacities, mass media, and the like, the Dionysians have set the *tone* for today's youth. This phenomenon has spread to conservative parochial schools (Langman et al., 1971). Conservative mass merchandisers like Sears' and Ward's attempt to cater to the "new" styles. The youth culture is no longer limited to colleges; it can be found in every major Western European or American city. Whereas initially the youth culture was an upper-middle-class phenomenon, this is no longer true.

We have now attempted preliminary definition and explanation of the youth culture (from an Apollonian perspective, of course; no genuine Dionysian would attempt it). We now come to the major task—what does the future bode for us? What can we say about the life styles of youth in the next decade, or even in the decades following? We first note that the forces which created the youth culture show no signs of reversal in the near future; in fact, automated production and disposable income are going to increase. More and better items lie in store for the consumer. Given the rapidity of change in our society, it may well be that a selective process is occurring and only the Dionysians will be capable of adjusting to a rate of change which may be approaching the limits to which men can adapt (Bennis and Slater, 1968; Toffler, 1970). The socialization patterns of every society attempt to pattern the motives and values of children in order to enable them to assume the adult occupational roles (Clausen, 1968; Inkeles, 1955; Kohn, 1969). When the occupational system is in a state of rapid flux, the only thing the young can be taught is flexibility and openness.

Given the persistence of the economic and psychological forces that created the youth culture, we can expect it to continue to grow. A major contributory (but not causal) factor in the emergence of the counterculture was the rapid proliferation of higher education and its availability to varied strata.[7] As even greater proportions of young people go to colleges and universities, more will be affected by the ideology of the counterculture. Therefore, barring major changes in the economic system—a depression or a major nuclear confrontation—the counterculture will continue to grow in strength and influence.

As has been noted, the diffusion of the new youth culture is no longer limited to the college campus. It can be seen in high schools—even in some grade schools. The Armed Forces have begun to accommodate themselves to the "new" kind of recruit.[8] This growth in numbers and influence will have important consequences in political, economic, and social trends.

Perhaps the most prevalent types within the counterculture are the hippies and the politicals.[9] The impact of youth on the political system is obvious—they kept Johnson from running again. While the number of genuine radicals and revolutionaries is really quite low, there are sympathetic numbers who will support many of these proposals. Yet many social scientists and large numbers of the young fail to realize a basic fact of industrial democracy—it is *centrist,* not fascist or communist. Further, industrialization *requires* and fosters democracy (Bennis and Slater, 1968). Therefore the political factions of the youth culture will and must work *within* the system. The modern state has a monopoly of violence that Weber would not have believed possible. No advanced industrial society will have a revolution. But the counterculture has already witnessed a good deal of success within the system; they reversed the trend in Vietnam; they helped defeat the SST; they have elected such representatives as Dellums and Abzug; they now control the city council of Berkeley. The Kabouters are a major political force in Amsterdam. The realization of Dionysian goals does *not* require violent political revolution. Therefore, we can expect the youth movement to become a *significant* force in the political arena, in a few years more significant than the labor or Black votes. All politicians will have to consider the counterculture. Conversely, the Dionysians will be *more* likely to run their own candidates, and many will be elected. Space does not permit elaboration, but some of the political consequences will be:

(1) Decreased military spending. The youthful sector of the peace movement is hardly going to be impressed with the Pentagon's annual spring horror story of new Soviet weapons.

(2) Genuine concern for the environment, the quality of goods and services.

(3) Increased expenditures on health, education, and welfare; subsidy for those who wish to experiment with life styles.

(4) Greater redistribution of wealth.

(5) An end to "victimless crimes," e.g., consenting sex acts, gambling, prostitution, drugs.

The economic consequences will be primarily in terms of residence, consumerism, and occupational structure. Until the fifties, most residential growth was in the urban areas. At that time, the suburbs began to grow. Suburbs, attempts to create a sense of community in an individualistic, fragmented society, were not only failures, but may have contributed to the emergence of the counterculture. The growth of the counterculture will probably see a return to rural settings, communes, and leisure-resort areas. All such efforts will attempt to create harmonious, shared relations with nature, allowing the person to do his (or her) thing.

As society undergoes the transition from consumer capitalism to postindustrial, a curious paradox emerges. As goods beome more plentiful, they become less desirable, at least to those who are used to having them. The youth culture of today who will reach maturity in a postindustrial society will *not* be avid consumers. Those products that *are* desired must be high in quality and safety. A larger portion of income will be spent on travel and leisure.[10] Those young people who grew up in affluence know how little material things matter. While they had cars, charge accounts, and money, they usually had "busy parents." The cult of Dionysus knows how much preferable warm, intimate relationships are to anything money can buy. As the Beatles proclaimed, "money can't buy you love, my friend . . . no, no, no, no, no, no."

The decline of consumerism does not portend chaos for the economy; perhaps it will have positive consequences for the environment. A much greater part of the GNP will be in services and leisure activities than in durable products (heavy or light manufacturing). The ever-growing technology will create an even greater diversity of jobs for those who want them. We can be sure that "profit" will decline as a basis for motivation, and humanistic concerns will become important in the functioning of the economy.

A major social consequence of the emergence of the Dionysian counterculture will be the transformation of the isolated, conjugal, nuclear family structure. While this may be the ideal unit for a mobile industrial society based on corporate capitalism, in a post-industrial society it may be more pathogenic than functional. It has been said that psychoanalysis is itself a symptom of the problems it purports to deal with. The nuclear family creates the "romantic love complex" based on an unresolvable Oedipus complex (Slater, 1970). The high divorce rate and the even higher rate of barely tolerable marriages questions the very future of this institution. The isolated conjugal nuclear family will be maladaptive in a postindustrial society. Therefore, alternative patterns of family life will emerge, and it seems as if several possible arrangements may occur:

(1) Communal living with group marriage, socialization practiced by all members, not just biological parents.

(2) Communal living with monogamous marriage, socialization by specialized members, such as in Israel (Spiro, 1958; Bettelheim, 1969) or the Soviet Union (Bronfenbrenner, 1970).

(3) Monogamous or serially monogamous marriage with communal socialization as above.

(4) Pseudo-extended families, several monogamous families maintaining separate residence yet shared socialization responsibilities, child-rearing co-ops.

Perhaps other patterns are possible. We can, however, be sure that the present family structure will be modified along lines of sharing, cooperation, and permanence. Individual members may come and go, but family life will no longer be an all or none, good or bad situation.

The youth culture of today is beset by many problems, not the least of which is the conflict between an Apollonian parental generation and their Dionysian offspring. Subsequent cohorts will experience less and less conflict, since the older brothers and sisters will have paved much of the way. Many of the battles over dress codes, birth control, relevant education, and the like have been fought. A long-haired male or bra-less female teenager is hardly noticed anymore; indeed, the crew cut of cheerleader types seems a rarity.[11] Because of the increased numbers of the Dionysians and the dying off or conversion of the Apollonians, the current crisis over the "generation gap" will decline.

Within about fifteen years, we will see the first of the second-generation Dionysians. They will have been raised with a good deal of love and attention, and little trauma, frustration, or conflict. Drugs, sex, and personal styles will be more of a bore than a shock. They will expect warm and meaningful relations with others—even if these relations are transitory. They will not be highly achievement-oriented. Much to the consternation of those academics who identify with or favor the counterculture, many are likely to be anti-intellectual.

The growth and possible social dominance of the Dionysian counterculture will affect the educational system of postindustrial society. There will be many ramifications which cannot be fully explored.

(1) Concern for "relevance" in curricula.

(2) Concern for individual psychological growth and humanistic perspectives, rather than the present system of education, which is modeled after a factory.[12]

(3) Ability rather than age grouping.

(4) Elimination of competitive grading systems.

(5) Greater integration of school and life experience.

(6) Greater emphasis on how to solve problems, rather than just the transmission of accumulated information, the half-life of information is decreasing while this amount is increasing. Preparation for assumption of more than one career.

The school systems will be radically transformed by computerized instruction. We will see a strong psychoanalytic influence (Niell, Redl, Bettelheim), as well as the cognitive theories and methods of such people as Piaget, Bruner, Kohlberg, and Montessori.

From all indications, the youth culture will grow and flourish; at some time in the future, "counterculture" will not be an appropriate designation. The counterculture will then be those hard-working, impulse-controlling, individuated Apollonians. If the transition of our society to a postindustrial one is to be without the bloodshed that has accompanied most social changes, we must be tolerant of all the styles—even those we oppose. An old, preindustrial document proclaimed a message that all men are entitled to life, liberty, and the pursuit of happiness. The past is relevant for tomorrow.

NOTES

1. Black Panthers, other Black Power groups, and the "New Left" seem to differ from traditional revolutionary movements which attempted to *foster* class consciousness as a prelude to revolution and redistribution. Today's groups question not only ownership of the means of production but production itself. While they may use Marxist rhetoric, we must not dismiss them as Marxists; they attempt to not only transform political and economic distribution, but to develop alternate life styles, new interpersonal relations, and new patterns of consciousness. Perhaps Marx in his early writings (1844) understood this.

2. This is not to deny a historic dimension to the youth movement. Today's counterculture was rooted in the "beat generation" of the fifties, whose ancestry goes back to the "Bohemians" of Greenwich Village, who in turn were cultural descendants of the Parisian Left Bank. The Utopian quest of the "New Left" (the political sector of the counterculture) can be traced to the French socialists like St. Simon or Proudon, and other Utopians like Robert Owens, Bellamy, Thoreau, and the like. Finally, student movements long predate Berkeley (compare Feuer, 1969). While there is historic *precedent,* we do *not* have historic *continuity* through intergenerational transmission; hence, the youth culture is not an independent culture. As we will endeavor to demonstrate, while the youth culture of today is a new phenomenon, it is at the same time the current manifestation of a perpetual dialectic between Apollonian and Dionysian patterns of Western thought.

3. As Weber (1905) and Bendix (1970) have shown, rationality as a normative value and pattern of social organization is unique to Western capitalism. Reason has always been challenged and seems only to have won a Pyhrric victory.

4. Keynes (1936) clearly showed the disastrous consequences of savings in a modern economy whose growth depends on spending—even if that spending must be done by the public sector with money it does not have.

5. Recall that in psychoanalytic theory, the acquisition of values (superego) occurs through introjection; in the nuclear family this also meant identification.

6. And the reaction of the Apollonians whose values were threatened was predictable: *stronger* adherence to the obsolete values of the preconsumer, industrial era (compare Slater, 1970; Toffler, 1970; Mead, 1970). The Apollonians hated and castigated their own children—only because they themselves so desired the freedom, spontaneity, sensual pleasure, and community of the youth. The reaction was especially vociferous among the lower-middle and working classes, who were still aspiring to what the counterculture was repudiating—e.g., respect for authority, sexual morality, private property, suburban homes.

7. College attendance has traditionally been associated with social class; therefore many of the students came from the affluent-permissive households. Students can explore ideas, while nonstudents must be more concerned with survival. College atmospheres are generally more tolerant of varied life styles than is society in general, especially for the political or hippie styles of the counterculture. Finally, it seems as if higher education, especially in the liberal arts, leads to more liberal political beliefs.

8. The ready availability of drugs to servicemen in Europe or Southeast Asia may also have contributed to the growth of the youth culture. The very stationing of young men in foreign zones without a "state of war" has led many of them to question basic values of the society which sent them abroad.

9. It is important to differentiate the hippies and politicals who, despite some similarities in appearance, represent *separate* patterns of response to the anomie of technological society—e.g., retreatists and rebels in Merton's (1957) schema.

10. In the past few days, the airlines have announced youth fares to Europe.

11. I must report a personal anecdote. In one of my courses, I ask students to analyze a long-term friendship. One group of three seniors included a recent snapshot and their pictures from their high school year book of four years ago. Needless to add, high school had marked their last hair cuts. It took me ten minutes to stop laughing.

12. The present model is basically designed to produce a labor force of manipulators (sales force), symbol users (managers), or tool users (workers) for the economic system. Future educational programs will attempt to develop the person in his own right.

REFERENCES

ABERLE, D. E. et al. (1950) "The functional pre-requisites of a society." Ethics 60: 100-111.

BENDIX, R. (1970) Embattled Reason. New York: Oxford Univ. Press.

BENEDICT, R. (1934) Patterns of Culture. Boston: Houghton Mifflin.

BENNIS, W. and P. SLATER (1968) The Temporary Society. New York: Harper.

BETTELHEIM, B. (1969) Children of the Dream. New York: Macmillan.

BRONFENBRENNER, U. (1970) Two Worlds of Childhood. New York: Russell Sage.

——— (1961) "The changing American child." J. of Social Issues 17: 16-18.

BRUNER, E. (1956) "Cultural transmission and cultural change." Southwestern J. of Anthropology 12: 191-199.

CLAUSEN, J. (1968) Socialization and Society. Boston: Little, Brown.

CROCKETT, H. (1962) "The achievement motive and differential occupational mobility in the United States." Amer. Soc. Rev. 27: 191-194.

DOUGLAS, J. (1970) "Youth in turmoil." Public Service Publication 2058. Chevy Chase: National Institute of Mental Health.

FEUER, L. (1969) The Conflict of Generations. New York: Basic Books.

GALBRAITH, J. (1967) The New Industrial State. Boston: Houghton Mifflin.

——— (1958) The Affluent Society. Boston: Houghton Mifflin.

GOULDNER, A. and R. PETERSON (1962) Notes on Technology and the Moral Order. Indianapolis: Bobbs-Merrill.

HSU, F. (1961) "American core value and national character," in Psychological Anthropology—Approaches to Culture and Personality. Homewood, Ill.: Dorsey.

INKELES, A. (1955) "Social change and social character: the role of parental mediation." J. of Social Issues 11: 12-23.

KEYNES, J. M. (1936) General Theory of Employment, Interest, and Money. New York: Harcourt, Brace.

KLUCKHOHN, F. and F. STRODTBECK (1961) Variations in Value Orientation. Evanston, Ill.: Row-Peterson.

KOHN, M. (1969) Class and Conformity. Homewood, Ill.: Dorsey.

LANGMAN, L. (1969) "Economy, motives, and values: a study of relationships." Ph.D. dissertation. University of Chicago.

——— R. BLOCK, and I. CUNNINGHAM (1971) "Radicals and Roman collars." Presented at the American Sociological Association, Denver.

MALINOWSKI, B. (1944) A Scientific Theory of Culture. Chapel Hill: Univ. of North Carolina Press.

MARX, K. (1964) "Economic and philosophical manuscripts of 1844," in T. B. Bollomire (ed.) Karl Marx: Early Writings. New York: McGraw-Hill.

MEAD, M. (1970) Culture and Commitment. Garden City, N.Y.: Doubleday.

MERTON, R. (1957) Social Theory and Social Structure. New York: Free Press.

MILLER, D. and G. SWANSON (1958) The Changing American Parent. New York: John Wiley.

PARSONS, T. and E. SHILS (1951) Towards a General Theory of Action. Cambridge, Mass.: Harvard Univ. Press.

PARSONS, T. and N. SMELSER (1956) Economy and Society. New York: Free Press.

REICH, C. (1970) The Greening of America. New York: Random House.

ROSENBERG, M. (1957) Occupations and Values. New York: Free Press.

ROSZAK, T. (1969) The Making of a Counterculture. Garden City, N.Y.: Doubleday.

SCHUMPETER, J. A. (1942) Capitalism, Socialism and Democracy. New York: Harper & Row.

SCOTT, M. B. and S. M. LYMAN (1970) The Revolt of the Students. Columbus: Charles E. Merrill.

SLATER, P. (1970) The Pursuit of Loneliness. Boston: Beacon.

SMELSER, N. (1956) Economy and Society. New York: Free Press.

SPIRO, M. (1958) Children of the Kibbutz. Cambridge, Mass.: Harvard Univ. Press.

STEWARD, J. (1955) The Theory of Cultural Change. Urbana: Univ. of Illinois Press.

TOFFLER, A. (1970) Future Shock. New York: Random House.

WEBER, M. (1905) The Protestant Ethic and Its Spirit of Capitalism. (T. Parsons, trans.) New York: Charles Scribner's. (English edition, 1920).

WHYTE, W. H. (1956) The Organization Man. New York: Simon & Schuster.

WOLFENSTEIN, M. (1951) "The emergence of fun morality." J. of Social Issues 7: 15-25.

7

THE FUTURE OF BLACK YOUTH

NATHAN HARE

To examine the future of black youth is to consider the future of the entire black race. Moreover, insofar as the future of the black race and black youth is a function of their projected position in society and its total conditions, to consider the question of the future of black youth is to take up the question of the future of society itself. It may be impossible to speak of a new future for black youth without speaking of a new society.

Black youth seeking a new future must change society. They must, therefore, be social innovators, agents of social change. For this reason, the future of black youth is a future of struggle for a new society. Indeed, there are those who would present evidence for the theory that without a fundamental change in American society, there can be *no* future of any kind for black youth (Yette, 1971; Walton, 1970).

Thus it is natural that the initiative in black rebellion is passing to black youth, the least accommodated of the most oppressed group, whose minds are less poisoned by the myths and passions of racism and whose social conditions persistently provoke them to rebel and seek a better society.

Historically, the rise to preeminence of black youth in the black rebellion was, like the rise of black male consciousness, simultaneous with the rise of revolutionary black consciousness as a whole. All these elements were mutually reinforcing; for the rise of black male consciousness in particular, with its tenet of restoring the male to supremacy in the family, meant that black men increasingly began to play a more prominent role in the socialization of black children. This was especially so in reference to the development of racial consciousness.

Shortly after the Supreme Court decreed desegregation of schools with all deliberate speed, the passive resistance movement sprang up within the context of intransigence and slow-paced change. Black children and women continued to occupy a salient place among test cases in desegregation endeavors (the Little Rock Nine, Rosa Parks and Artherine Lucy being among the most famous but by no means the only ones). Ministers of the Gospel (notably the Rev. Martin Luther King), who still reigned at the apex of the black movement's power structure, came more flamboyantly to the fore with a philosophy of nonviolence. They were soon joined in droves by black youths, particularly college students.

Contrary to popular belief, however, the sit-in movement did not begin with college students; they merely escalated it. Among others, there was a movement launched in Oklahoma City in the late summer of 1958 by black youths from six to seventeen years old. It spread from town to town, but soon died when their elders agreed to form a committee to "study the matter"; the children reluctantly returned to school after a sit-in wave in Oklahoma drugstores—in at least one drugstore-restaurant, the proprietor removed the chairs and served black kids and white customers standing, in the manner of Harry Golden's suggestion of "vertical" equality in *Only in America.*

These youth received headlines in Oklahoma and small notices on, say, page nineteen of national newspapers such as the *New York Times;* but Arkansas Governor Orville Faubus' threat to refuse to reopen Little Rock schools if they were desegregated and the success of Sputnik and America's own erratic efforts to get Vanguard up took front-page headlines and robbed the children of the *social contagion* which later characterized the sit-in of merely four college students in Greensboro, North Carolina, in winter of 1960.

In the latter movement, social contagion was apparent in the comments of typical student leaders.

At Tuskegee Institute: "From now on, whenever Alabama State sits in, we're going to sit in too."

At Shaw University, North Carolina: "We didn't want to be caught doing less than our part."

But black college students as a group were emulative mainly only of one another and soon escalated the non-violent tactics of their more passive elders, whose tactics they incorporated to "take the initiative in a disciplined manner, achieve cooperation between white and Negro youth, and dramatize the realities" of white injustice (Boggs, 1963: 82).

King did not draw the dialectical conclusion of his movement. This was the historical contribution of the young Blacks in the Student Non-Violent Coordinating Committee who pursued his strategy in every state of the South. Thus, in 1966, the Black movement arrived in practice, before the eyes of the whole nation, at the concept of the struggle for Black Power which Malcolm X had been developing before Black audiences in the North since his break with the Muslims in 1963 [Boggs, 1971: 6].

Subsequent to the Birmingham confrontation in 1963, the struggling youth had moved north, where ghetto blacks had de jure rights but remained victims of de facto white oppression in the crucial areas of jobs, housing, schools, and police brutality. When they turned again briefly south on the Meredith March in the summer of 1966, they returned to the ghettos with cries of "black power." But they infused "the slogan of Black Power with a revolutionary political content very different from the chiefly cultural content cultivated by an earlier generation of Black Nationalists" (Boggs, 1971). Indeed, in the words of a white intellectual, "all Americans owe them a debt" for exposing the hypocrisy of a nation which had not recently, as of that writing, been subjected to a social upheaval.

> Theirs was the silent generation until they spoke, the complacent generation until they marched and sang, the money-seeking generation until they renounced comfort and security to fight for justice [Zinn, 1964: 2].

In any case, this was "the first time in our history" that "a major social movement, shaking the nation to its bones" was being "led by youngsters" (Zinn, 1964: 1).

"The emergence of the slogan Black Power was the turning point for the black student community. The concept of black power challenged the whole value structure of the Negro community." Soon it was to spread to other youths beyond the borders of this nation until by 1969, when all Africa turned toward Algiers in a "Pan-African Cultural Festival," the "black power salute" (the fist held aloft) was universally known, and Algerian (Arab) cab drivers addressed black American passengers with "pouvoir noir" (black power) and frequently refused to accept fare for their transportation.

Although there were flames of angry revolution among many segments of the festival delegates, they were

> hotter still in the hearts of the Pan African Movement for Youth. Early in the Festival, the youth had been rather suspicious of their revolutionary elders and took pains at once to see "that solutions [coming out of the Festival] conform to the aspirations of the youth." They watched impatiently the too-ready accept-ance of neo-colonialist domination and imperialist aggression on Africa's immense land and riches. And they "parry and thrust" against colonial conspiracies "on the military, political and economic plane rather more than on the cultural" [Hare, 1969].

Of course, this generation gap is not unique to black and oppressed peoples; but, if there is in white America a generation gap, we might say that there is in black America a generation gulf, though in many respects less conspicuous and more subtle. We have, on the one hand, black youths who sincerely believe that they invented the black struggle, instead of merely escalating it and evolving new horizons. On the other hand, many of the older generation too often lack the sensitivity and liberalism sufficient to enable them to silently steal away whenever they cannot keep pace with the new pace of the young.

> these young Blacks are not only a challenge to white authority. They are also a challenge to all those inside the Black community, including their parents, who still have their little jobs and dream of peaceful coexistence with white America. With their Black Pride, their rejection of white values, and their expendability to the economy, these youth represent the future of Black people —*one way or the other* [Boggs, 1971: 8].

One striking case of the wideness of the black generation gap was only recently reported in a documentary travelogue through black America (Selby and Selby, 1971). It involved a black U.S. congressman and gold medal winner in the 1936 Olympics and his son, a recent college graduate.

The congressman:

> If you ask me for the proudest moment in my life, I think it was after I had won the Olympic tryouts and I was called over to be measured for my uniform, with the red, white and blue slash across the jersey. I was going to represent the entire United States on the track, and I felt proud of myself and my country.

His son:

> I am a black revolutionary. I support the Vietcong, the Palestinian guerrillas, and I was for Nasser. If I were to be drafted, I certainly would not fight on the side of those I consider to be my enemies. As a matter of fact, I think my role is to work toward overthrowing the type of system we have in this country.

Looking to the future, however, neither the generation gap between blacks nor the generation gap between whites is likely to be as consequential as the racial gap now emerging. By this, we do not mean to imply the traditional separation of racial sentiments (for this has always been present and has probably increased less in recent years than is popularly believed; there is, in these days of separatist cries and sloganisms, more integration in America than ever before). The racial gap more relevant to our discussion is that among the progressive elements, those blacks and whites who seek to change society and rectify its conditions.

Within the black movement, increasingly among youth, there is much confusion and consternation over the role, if any, white radicals can play in the struggle for black liberation. The trend of thinking now is, at least superficially, toward a narrow, monolithic approach, with the notable exception being the Black Panthers. But it is significant to note that the Panthers, in their efforts to keep open alliances with white radicals, have alienated themselves from the black militant movement. This fact is either unknown or overlooked by most white observers. Thus, the possibilities of a strategy of integration seem dim for the near future and may even risk being supplanted by open, even violent, conflict.

All this poses very fundamental questions not only for American society as a whole but for American revolutionaries. The old slogan "Black and White, Unite and Fight" has been proved false and obsolete. . . . What is involved is not only the likelihood of open and armed revolt of the Negroes against the state power in the South. The Negroes are now posing before all the institutions of American society, and particularly those which are supposedly on their side (the labor organizations, the liberals, the old Negro organizations, and the Marxists), the same questions that have been posed by the Algerian Revolution to all of French society, with this difference that Algeria is outside France while the Negroes are right here inside America. But in the same way that, during the course of the Algerian Revolution, Algerians fought Frenchmen, and Algerians fought Algerians, and Frenchmen representing the national government eventually had to take over political power and now have to expropriate the property of Frenchmen—so in the United States the Negro revolt will lead to armed struggle between Negroes and whites, Negroes and Negroes, and Federal troops and armed civilians, and will have to move to political power and economic power [Boggs, 1963: 84].

All this was written by a leading black revolutionary theorist almost a decade ago, but the interpretation has grown increasingly sound through the years and now promises to intensify. This is not an alarmist theory; as a matter of fact, it is merely a necessary stage in the direction of an ultimate and more permanent solution.

Still, in these times, it may be difficult for many white individuals to imagine the frustration of black youth. Many may know well enough the statistics involved and may have, on occasion, observed firsthand the socioeconomic degradation of the black race in America, but it remains for blacks to live and suffer the conditions whites experience only vicariously at worst.

A survey of a national sample of young white men reported "racial tensions and civil rights" as the second most frequently mentioned problem facing America. When responses were rated on a scale of six "most important national problems," pollution came in first as "very important or extremely important," while race relations emerged as far down as fifth. Few of the white youths advocated more government activity as a solution to racial strife; only one-fifth could independently think of a solution at all. Thirty-two percent checked that the solution depends merely on individual good will (with 17% more checking relations related thereto), and only 4% advocated government force (Bachman and Van Duinen, 1971).

More subtle contrasts in the basic motivations of black and white youth rebels (though there are notable and well-known similarities) are apparent particularly among student militants in the nature of their "withdrawal" or "avoidance behavior."

For instance, in the use of drugs, we may discern a sharp difference. Despite the high cost of hard drugs and the relative poverty of blacks, young blacks are more given to their use. But the contrast is not lost even in the use of marijuana.

> A University of California team sent into the East Oakland (California) ghetto to study marijuana use at firsthand discovered just the opposite [among black and white youths]. Among the young ghetto people, marijuana is a social cohesion factor. It is used in conjunction with the group; to use marijuana is to belong, and its use is a factor in group acceptance. Thus it is exactly the opposite of an escape or a withdrawal, and the findings of the team contradict the traditional literature and attitudes on the subject [Jones, 1970].

The alienation of black youth is not only more poignant and acute but also more steeped in contradiction. Even those who do not rebel outright are "rebels without a cause," withdrawing into and courting nothingness while ostensibly adhering to society's norms. It is no exaggeration to say that a card game, bid whist, is, more than anything other than educational irrelevance and emptiness, contributing to the flunkout rate of black students across the country. Many may be seen huddling in a corner of the cafeteria, now and again playing bid whist even in the school, let alone elsewhere at other hours of the day and night. They are stymied by the sharp transition between two worlds and confused by their own mental anguish, on the one hand, and a kind of newfound economic comfort on the other. A recent criticism of such a syndrome in a militant black student newspaper was no isolated occurrence:

> We should admit to ourselves, regardless of our real or professed socio-economic backgrounds, that life at Lake Forest College and similar institutions is very alluring and comforting—it makes you want to lay back and be a student all your life (talking shit, doing nothing)!—cause it's so damn easy!! The contradictions wherein

an institution can be so much a part of a destructive society and at the same time alluring to those it oppresses is very dangerous. We should learn and keep what parts of this education which may be useful to us as a people, discard the rest (including its destructive values) and keep on dealin' [Black Rap, 1971].

Nevertheless, although black students may be impelled to spend much time and passion on such compensatory behavior as bid whist, conspicuous costumes, and symbols attesting to the fact that they are "together" (aware and militant), they are not uncommonly moved at various points to turn their backs on adolescent distractions and act outright to reject the more staid but no more functional trivia of their elders.

At one Southern Negro college, 47 black students were expelled as early as 1967 for rebelling against the college's traditional preoccupation with athletics to the point of deemphasizing scholarship. A & M colleges (agricultural and mechanical), as Negro colleges are frequently dubbed by their founders, are mocked by their students as "athletics and music" colleges; A & I colleges (agricultural and industrial), "athletics and ignorance"; and A & T (agricultural and technical), "athletics and tomism" (Hare, 1967).

In the same year, 1967, a young student barricaded himself in a corner window of a dormitory and, with the help of his fellows, seized the dormitory until the arrival of the National Guard. Seizing buildings is no longer unique nor new to black students, but the killing of protesting students by law officers is newer by far with white students than with blacks, who were being killed as early as 1967 and 1968 at Southern Negro colleges (Hare, 1967).

Even in their own strategy and approaches, black and white students may differ. White students typically follow mass tactics, whereas black students, even at colleges where they predominate, more prevalently are given to symbolic behavior. (Note the similarity of the behavior of black students at Cornell, a predominantly white university, and Vorhees, a predominantly black college in South Carolina, where in each instance they posed with carbines and ammunition visible but with no ammunition in the unloaded guns.) They operate both underground and in conspicuous public demands and press conferences, but seldom in mass. This is, in part, a product of the duality of their quest for belonging and identity.

The latter word, *identity,* is a crucial word in the black youth's quest for freedom in an alien world.

You hear it over and over again. On this word will focus, around this word will coagulate, a dozen issues, shifting, shading into each other. Alienated from the world to which he is born and from the country of which he is a citizen, yet surrounded by the successful values of that new world, and country, how can the Negro define himself? [Warren, 1965: 17].

While some continue to disidentify with their race and many strive to lose themselves in superficial bliss, the corrosion of self-hatred and feelings of inferiority among black youths in the growing era of black pride and consciousness have been indicated by a number of recent observers (Noel, 1964; Maliver, 1965; Johnson, 1966). This is bound to increase. Not only do black youths active in political rebellion exhibit more favorable self-images and attitudes toward other blacks, but psychiatrists have early discovered that black communities with high rates of youth activism exhibited lower crime rates (Fishman and Solomon, 1964). Many youths previously engaged in criminal behavior

no doubt, often defended whatever identity elements were available to them by revolting in the only way open to them—a way of vicious danger and yet often the only way of tangible self-respect and solidarity. Like the outcast heroes of the American frontier, some antisocial types among the Negroes are not expendable from the history of their people—not yet [Erikson, 1968].

In a systematic scientific survey of black consciousness among two samples of high school and junior college students, the following beliefs were found to be directly correlated with the level of black consciousness (Banks, 1970):

(1) We should organize in an effort to free ourselves from American society.

(2) In the United States, freedom for my race can *only* be achieved through integration.

(3) The Christian idea of heaven and hell has slowed down my race's fight for freedom.

(4) For my race, equality and integration are *not* the same thing.

(5) When assigned to "riot" duty in the so-called Negro ghettos, soldiers of my race should fight the police and the other white soldiers.

(6) We should fight for freedom by any means necessary.

(7) Members of my race need to buy weapons.

Among the responses which were negatively or inversely correlated with black consciousness among black youth studied were the following:

(1) Through education, my race will be accepted into the mainstream of American society.

(2) There is no need for my race to buy guns.

The new mood of black youth is merely indicative of the fact that the black struggle increasingly "has the combined force and drive of a *national* revolution and a *social* revolution" (Boggs, 1971: 5) leading to a cultural, if not a political, revolution and a revolutionary culture.

A poll taken by *Newsweek* magazine in 1969 (when nationalist and separatist sentiments were on a lower level than they are today) indicated that 21% of black people longed for a black nation of their own and an additional 12% "quite seriously expect it" (Thomas, 1971: 18). The irony is that separatism as a strategy not uncommonly leads to more integration than an outright strategy of integrationism. Witness black students at white colleges and the separatist cries for black studies bringing more black students and black professors to white campuses than decades of integrationist tactics had achieved. Black students at one white college recently gained a greater voice in the regular student newspaper by merely threatening to establish a black newspaper of their own. At another college, where black students, as is typical, were excluded from white Greek social fraternities, a conflict arose because black students demanded a fraternity of their own. This was integration in bloc form, a last-ditch effort on the part of the black students, however unconsciously, to assimilate. They were demanding not an Egyptian or Ethiopian fraternity, but a Greek fraternity just like their white counterparts (Baldwin-Wallace College, 1970-1971).

Thus, separatism and assimilationism among black youth increasingly are evolving as diffused orientations. This is not surprising since separation and integration merely constitute approaches and strategies in the struggle for freedom and lose their effectiveness when they become goals in themselves. It will be an irony of recorded history that segregation (involuntary separation) was used in the first half of this century to hold the black race down, whereas the ideal of token integration is being used in the second half.

In the search for new solutions to the paradoxes and adversities they face, black youth will challenge and confront the very foundations of American society. For instance, the greatest contribution of black studies up to now, perhaps, has been its impact on the educational arena at large. Such an impact will increasingly be felt in the educational arena as well as other institutions of society, including even the family where the shortage of males is far greater for blacks in the age groups of marrying adults and is further aggravated by higher rates of attrition in the Vietnam War. But, although the almost axiomatic fact that black youths, an oppressed minority, will be the catalysts for change which will indirectly benefit the oppressive majority is ironic; the significance of youth in struggles for change is not unique to the black movement in this country. The parallel is already heard around the world. For

> youth must become what we all dreamed for the future . . . what we all hope the people of tomorrow, the country's new generations, will be. This youth must become what all of us would have wanted to be, to lead the lives that all of us would have wanted to live. In short, with this youth the future must be built [Castro, 1969].

This is especially true of black youth in America.

REFERENCES

BACHMAN, J. G. and E. VAN DUINEN (1971) Youth Look at National Problems. Ann Arbor: University of Michigan Institute for Social Research.

Baldwin-Wallace College (1970-1971) "The conversion of a campus: final report of Baldwin-Wallace panel on race relations." Berea, Ohio, June-April.

BANKS, H. A. (1970) "Black consciousness: a student survey." Black Scholar 2 (September): 44-51.

Black Rap (1971) May/June: 3.

BOGGS, J. (1971) "Manifesto for a black revolutionary party," Black News 1 (May 29): 3-8.

––– (1963) The American Revolution: Pages from a Negro Worker's Notebook. New York: Modern Reader.

CASTRO, F. (1969) "The revolution must be a school of unfettered thought." Speech at University of Havana, June.

ERIKSON, E. H. (1968) "Race and the wider identity," pp. 295-320 in Identity: Youth and Crisis. New York: W. W. Norton.

FISHMAN, J. and F. SOLOMON (1964) "Youth and social action." J. of Social Issues (October): 1-27.

HARE, N. (1969) "A report on the Pan African cultural festival." Black Scholar 1 (November): 2-10.

––– (1968) "The legacy of paternalism." Saturday Rev. (July 20).

––– (1967) "Behind the black college student revolt." Ebony (August).

JOHNSON, D. W. (1966) "Racial attitudes of Negro freedom school participants and Negro and white civil rights participants." Social Forces 45: 266-273.

JONES, M. H. and M. C. JONES (1970) "The neglected client." Black Scholar 1 (March): 35-42.

LLORENS, L. A. (1971) "Black culture and child development." Amer. J. of Occupational Therapy 25 (April): 144-148.

MALIVER, B. L. (1965) "Anti-Negro bias among Negro college students." J. of Personal and Social Psychology 2: 770-775.

NOEL, D. L. (1964) "Group identification among Negroes: an empirical analysis." J. of Social Issues 20: 71-85.

SELBY, E. and M. SELBY (1971) Odyssey: Journey Through Black America. New York: G. P. Putnam's.

THOMS, T. (1971) "Is separatism revolutionary?" The Militant (June 18): 18.

WALTON, S. (1970) "Census 70: blueprint for repression." Black Scholar 1 (March): 28-34.

WARREN, R. P. (1965) Who Speaks for the Negro? New York: Random House.

YETTE, S. F. (1971) The Choice: The Issue of Black Survival in America. New York: G. P. Putnam's.

ZINN, H. (1964) SNCC: The New Abolitionists. Boston: Beacon.

8

THE FAMILY IS DEAD
—LONG LIVE THE FAMILY

NED L. GAYLIN

Mister, remove your shoulder from the wheel
And say this prayer, "Increase my vitamins,
Make my decisions of the finest steel,
Pour motor oil upon my troubled spawn,
Forgive the Europeans for their sins,
Establish them, that values may go on."

—Karl Shapiro from Boy-Man

In discussing any American institution, particularly one as central as the family, it is necessary to expose and face squarely the growth of our historic ambivalence—that which (some 25 years ago) Gunnar Myrdal (1944) called "the American dilemma." By that he referred to our inability and frustration at matching our actions with our ethos. Although Myrdal was addressing himself primarily to racial problems in the United States, his observations are no less cogent with regard to other of our interpersonal behavioral patterns. And this dilemma sits squarely in the family rooms of our American homes, like a cricket on the hearth, chirping louder with each succeeding generation.

[171]

Recently, this blatant paradox between our practice and our preachments has been brought home to us rather dramatically by the much publicized activities of our young people. These activities, beginning with the civil rights movement in the early sixties and continuing through the resistance to the war in Indochina and the current widespread concern with our polluted environment, have focused on our value system with such force that the impact is constantly with us. No newspaper or journal (popular or esoteric) has failed to deal with the issues of the "generation gap" and its implications. Indeed, the apparent hiatus has become a national priority.

It is perhaps ironic (though not purely coincidental) that the beginning of our young people's activism dealt with our longest-standing major hypocrisy—de facto slavery of the blacks—that upon which Myrdal most specifically focused. The Mississippi sit-ins were pacifist action protests which were the logical forerunners to the peace marches of a decade later. And in between—the demands and demonstrations for students, women, homosexuals, and so on have all stemmed ,from a concern for individual rights and freedoms.

Examining the basic moralistic underpinnings of our secular ideology, two seem most glaringly contradictory: the first is our earliest value of the right to individual and different life styles (e.g., the "four freedoms"). Our first settlers sought freedom to worship as they chose when they immigrated and generalized this notion a century later in our Constitution. The second and somewhat more recently acquired (though less articulated) value is the constraint to conformity (the "melting pot" myth) which began crystalizing during the time of industrialization and the second wave of major immigration from Europe (circa 1900).

With the complexity of that which many writers have called posttechnological society, we rarely dwell upon these ideologies. They tend to be seen as a bit sentimental and simplistic for our sophisticated, computerized, complex society of today. Yet they are evident in the teachings and preachings conveyed to our children both by interpersonal behavior and as these values are depicted in our modern folklore (television, for example). Although we do not examine these values openly, this is basically what our young people are doing when they march (bearded, long-haired, and unisexually clad) seeking life styles different from those of their parents. They are challenging and exposing those which they consider to be some of our major hypocrisies.

Sadly, their quest for honesty has had deleterious side effects. When the word hypocrisy is used by youth it is alienating and insulting. It often results in defensive maneuvering by the adults to combat that which they regard as vituperation—and the name-calling begins. Given an atmosphere less emotionally charged, both sides might concede that the situation is one of moralistic confusion enhanced by a burgeoning technology advancing faster than cultural values can absorb it. Nonetheless, the confrontation is before us, and the consequences of the battle are typically American—a search for somewhere to lay the blame. Perhaps that is a bit harsh. It might be fairer to use another model—that of the clinician. We search for the root of the pathology in order that we may remediate—cure it. But often, in using a disease-cure model, we focus upon a symptom rather than the cause. And one of our favorite mistaken symptom-scapegoats is the already overworked and overburdened American family.

The family is a natural whipping boy for both professional and lay observers of the American scene. In part, this is because all of us have had familial experiences and have observed those of others. But perhaps more important is the family's position as interface between the individual and society. The family has first contact with the child and begins the socializing process. If the child does not seem to be adjusting to the society of which he is a part, the first source of blame—the transmitter of disease—is often seen as the family. And when an entire generation through its actions seems ill-adjusted and abrasive to the larger society, parents, politicians, and social scientists look for causative forces and corrective measures.

The increasing and alarming number of young people who are prematurely striving for independence from their families by running away adds further credence to the hue and cry that the American family is failing to fulfill its function adequately. That previously supermotivated middle-class youths are opting out of the educational marketplace before completing their credentialing causes some serious questions to be raised with regard to their parents' child-rearing practices. When more and more of these young people are turning to drugs as a way of life, then even the previously respected and revered advice givers to the parents of these young are castigated, and Benjamin Spock, for example, the one-time darling of the middle-class mother, is dethroned from his position in one fell swoop!

It would therefore seem to be more than coincidental that professional interest in the analysis of family dynamics has increased enormously in the last twenty years, but particularly in the last decade. Once primarily the purview of the sociologists and the cultural anthropologists, such as George Murdock (1949), Margaret Mead (1950), and Talcott Parsons (and Bales, 1955), the family is under scrutiny by behavioral scientists of all persuasions. Family therapy, a field previously dominated by but a few vanguards such as Nathan Ackerman (1958), Erika Chance (1959), and Murray Bowen (1961), is now a means of intervention practiced by social workers, psychologists, and psychiatrists in most community and child guidance clinics across the country. But, as yet, the bulk of the studies and research of the American family is dominated by sociologists, who in ever-increasing numbers are joining the fold of critics of the modern American family.

As is to be expected, the early sociological views of the family were relatively simplistic and filled with generalizations and abstractions. The family was thought to be the most basic of all institutions and the "primary" of all primary groups (Biesanz and Biesanz, 1964). Despite variations on the theme, the notion of the universality of the family went much unchallenged until fairly recently. This thinking was perhaps best embodied in and crystallized by Murdock (1949: 10), an anthropologist, who summarized the four necessary and sufficient functions of the family in all its permutations in all cultures as:

(1) socialization,

(2) economic cooperation,

(3) reproduction,

(4) sexual relations.

Later, Aberle (1950: 110) coined the notion of "functional prerequisites" regarding these four functions, using them as a shibboleth for the universality of the family.

Parsons and Bales (1955: 16-17), in examining contemporary American society, have suggested that family functions may be reduced to two:

(1) socialization and acculturation of the young,

(2) the stabilization and articulation of the adult members of that society.

Most recently Ira Reiss (1965) has thrown the entire matter up for grabs by suggesting only one basic universal function of the family—"nurturant socialization." He goes one step further by asserting that the "nuclear family itself seems either absent or unimportant in some cultures."

Although, at times, the exercises of such theorists may seem a bit removed from the everyday problems facing us, their theorizing attempts, through analysis, to delineate the causative forces over time which shape and change our institutions, their individual components, our society, and our world.

At present, the situation is at best confusing with regard to what the social analysts think about the future of the family. There are those who see the American family as a progressively dysfunctional appendix to the postindustrial societal body. Even the more optimistic are suggesting a narrowing and specializing of the family's role in society (Rodman, 1965), so that, in the view of some, it has become primarily a "giant shock absorber" for postindustrial man (Toffler, 1970)—and an overloaded one at that.

By dint of action, the behavioral scientists concerned with therapeutic intervention may be agreeing with their sociological colleagues. The growth of family therapy in the last decade may attest to this. The clinician's approach is far less abstract that that of the sociologist. Indeed, the clinician is most concerned with the active, day-to-day functioning of the individuals within the family. His emphasis is upon the interpersonal relationships within the family, the functioning of the individual members within the unit, and the workings of the unit as a whole. Most of these clinicians have their moorings in the more classical area of individual psychotherapy (e.g., psychiatry, psychiatric social work, and clinical psychology). Many began their work with children, discovering often that the disturbed child was merely an outward manifestation of a disturbed family (e.g., Fritz Redl [and Wineman], 1951: Nathan Ackerman, 1938). Treatment of the referred child often disclosed even more severe pathology in other children within the family or was considered relatively ineffective without the advent of the other family members. Others (e.g., Murray Bowen, 1965; Donald Jackson, 1961; Carl Whitaker et al., 1965) started with severely disturbed adult patients (i.e., schizophrenics), noted little gains employing classical individual techniques that did not include patients' families, and began using the family as their primary interventive approach. Despite the differences in origin, and the "bewildering array of diverse forms of family treatment" (Ackerman, 1970: 123), the emphasis is virtually entirely concentrated upon the internal workings of the family. (For a detailed explication of the state of the art, see Olson, 1970).

Thus, the activity from two different camps of social science seemed increasingly focused upon the family, but for both groups, the sociologist-anthropologist, and the clinician-therapist, the situation is disorganized and confusing. Compound this with the lack of *joindre* between these groups in coalescing their work in a consistent body of knowledge; one becomes aware that the situation is more and more like an ivory tower not unlike that built in Babel.

There are, however, more insidious dangers than confusion resulting from such analyses. Diagnosis and prognosis without recommendations for remediative actions are primarily intellectual athletics—a stance for which the social sciences have been under heavy fire most recently. And while the clinicians may disclaim debt on this account, their approach borders on band-aid psychology. That is, it is tantamount to putting band-aids on cancers. Not only does the basic problem go untreated, but the sore spots are hidden from view—neatly covered, until such time as the pathology has swept through and annihilated the system.

The present concern with the family tends to encourage the inference that the structure and function of the family are the root causes for difficulties within the larger society, when in reality the family is but a responsive institution grown overtaxed and overwhelmed by the many conflicting demands made upon it. We must begin to recognize (and pay more than lip service to the notion) that our familial structures do not shape society, but rather reflect and respond to it. To do otherwise is to place the cart before the horse and then maliciously castigate and beat the horse for not moving ahead—frustrating it in the process.

The family is indeed still the primary socializing unit within this society. When things go amiss, rather than condemn, should we not, instead, question whether the family is adjusting perhaps *too* well, whether it is performing its functions too efficiently in grooming its children for society, the values of which may be somewhat askew? Such was the case in Nazi Germany before and during World War II, where families either groomed their children for the state or were destroyed. The basic question being raised is whether the social sciences any longer can afford the luxury of taking a stance of "scientific neutrality," of social relativism with regard to the society of which they are a part, while examining the institutions of that society. The answer seems apparent that social science must face its responsibilities as change agent and advocate, and therefore it must be prepared to examine and evaluate the values of that society in which it operates.

When Aldous Huxley (1932) and George Orwell (1949) proposed their societies of the future based upon technocracy and the assembly-line efficiency of Henry Ford, it is dubious they anticipated that their "Brave New World" of "1984" was so close at hand or that we would be rushing to greet it with such open arms. When translating efficiency into human equations, we have translated means into ends without regard to the repercussions. Efficiency and the profit motive have made us callous—and have given us the power to do so with significant ease. Child-rearing—the process of socialization and education—has become mechanized to a point where our children have become commodities—things to be groomed and displayed. Mass production and assembly lines may be fine for the manufacturing of goods and machinery, but the corresponding lack of quality controls and planned obsolescence, when translated into human products, cannot be tolerated if we are to continue to maintain that we are truly a nation invested in seeing a democratic, humane, and concerned citizenry developed through our young people.

It is at this crossroad that the conflict between our concern for the individual and our constraints to conformity creates stress. In our quest for efficiency in child-rearing and development, we have turned to assembly-line methodology. Under such ideology, the individually produced commodity is economically unsound. Education, in its attempts to serve larger and larger numbers, has resorted to these techniques. The American families and the communities which house them have become primarily the suppliers of raw material for our educational assembly lines, which attempt to process greater and greater numbers. The consequences have had severe effects upon our age-grading systems. We have become a nation of horizontal, tightly knit peer cadres. In addition, our system of planned obsolescence has aggravated the situation so that the process of aging has become stigmatized. Unlike the older nations of the East (China and Japan, for example), our system of age-grading is not a relatively straight ascending line whereupon the older one becomes, the more status and respect one attains. Rather, our system resembles more the normative, or bell-shaped curve of which we have become so enamoured. The relatively narrow age band (roughly 30 through 50 years of age) is seen as the pinnacle power years. These are the years when a man reaches his acme in the production-consumer society in which we live. Those on either end of this age range are often seen as dependent in some way or another. Edwards (1967: 509) has phrased the situation succinctly if perhaps somewhat brutally:

> In many instances, it is not too much of an overstatement to consider as objects those that have not yet developed exchangeable resources (the young) and those who have exhausted theirs (the elderly). Even those occupying the middle ground, however, are not necessarily in an enviable position, for their relationships often lack all but a vestige of emotional interchange.

Thus, maturing, for a third of our lives, means gaining independence, power, and respect. This is the phase that we refer to as "growing up," and it is imbued with the dreams and expectations of becoming a person. Despite a relatively momentary plateau, the next two-thirds of our life span are basically a downhill slide with little to look forward to: retirement, pension, grandchildren—all words loaded with the onus of dependency and lack of productivity.

Our children's transition into their teens and twenties and their subsequent autonomy (that which has been referred to as the "empty nest" phase) have become, in our society, the prelude to their parents' disenfranchisement—this process we refer to as "growing old." This is the age where desperation often sets in. Men become concerned about having "done their thing," and women begin forgetting birthdays and dyeing their hair. Youth fetishism becomes the order, and commercials for everything from cosmetics to breakfast cereal zealously drive home our psychological quest for the fountain of youth. We continually emphasize our unique tradition of anti-tradition in this way—that which is new (i.e., young) is better.

Other ramifications of condensing the productive years into roughly two decades are manifold. There is a frantic need to "make it," and one must do it quickly. As a consequence, families often make many geographic moves to maintain and jockey for position and power in the economic marketplace. This, in turn, encourages a necessity for consistency and conformity in our educational systems as children are frequently introduced to different schools. Furthermore, as concern with climbing the vocational ladder intensifies, parents are often more than willing to entrust much, if not all, of their children's education and socialization to the professionals—the educators. Our overworked and underpaid educators are, in turn, forced to look for more efficient methods in order to process more children faster, through our school systems. Furthermore, they often feel harassed and annoyed when parents, out of concern for their young, siphon time away from already overburdened educational and administrative schedules by requesting counsel and advice. Attempts to ameliorate this trend are made through organized PTA groups, but their lack of effectiveness is, by and large, notorious, and the "association" becomes a travesty of the word.

As many authors have pointed out recently (Goode, 1963; Bronfenbrenner, 1970; Slater, 1970), the geographic mobility is usually at the expense of extended family ties and the loss of a spirit of community as we had known them in the past. Anonymity and a lack of commitment isolate the family further from a sense of belonging, of rootedness and tradition. Emotional interchange between generations is primarily expressed among the few people in the nuclear family, again enforcing a locking into peer group or horizontal social structure.

Grandparents, aunts, and uncles become people to be called on the phone and visited perhaps once or twice a year. They are nonpresent. Though investigators like Litwak (1960) and Sussman (1959) argue that extended family cohesion still exists, their argument stresses the helping relationships of adult siblings even over distances. The effect of increased horizontal association and lack of cross-generational ties is still enhanced. Interviews with runaway adolescents (Haro, 1971) indicate that these young people have few adults with whom they can share and discuss their problems and concerns. Friends or siblings are their primary avenues for expression.

Grandparents command little respect because they do not contribute to the economic status of the family (except in rare and special instances). They are no longer sought for counsel, advice, or decision-making. They have been encouraged to let their children lead their own lives, and instead of the working mother using her mother to help raise her children, she turns (once again) to the professional (e.g., nursery schools, day-care centers, professional babysitters, and so on).

Our children are thus prepared for our peer-oriented culture and we begin the countdown for orbit the moment they leave the breast. Home has become the place where you sleep, eat breakfast and dinner, and watch a little TV—often in your own room (as we become two- and three-set families). It is the place from which you leave for school (nursery, elementary, high, college, and graduate)—the place you return to after commuting to work (vocational or volunteer), women's clubs, or Little League. Most American parents spend less time with their children than do their teachers, and that time is often nonrelational in nature after the first three or four years of life. The modern American family stresses what Talcott Parsons (and Bales, 1955) has referred to as the "instrumental" (as opposed to "expressive") cogwheeling of the corporation: the distribution of funds and commodities, the planning of extrafamilial schedules, and the like. The peer group becomes ubiquitous as our emotional support system. From nursery school through graduate school, close association with anyone but your nearest agemates is exceptional.

This sytem has interesting consequences. For one, it severely delimits the choice of experiential models to emulate. For the male child, the process is devastating. Father no longer does work that is visible, with the exception of a few minor, incidental chores around the house. For our girls, there exists a more insidious danger. Their model is the high-powered house manager known as mother: the supershopper, megamaid, cook, clubwoman, and PTA organizer. The only other live alternative model is the teacher-expert, who, for both boys and girls in the early formative years, is predominantly female.

Beyond that, the field is left open to the ever-present media for emulative objects. The TV industry has taken over that which the movie industry began and with a vengeance. Unrealistic fantasies about love, marriage, and family life are voraciously gobbled up by our experience-hungry young, incorporated into their beings, and stored in their private video tape banks for instant replay when necessary. Such pap becomes encouraged viewing by parents who have little option between the "family shows" and some of the more violent offerings. There is, of course, the Western, which continues to emphasize our pioneer heritage, and with it the ruggedness and vigor of youth—the young adult. (The image of the sage old grandfather is not to be found in our fables.) This kind of programming is constantly injected with the machine-gun selling approach of the advertisers who stress the need to acquire—the desirability of newness, and the be-like-everybody-else-on-the-block mentality. (The hazards of these approaches with regard to our children's notions about life have been discussed most recently in a report of the 1970 White House Conference on Children.)

Another danger of increased horizontality lies in the lack of individuals who can offer emotionally supportive dependency relationships. From three years on, our children are thrown into an awareness that the "Robins" are much better than the "Bluebirds" in reading, that an "A" is much more meaningful than just being the first letter of the alphabet, and that teachers are as much (if not more so) judges as they are purveyors of information. They are certainly not people of whom to ask questions, for to do so would lay you open to judgment as a fool, and besides, hands are only to be raised in *answer* to questions (or, perhaps under dire straits, to get permission to go to the lavatory). Our five- and six-year-old preprofessionals and junior homemakers quickly learn that parents are very concerned about how many first letters of the alphabet they can log on the slips of paper that with great regularity are carried home from school. They soon learn to figure out that some of their friends are far better in the game of collecting certain letters than are others—and almost with mother's milk they imbibe that good old American tradition called competition—and what's worse, it begins to taste good! Indeed, what could be more American than competition?

Who then is there left to give some measure of unconditionality to their positive regard? Teacher judges in the form of grades; parents deliver sentence in the form of withholding rewards or meting out punishment; peers are competitors, and grandma and grandpa are 500 miles away. The answer, more and more often these days, tends to be child guidance clinics and professional psychotherapists. Again—we return to the professional, who for a fee will attempt to patch up the wounded egos and send them back on their developmental road to their American destiny. As more clinicians are called upon to intervene, their function begins to resemble that of professional grandparents—an interesting irony.

But, it might be said, the American parent in rearing his young *has* followed the advice of the expert. During the past three decades, the advice givers have offered numerous books on child-rearing and have stressed the psychic development of the young–particularly the importance of the first five years. Parents are aware that this is the same short time period in which they have to do their job before society (i.e., the school and the peer group) takes over. The effect is to instill anxiety and fear in our young parents who, because of the horizontal nature of *their* rearing, have had little firsthand experience with children, and now, when needed, little contact with their own parents and older siblings of greater experience. So they turn to the nonpresent authorities–the books. Books are filled with formulae and warnings: "do's and don'ts." Because all unique situations and relationships cannot be covered, parents must interpret and extrapolate. The terrible responsibility looms before them that they have a life in their hands–a being to whom they can do either considerable psychic harm or enormous good. The effects of rigid schedules in feeding and toilet training can create "neurotic" behavior patterns in adults; stultify and stunt creativity, and so on ad infinitum. So to be on the safe side, parents often interpret encouraged flexibility to mean a policy of laxity or laissez faire, and freedom to mean license. The infant becomes an unsuspecting tyrant ruling by the cudgel of guilt instillation in his confused and isolated parents.

When the infant tyrants reach preadolescence and adolescence, they are no longer strangers to their parents, nor are their parents strangers to the child-rearing experience. At this time, after having ensured that the children will not be restricted, hampered, uncreative individuals, we reverse ourselves and begin enforcing more authoritarian behavior patterns. As parents, we then become shocked and indignant that our children do not and will not heed the rules of the road, nor do they look to us more often for advice and counsel. They resent the imposition by adults of standards which seem to them suddenly and arbitrarily established. But what is worse, we are hurt that we have little part in their lives. Just as we have put the finishing touches on the horizontal independence of our young, we recognize, too late, that we have created a gap between us. And in our puzzlement, hurt and indignation, we blame and attack poor Dr. Spock (1971).

We have, as parents, turned the child-rearing process topsy turvy. We have not afforded our young the benefit of structure and controls—of psychic protection in infancy and toddlerhood when it is most needed, but rather have delayed the process until the later years, the time when we should be granting more freedom and expecting more decision-making on the part of our youth. An interesting study comparing Danish and American child-rearing practices makes just this point, concluding that, "the discipline exercised at an early age would create a child who as an adolescent is far more disciplined and one to whom, as a consequence, the parent can afford to give more freedom" (Kandel and Lesser, 1969: 357).

Others have tried to make the distinction between love and license and the need for a consistent notion in parenting (e.g., Bettleheim, 1955; and, more recently, Chess et al., 1965), but their advice, again, has been interpreted in light of our own cultural values and anxieties. In our consumer-commodity society, this often means the doling out of goods. Then we wonder why our young have become so materialistic, when by the most subtle form of behavior modification we have trained them to prize the things that we, as parents, have been supplying in substitution for discipline, guidance, time, and understanding in order to assuage our own remorse (only dimly, though gnawingly felt, because we too are products of the selfsame system).

Because we *are* aware at some level, we try to correct for our brave new world. We try in the only way we know—by structuring time away from the home in planned activities. The activities often attempt to simulate models of old. And we appeal to the experts to help us design these models. The YMCA Indian Guides program is one such example. It tries to structure the father-son relationship by having the "men" (seven-, eight-, and nine-year-old boys and their fathers in small groups) in Indian regalia sitting in a circle, repeating the slogan "pals forever." This program has grown so popular that it has been extended to a father-daughter program called the "Indian Princesses" and even more recently a mother-daughter program—"The Indian Maidens." In the past, *Ladies' Home Journal* has talked about "togetherness," suggesting bowling, family vacations, and hobbies as a means of fostering this idyllic family scene.

But despite their popularity, such efforts are by and large most often futile in their attempts to create greater verticality—more bridges between the generations. Because, despite the obvious and felt lack and the needs for some kind of supportive shoring up or redefinition of the family, we are attempting to constrain our modern technologically dictated life styles into Procrustean beds of nostalgic fantasy, that which William Goode (1963) has referred to as "the classical family of Western nostalgia." However, we constantly find out (though never really learn) that we cannot go home again—because that home to which we want to return never really was except in our Proustian reveries.

Goode described well the stereotypes we cherish, but does not explore the reasons they persist in our fantasies. More recently, however, Bronfenbrenner (1967) and Slater (1970), in examining these stereotypes, spell out the need—a hunger and a wish for connectedness and belonging—for affiliation.

Our children are being raised in essentially noncommunity communities, where carbon copy anonymity and the constraints toward conformity are the order of the day. There is no longer a spirit of neighborhood. As these communities grow larger and larger, and along with them our schools and universities, they become more like horizontal high-rises. Anonymity increases. The quest for individuality is mistakenly perverted into the pursuit of privacy, which becomes almost obsessional. The result is increasing isolation and a growing sense of anomy.

The young, having been trained in the model, associate with their peers—the old withdraw. We become Johnny's father and Sally's mother to one another. We shake our heads when we see our children playing with matches and chasing their balls in the street, rather than taking the time to correct their behavior. That is, we say, "These are not our children and we have not the right to castigate them, just as we would not expect our neighbors to reprimand our own children for their behavior." Only in times of great stress or emergency (when snowbound or during power failures) do glimmers of that spirit of neighborhood return.

What happens to our affiliative needs the rest of the time? To a large degree, we place the burden on the nuclear family, and like the obliging scapegoat, it desperately attempts to meet the need without questioning the role it is being asked to fulfill, or recognizing the impossibility of the task and the unreasonableness of the request. Then the critics step in and condemn the family for its failures, using the example of modern youth. Their search for new life styles—the burgeoning of communal living, "free communities," and so on have all been used as arguments that the modern American family has failed to meet the needs of postindustrial man. The introduction to a recent compendium on the family contends: "Not only is the nuclear family a faultily constructed piece of social engineering, but it also, in the long run, contains the seeds of its own destruction" (Skolnick and Skolnick, 1971: 29).

The danger of this kind of argument is that of throwing out the baby with the bath. Indeed, it well may be that despite the inability of the family to cope with all the excessive demands made upon it, it has nevertheless somehow managed to inculcate in its young members a desire for that sense of community toward which they strive in ways outside their present family structures. Curiously enough, at the same time that many of our youth are looking to forms of group and communal living as alternatives, there are indications of a gradual return to the more traditional forms of family life in those societies which have attempted to mandate or legislate communal rather than nuclear familialism. Both Russian and Israeli parents seem to want a more important share in the rearing of their young (Goode, 1964: 5; Wells, 1971: 3).

Thus we must be wary of the typically American penchant for panacea solutions. Particularly regarding our social policies, we are far too prone to let things ride, to work themselves out until the crisis arises. We then frantically rush in with a dearth of well-thought-out models, spend large (though still inadequate) sums of money, and finally throw up our hands in dismay when their effectiveness is less than miraculous.

This is the process by which we create self-fulfilling prophecies. For example, if the family is not, in our judgment, preparing its offspring adequately for our times, we propose downward extensions of our presently over-strained educational networks, suggesting forms of institutional education of three-year-olds (or younger). Not that Headstart or nursery schools are, in and of themselves, bad, but the protracting and extending of our already overlong credentialing process both upward and now downward, has the effect of eroding and disenfranchising the community and the family unit from its training and educational responsibilities. Will we ten years from now castigate the family for not fulfilling our same expectations in eighteen months that we now blame it for not being able to accomplish in four or five years? Furthermore, are we so pleased and complacent with the effectiveness of our educational systems that we are willing to substitute one overtaxed institution for another?

But most important, we must recognize that if an institution is not meeting the needs of a society, there may be at *least* two reasons:

(1) the institution is inadequate (our usual assumption), or

(2) the ideologies, values, and priorities of that society in which the institution is operating may be awry.

It is the second of these alternatives, I am firmly convinced, that we as scientists and citizens have not explored adequately. We are a young nation grown fast—indeed, an adolescent "Boy-Man" in time, struggling with our identity. If we are to mature into a great society, it will be not because we have augmented our technology into an uncontrolled, voraciously destructive behemoth, but because we have used that technology to enhance a moralistic philosophy which cherishes the rights and uniqueness of the individual while encouraging his relationship to those around him. Unless we take the time and energy to do so, Ralph Linton's (1949: 38) apocalyptic prediction may prove to be more than ironic rhetoric: "In the Götterdämmerung which overwise science and overfoolish statesmanship are preparing for us, the last man will spend his last hours searching for his wife and child."

REFERENCES

ABERLE, D. F. (1950) "The functional prerequisites of a society." 60 (January): 100-111.
ACKERMAN, N. W. (1970) "Family psychotherapy today." Family Process 9: 123-126.
––– (1958) The Psychodynamics of Family Life. New York: Basic Books.
––– (1938) "The unity of the family." Archives of Pediatrics 55: 51-62.
BETTELHEIM, B. (1955) Love Is Not Enough. New York: Free Press.
BIESANZ, J. and M. BIESANZ (1964) Modern Society. Englewood Cliffs, N.J.: Prentice-Hall.
BOWEN, M. (1965) "Family psychotherapy with schizophrenia in the hospital and in private practice," in I. Boszormenyi-Nagy and J. Framo (eds.) Intensive Family Therapy. New York: Harper & Row.
––– (1961) "Family psychotherapy." Amer. J. of Orthopsychiatry 31: 41-60.
BRONFENBRENNER, U. (1970) Two Worlds of Childhood. New York: Russell Sage.
––– (1967) "The split-level American family." Saturday Rev. (October 7): 60-66.

CHANCE, E. (1959) Families in Treatment. New York: Basic Books.
CHESS, S., A. THOMAS, and H. G. BIRCH (1965) Your Child is a Person. New York: Viking.
EDWARDS, J. N. (1967) "The future of the family revisited." J. of Marriage and the Family (August): 505-511.
GOODE, W. J. (1964) The Family. Englewood Cliffs, N.J.: Prentice-Hall.
––– (1963) World Revolution and Family Patterns. New York: Free Press.
HARO, P. J. (1971) "A descriptive analysis of the runaway adolescent and his family." Master's thesis. University of Maryland.
HUXLEY, A. (1932) Brave New World. New York and London: Harper.
JACKSON, D. D. (1961) "Family therapy in the family of the schizophrenic," pp. 272-287 in M. I. Stein (ed.) Contemporary Psychotherapies. New York: Free Press.
KANDEL, D. and G. S. LESSER (1969) "Parent-adolescent relationships and adolescent independence in the United States and Denmark." J. of Marriage and Family (May): 345-358.
LINTON, R. (1949) "The natural history of the family," pp. 18-38 in R. Anshen (ed.) The Family: Its Function and Destiny. New York: Harper.
LITWAK, E. (1960) "Geographic mobility and extended family cohesion." Amer. Soc. Rev. 25: 385-394.
MEAD, M. (1950) Sex and Temperament in Three Primitive Societies. New York: Mentor.
MURDOCK, G. P. (1949) Social Structure. New York: Macmillan.
MYRDAL, G. (1944) The American Dilemma. New York and London: Harper.
OLSON, D. H. (1970) "Marital and family therapy: integrative review and critique." J. of Marriage and Family (November): 501-537.
ORWELL, G. (1949) 1984. New York: Harcourt, Brace.
PARSONS, T. and R. F. BALES (1955) Family, Socialization and Interaction Process. New York: Free Press.
REDL, F. and D. WINEMAN (1951) Children Who Hate. New York: Free Press.
REISS, I. L. (1965) "The universality of the family: a conceptual analysis." J. of Marriage and Family 27 (November): 443-453.
RODMAN, H. (1965) "Talcott Parsons' view of the changing American family." Merrill-Palmer Q. of Behavior and Development 11 (July): 209-227.
SKOLNICK, A. S. and J. H. SKOLNICK (1971) Family in Transition. Boston: Little, Brown.
SLATER, P. (1970) The Pursuit of Loneliness. Boston: Beacon.
SPOCK, B. (1971) "Don't blame me!" Look (January 26): 37-38.
SUSSMAN, M. B. (1959) "The isolated nuclear family: fact or fiction." Social Problems 6: 333-340.
TOFFLER, A. (1970) Future Shock. New York: Random House.
WELLS, C. A. (1971) "Women's lib and the USSR experience." Between the Lines 30 (May 15): 6.
WHITAKER, C., R. E. FELDER, and J. WARKENTIN (1965) "Countertransference in the family treatment of schizophrenia," in I. Boszormenyi-Nagy and J. L. Framo (eds.) Intensive Family Therapy. New York: Harper & Row.
White House Conference on Children (1970). Report to the President: Washington, D.C.: Government Printing Office.

9

YOUTH AND THE DRUG CRISIS

JOEL FORT, M.D.

There are differing points of view on evil as illustrated by the anecdote about the young boy who regularly attended Sunday School. One Sunday morning his teacher said to him, "Are you troubled by evil thoughts?" He said, "No, I enjoy them."

In approaching the matter of drug use and abuse and youth behavior, we have taken for granted a great many things that really need to be reexamined. What is a drug? When does use become abuse? Who uses drugs and why? What do we mean by "youth"? How can we define problems objectively?

We start off with the basic misconception about what drugs are. We have been taught by the selective omissions and preoccupations of the mass media, politicians, and other "authorities" in our society that there are only a few drugs and a few drug problems—namely, marijuana, LSD, and narcotics.

If I were to hold up a glass of a liquid substance and talk to you about a beverage in referring to alcohol, you would have quite a different reaction than if I were to talk to you about something I called a *medication;* still a different and more emotional reaction if I talked to you about a *drug;* and, finally, you would probably have the most intense reaction if I called that substance a narcotic, because that is the foundation for our emotional attitude about certain phenomena—the stereotype of the dope fiend. Parenthetically, we use very endearing terms to refer to somebody we do not like who uses a drug of which we disapprove. We call them heads, freaks, fiends, rummies, and a variety of other terms that drive people deeper into a drug culture.

We doom ourselves to ignorance and fear by conjuring up these stereotypes and by misunderstanding the proper context of drugs. "Drug" actually means any biologically active substance, whether used in the treatment of illness or disease or used for nonmedical recreational purposes, and it includes aspirin, penicillin, antihistamines, and the mind-altering drugs that are part of the broader drug context. This includes, or starts with, the most widely used and abused of these drugs, by young and old, legally and illegally (if you remember the age prohibitions), the drug alcohol. The true psychoactive drug context then goes on to the most widely used and abused mind-altering drug by young and old, legally and illegally, the stimulant drug nicotine (also an insecticide and vasoconstrictant), which is accompanied by such "healthful" ingredients as arsenic, cyanide, formaldehyde, carbon monoxide, coal tars, nitrogen dioxide, and a variety of other things. Thus alcohol and cigarettes (tobacco) are by far the most extensively used illegal drugs by the young. Then you come to the drugs that are between full social approval and encouragement and some degree of official concern: sedatives, stimulants, and tranquilizers. These are used by about 35 million Americans; not quite the 70 and 100 million each using the first two drugs, but still with massive abuses.

Only then can an honest person come to a discussion of those substances that get all the attention as *the* drugs and *the* problems. There are the *LSD-type* drugs, a list of which reads very much like a list of the federal bureaucracy: STP, MDA, DMT, one named in honor of the FDA, and a variety of others. *Narcotic,* which is a very much misused term, scientifically means opium, morphine, heroin, codeine, methadone, Demerol; drugs used medically to treat severe pain, cough, and diarrhea.

There is no such thing as a "soft narcotic" any more than there is soft pregnancy. A drug is either a narcotic or is not a narcotic, and it should certainly not be controversial for anyone to talk about drugs by their precise names. Thus, to talk about alcohol as alcohol instead of "demon rum" would help to prevent a great deal of misunderstanding and confusion that our past sources of drug education have fostered.

Then we have *marijuana* in this context, used by some 20,000,000 Americans of all backgrounds, and an enormous range of miscellaneous substances that are particularly important in showing the impossibility of ever dealing with this phenomenon through any one oversimplified approach such as blanket criminalization. We have morning glory and other plant seeds, nutmeg and other kitchen spices, catnip, nitrous oxide (in aerosol cans of whipped cream or in tanks), belladonna (scopolamine) in over-the-counter pseudosedatives, and many others. Therefore, if a person is forced to give up one substance, he easily turns to another that may be equally as or more dangerous unless the motives or causes of drug use are attacked and more positive alternatives presented.

Let me also use other examples to try to communicate to you the absurdity of our present approach to certain drug problems. After the *Wall Street Journal* published an article about ten young people turning on with catnip, a legislator in Ohio introduced a bill to make it a felony to possess catnip. As the construction industry presumably geared up to build more jails and prisons for all cats and their owners, the bill fortunately died in committee.

Then we have two Congressmen who gained great mileage in their districts for being "hard" on airplane hijacking. I am sure that all of us are concerned about the large number of airplane hijackings. I certainly am because I lecture and consult a lot around the country and have to fly frequently. These legislators called for harsher penalties as the answer and introduced bills to bring this about; however, few people were aware that the death penalty is already provided for. It is difficult to understand how one can be harder in penalties than death. If problems could be solved that simply, we would have far fewer difficulties in society than we have now. If simply passing a law against something is all that is necessary to stop it, we could pass laws against poverty, disease, war, and a variety of other things.

Despite this, those who call for reform, in this field that has become much more controversial than it should be, are usually labeled "soft on drugs" with the explicit assumption that the present approach has been "hard on drugs." Actually, the current American system has led to far more drug use by more people, including more dangerous drugs than ever before, and, therefore, objectively it has been soft on drugs while being hard on *people*. What we need is a reversal of our values—to be hard on drugs in some humane, effective, and rational way while being soft on people. Our society should place the greatest emphasis on human beings and not on drugs.

With that in mind, recognize that you must distinguish between the use and abuse of a drug. You certainly can disapprove of anybody using, under any circumstances, certain substances, but there is a clear difference between a person who *uses* alcohol, marijuana, or other drugs one time, occasionally, or even regularly—once a month or daily. There needs to be a distinction between moderate doses and heavy doses, and a major distinction between drug use and drug abuse.

Most people define drug abuse, insofar as they define it at

all, as any illegal drug use. In addition to that being generally inadequate, it is also very hypocritical because the most widely used illegal drugs, as I have already pointed out, are alcohol and tobacco, which are ignored. If we were, however, to fully, justly, consistently enforce all existing drug laws, we could, for the first time, eliminate overcrowding in all our high school classrooms. Ninety-five percent of the students, by twelfth grade, could be sent to jail or prison for the illegal possession of alcohol or tobacco, first of all, and then as a distant but significant third, marijuana, and finally other drugs.

The other common mid-definition of drug abuse is: anyone you do not like who uses a drug you disapprove of, particularly if that person has not visited the barbershop recently or is not appropriately dressed in terms of your values. That all such people are drug abusers is what we are led to believe by some of our current sources of information.

Drug abuse is the excessive use of any drug that measurably impairs health or damages social or vocational adjustment. Obviously, use is related to abuse, and, obviously, we want to try to deal with the total context. But the highest priority certainly should go to reducing drug abuse, particularly through treatment and education. We do not understand that any drug—caffeine, nicotine, alcohol, marijuana, or the rest—can produce psychological dependence, which is the same as the layman's term, habituation. We have all been taught that, if somebody uses polysyllabic language and a pathological frame of reference, the thing talked about is much more significant and dangerous than if he just used ordinary language. So if I talk about one drug and say it produces psychological dependence, that sounds very serious unless you understand that any and all drugs can produce habituation, as can many other things in our society. The only way to determine whether that habituation is a problem is to use some objective definition of drug abuse applied individually. There are many millions of Americans who are psychologically dependent on television, so that when the tube suddenly burns out after years of their spending five hours a day in front of the set, they become restless, irritable, out of sorts, and do not know what to do with themselves. That is a somewhat fuller context of habituation than is usually talked about, and, depending upon your value system, you may feel as I do that such TV dependence can be as detrimental to the individual self-development and the society's welfare as habituation to any drug, whether alcohol, marijuana, or another.

The most important concept for understanding the drug scene is really the concept of the *drug effect;* how these drugs exert their actions on people. We are stuck between two polarities in most people's discussion of the political drugs. On the one hand, there are those who tell us that within minutes of exposure to drug X or Y everyone would become a murderer, rapist, heroin addict, or lifelong inmate of a mental hospital. On the other hand, there are those who tell us that within a short time of such exposure everyone would become a fully self-actualized, creative genius living happily ever after. I hope that seems absurd when put that way, but if you think about it, that is the way most people are talking or responding when they discuss certain drugs today. They are not thinking in context, not thinking about the pharmacology, psychology, or sociology of that particular drug and how it relates to other substances but, instead, talking in a way that is very well rewarded in our society, using the one-dimensional, viewing with alarm, out-of-context approach which is the technique of the advertising industry, the politician, and anybody who wants to get headlines. If I were to talk to you about alcohol on this basis, using my experience in treating skid row alcoholics, I would try to get you to believe that all users of this drug were derelicts with severe liver and brain damage, undergoing delirium tremens. Of course, you would immediately recognize that I was only talking about a small part of the picture and that I was distorting the full reality of the use and abuse of this drug.

But when that is done with certain other drugs, you have been taught not to think through the broader picture and to accept uncritically this one-dimensional view. Thus, we have headlines to lead us to believe that the only cause of violence, massacre, or whatever in Vietnam or other areas is that a certain squad of soldiers used marijuana 24 hours before. At the same time, we have headlines that leave out the use of other kinds of drugs. Thus, we do not have a headline that says "Drunk Richard Speck Kills Eight Student Nurses in Chicago." Yet, the use of alcohol was so much involved that the families of those girls killed have won a suit against the people who dispensed the large quantities of alcohol to Richard Speck on that particular day. Alcohol was selectively omitted because we do not think about it in the same way we do other drugs. In either instance, however, it would still be magical thinking to assume that alcohol or pot by themselves produced antisocial behavior. The way mind-altering drugs really exert their effects is best demonstrated by the most common drug experience in our society, the cocktail party. People of the same backgrounds, values, and body size consume identical amounts of this particular drug, and, far from everybody behaving in the same way, they act in quite different ways. Some become boisterous or aggressive; some become passive, withdrawn, or sleepy; some become amorous, flirtatious, or even lascivious. Same drug, same kind of people, yet quite different effects. This illustrates what is true of all mind-altering drugs—the basic ingredient in the drug effect is what you are as a human being—your personality, character, mood, attitudes, and expectations, all of which interact with the pharmacology of the drug and the social setting or environment in which that drug is consumed. Mainly what comes out is what you are as a person.

If you understand that concept, you can demythologize drugs for young people and also older people. You can convey that there is no drug—alcohol, marijuana, or any other—that will revitalize your school, improve your family life, or rebuild your neighborhood by your going on a trip with it. Drugs simply do not work in this way; they do not make ignoramuses into creative geniuses or geniuses into monsters. Just as many of the dangers of some drugs have been lied about, so have many of the benefits of some drugs. Both have to be put into perspective for our society, rather than a continuance of this sensationalism, glorification, and mythologizing.

To analyze sexual behavior in relation to drugs, as we might want to do because there is a lot of talk today about young people supposedly engaging in "sexual excesses" after using marijuana, you might think of a person sitting in front of his television set deeply enjoying one of his favorite programs, such as "Beverly Hillbillies," "Bonanza," "Gunsmoke," or "Mission Impossible," perhaps hoping that the whole program will self-destruct. There is no drug that will magically stimulate him to engage in sexual behavior in preference to watching his favorite program, whether that sexual behavior is preferred to watching TV forms of sexual interaction, whether the drug be a martini or grass brought by his wife. If, on the other hand, you have a person who, because of biology and psychology, has some already existing interest in sex, as many Americans do, he can certainly use a mind-altering drug in association with that. Most commonly used is alcohol—but remember what Shakespeare pointed out in *Macbeth* about that drug—that it may stimulate interest but diminish performance. The drug in itself does not produce the sexual behavior. That stems from more complex conditioning and learning. The drug can play a role in reducing whatever inhibitions, anxieties, or guilts the person might have about sexual relationships, but it does not produce it, and it certainly cannot be counted upon to give an enhancing effect to the sexual relationship. Sexual excesses seem to be a successful concept for arousing all kinds of fantasies in older people's minds about orgies that young people are supposedly engaging in. Perhaps the fantasies arouse a touch of envy in the older minds as well.

The same thing applies to crime. If you have dedicated your life to burglary as a profession, you can certainly use a drug in association with that already existing vocation, but, fortunately, there is no drug that will make somebody commit burglary if he would never otherwise do so.

We must look at why people want to believe such mythologies. It is understandable that we all crave a simple explanation for everything, that we have low tolerance for ambiguity and complexity, and that our media, the advertising industry, and our political process all foster the idea that there are oversimplified pseudosolutions for all human problems. We have to get beyond that to really teach people from early childhood on to think and to be immune to this type of propagandizing about drugs or about other things in the society.

Drug education, in the past, has been done by people without training or experience in any of the relevant disciplines—pharmacology, psychology, sociology, education, and a variety of other things that in any other field we would consider essential but have totally neglected in this field, Thus, we have had, first, temperance lecturers come into a classroom, hold up a glass of pure alcohol, drop a worm in it and, as the worm shriveled up, say to everyone in the room that this is what happens to the brain from use of this drug. Next, we have had drug policemen come in and say that use of marijuana or certain other drugs rots the brain. What happens is that, as people discover through their own research or that of others, these horrible things do not happen, and they (rightly) conclude that they have been lied to. Then they assume that even when a more knowledgeable, more responsible person tells them about certain risks or dangers with a given drug, he is also lying. They conclude that the drug is harmless, and they also tragically conclude that what is said about drugs such as heroin, amphetamines, barbiturates, LSD, glue, and gasoline is as distorted as what was said about alcohol and marijuana. This has been one of the major causes of the rapid escalation of drug use in our society and, thus, creates "softness on drugs." Effective drug education has to discard this kind of approach and institute a program that deals in context with all the drugs, attempts to be honest and objective, and desensationalizes and demythologizes drugs. It should be done by specially trained classroom teachers, not by former narcotic addicts presumed to be expert in pharmacology, sociology, and in all the other drugs that they did not abuse, or by an English teacher who is suddenly called in by a principal and told to give a lecture next week that will solve all the drug problems.

Actually, we have never tried drug education if we define drug education in the same way education would be defined in other areas. There has been a great deal of talk about drug education, but most such programs have been of the kind I have described above and have not really attempted to deal with the problem with the kind of perspective, commitment, honesty, or the knowledge that is needed.

The question of why people use drugs should be asked not only about the young, but also about the society as a whole. I am not sure, among other things, what the exact definition of youthfulness is. That is another concept we take for granted. We might all agree that we would set the lower range about age 15, but as we ourselves grow older, the upper range of youthfulness steadily changes, so that many people might define the upper boundary at 35, 40, 50, or even 60. It is more, I think, a spirit than it is a biological age, but certainly there are major differences in the way people think based upon their age group. In any case, why do people, young and old, rich and poor, black and white, use drugs?

We live in a drug-ridden, drug-saturated, drug-obsessed society. Almost from the moment we pop out of the birth canal and are placed in front of a television set in the maternity room, we are inculcated with the idea that every time we have a pain, problem, or some trouble we should drop a pill, take a drink, or smoke a cigarette, particularly one that is one millimeter longer than another and, therefore, will kill us two years sooner. This age of chemistry is particularly fostered by the alcoholic beverage and tobacco industries. Each of these spends $1 million every day in the United States alone to foster the earliest possible use of these drugs in the greatest possible quantities and, indirectly, of other drugs, too. They stress three images (if you think about what you see on television, in magazines, or in newspapers)—images of sexual pleasure, of eternal youth, and of happiness—somehow magically to be obtained from a chemical. They beam this imagery particularly to programs watched by large numbers of young people. If you watched or listened to recent Super Bowl football games, it is obvious that if Len Dawson or Joe Namath and their teammates buy the beer and tobacco it was implied by the commercials they regularly used, they would not even have been able to stagger onto the field, let alone win those championships. That is the way we teach drug use in our society. It is institutionalized and taken for granted, rather than being deliberate behavior. Twenty-two thousand hours are spent by the average American child by age 18 watching TV—more hours, by the way, than are spent in classrooms—to progressively inculcate pro-drug attitudes.

Every time children see their parents or other adults socialize with other people or seem to be having a good time, they see that apparently they must depend upon alcohol, tobacco, or other mind-altering drugs. This communicates that people cannot relate or be happy without chemicals. How often do you see people sit down and "turn on" to each other's personality, interests, and activities rather than defining hospitality or pleasure in terms of how much alcohol they can consume in a concentrated time period (just before going out into their cars to drive on the highway) or how many cigarettes they can smoke. Strangely enough, people can have a good time or be happy without depending upon drugs. I know of several instances where people have thought they were consuming alcohol or marijuana and actually were not, generally behaving in exactly the same manner as of they had consumed the active drug because of their expectations. Thus, people know they can talk louder, they can use four-letter words, they can pinch their neighbor's wife, or they can do a variety of things that they usually cannot do in the office or in other kinds of situations. That expectation of what is appropriate for a drugged setting leads people to do it or get a contact high from each other even when the drug is not involved.

Peer-group pressure is certainly a key factor in drug usage. Young people correctly point to the conformity and over-conformity of the older generations, while at the same time, being human, they ignore their own conformity. Far from being individualistic in their use of chemicals, they have accepted the basic definition that chemicals or drugs are "where it's at" and the more general messages that technology equals progress and quicker "solutions" are superior to those that take time. The best example of peer-group pressure, in regard to drug use, is the cocktail party. The nondrinker at such a social event is a major source of anxiety to everyone else present. Considerable pressure is exerted to get him to conform to the other people's pattern of drug usage and, at the very least, he comes to be seen as that most dangerous of Americans—the nonconformist. The young, particularly in a society that emphasizes popularity beyond everything else, when they see popularity defined in terms of the use of alcohol or tobacco, as it has been for decades or, in more recent years, marijuana or certain other drugs, it is little wonder that the majority of them accept this definition. They, too, want to be in, accepted, and part of their crowd. The most valuable lesson we can learn is that we are not creating or helping to develop a culture of inner-directed, individualistic people. We are fostering outer-directedness or "keeping up with the Joneses." What we most need to do is help people make far more independent decisions than just accept other people's concepts of the importance of drugs. They should ask the question "why" rather than just reacting and saying "why not" after becoming aware of the distortions about danger that have pervaded this field. Each individual should start with a fresh approach where the whole matter is put in context.

It is difficult for any group to face up to basic questioning of what they have accepted for decades or generations. But if we do want to deal successfully with drug use and abuse, we have to look at the roots. As Thoreau said, "There are a thousand people hacking away at the branches of evil for every one striking at the roots." Certainly, we should all be concerned with the indiscriminate use of alcohol, tobacco, "reds," marijuana, and a variety of other drugs by thirteen-year-olds or seventeen-year-olds in our schools, but, while being concerned, we should also wonder why so many millions of young people in our society are so "turned off" by going to school, so bored by it that they would prefer to be under the influence of a potent chemical rather than being attentive to what is happening or being involved in the curriculum. That is a more difficult question to raise and to remedy; unless we take steps to change the way education is coming across to the young today, we will never solve the problem of drug use and abuse or many other social problems. Positive alternatives have to be provided as the best approach to anything considered deviant, not only drug use, but also violence and bureaucratic excess.

Other causative factors in drug use include the tremendous sensationalism and glorification by certain agencies and the mass media of drugs like marijuana, which makes headlines practically every day and is seen totally out of proportion to its real significance or value in the society. This naturally arouses curiosity, and young people are expected to be curious about things, except the things they "should" not be curious about. We make diamonds or pseudo-events out of trivia and then wonder why people become so involved in them. We also have the criminogenic effect of the law with what sociologists call crimes without victims: private sexual behavior, most of which is illegal in America; private use or possession of alcohol or tobacco by those under age, or marijuana at any age; gambling, and the things that we often refer to as vices or immoralities when engaged in by other people. With these things, paradoxically, when you define the behavior as forbidden, abnormal, deviant, or illegal, you often make it more interesting and attractive to many people, particularly to those who see themselves as disaffiliated from, or in revolt against, the broader society, as do a large and increasing number of the young. To quote the President, however, "Let me make one thing clear." Because the criminal law does not work and is destructive with this kind of behavior does not mean that people have to be totally permissive or accepting of that behavior and does not mean that it is harmless or desirable. In regard to drugs, there is no mind-altering drug—including alcohol, nicotine, marijuana, and the rest—essential to human life, magically or automatically life-enhancing for all the people who take it, or harmless. But there are many ways of responding to real or alleged evils, and we must become more sophisticated, rational, and humane in our form of responses if we are to solve these complicated problems.

The criminogenic effects also involve driving the phenomenon underground, making it far more interesting and profitable to the purveyors of vice, and making the person who has a drug-abuse problem less likely to seek out help, treatment, or rehabilitation for fear of being arrested or reported. It also leads to the arrest each year of hundreds of thousands of people with the consequences of stigmatization, the barring of many job opportunities in the future, legal expenses, and expulsion from school. For some tens of thousands each year, it leads to even greater destruction of lives in juvenile halls, jails, or prisons.

Out of our frustration and out of our being taught that

there is only one approach to drug use and abuse—this blanket or indiscriminate criminalization—we have accepted the idea that when you send somebody to jail, you are rehabilitating him. Image does not always correspond to reality. Just because we build a multi-million-dollar facility, staff it with expensive administrators and guards, and put a label on it stating that it is a correctional or rehabilitation facility does not mean that people automatically benefit by going there. There is really no disagreement among criminologists or penologists about the majority of people's experiences through that process. Contrary to their or society's being benefited, they are given a postdoctoral course in real crime; they are taught how to use heroin and where to obtain it; they are given an aggressive introduction to homosexuality and dehumanized to be sent forth with the labels "ex-convict" and "drug offender," which make jobs and social acceptance difficult. This is what many people have been taught to think of as progress because of a false definition of what can or should be done about drug use and abuse in our society.

We, furthermore, have the misuse of drugs and the drug scene playing a smokescreening role in America, so that the more some people talk about drugs, the less they have to talk about more significant (but vote-losing) things. It is a very effective political technique. Anyone can become a "household name" by blanket condemnation of certain groups or certain "deviant" behaviors. There is far too much of it going on in our society, and it is dangerously fragmenting a society that is already torn asunder in many ways.

It takes no real ability to talk of drugs and their users as evil monsters who should be wiped out or, on the other hand, to tell people that drugs are harmless and inherently desirable. These are the two most popular techniques of public discussion of drugs. Neither one of them leads to anything socially beneficial, and both of them are destructive in many ways, but both techniques of distortion cater to the human need for oversimplified pseudosolutions. No drug is totally harmless, essential for life, or inevitably pleasurable. We have far more choices than the polarization we have been taught between legalization and criminalization—the American system which was first used in prohibition with great detrimental effects and has been used since then for a variety of other drugs. It is very much as though we had accepted the idea that when a child does something we disapprove of, as a teacher or a parent, we have only two ways of responding. We either ignore it entirely and let the child do anything he wants, or we smash the child in the face and throw him out of the house permanently. That is directly analogous to the opposites of legalization and criminalization. There are many other things that can be done which are more sophisticated and effective.

Starting with the criminal law, which people have been taught is the only approach (when in doubt, legislate), we should certainly make a distinction between the private use and possession of a drug of which we can certainly disapprove, whether it be alcohol, nicotine, or marijuana, but we should see that as a public health matter with emphasis on education, prevention, and treatment, rather than as a police matter. This, then, involves decriminalization (not legalization) of the user while shifting the priority of the criminal law to the mushrooming crimes against the person—murder, assault, rape, manslaughter—and crimes against property—embezzlement, burglary, auto theft—and then to major distributors of drugs considered unacceptable by the society. Most crimes do not involve drugs, and when they do, most involve alcohol, remembering that the alcohol by itself does not produce the crime but plays a role secondary to the personality and character of the user.

There are many hard drugs. When somebody drops that term out the side of his mouth, we have an instinctive knee-jerk reaction of fear and anger without ever defining what a hard drug is or to what we are reacting. Many drugs

produce death and disability, particularly alcohol and tobacco—tobacco alone killing 400,000 Americans prematurely
every year—but also barbiturates and others. I believe both
the John Birch Society and the Weathermen would have to
agree that death is a hard phenomenon, so that any substance
significantly involved in death has to be considered a hard
drug. In terms of addiction, a second dimension of hardness,
there are also a number of drugs involved: heroin and
morphine, sedative-hypnotics, and alcohol. Third, there is
psychosis, involving many drugs including amphetamines,
LSD, and alcohol, capable of causing acute or chronic
psychoses. This list is meant to be illustrative, not exhaustive,
but it demonstrates that there are many drug problems
involving many different drugs, and we must be concerned
about all, rather than a few.

The problem should be conceptualized as a human
problem, not a drug problem: what do you do with human
beings—including your own sons and daughters, brothers and
sisters—who do things that you consider evil? What do you
do that will be effective in changing their patterns of
behavior, moving them in a more constructive direction and
not being more destructive than the "evil" you are com-
bating? What will be moral, rational, and civilized?

Certainly destroying them through criminalization in the
name of saving them is not moral and is not effective, so the
priority must go to reforming all the drug laws (not just those
for marijuana). Along with this, we should certainly ban all
advertising and promotion of dangerous drugs such as alcohol
and nicotine. We should prominently label all bottles,
packages, and containers of these drugs, at least for educational purposes, to communicate to people the relationship
between the amount they consume and such things as drunk
driving, lung cancer, high blood pressure, and fires. We should
also be aware of the interdependence of many different drug
problems. If, for example, we had not been taught, as a
society, that it was somehow desirable, beneficial, and

harmless to put a dried plant leaf in our mouth—as in the case of tobacco—search for a match, ignite the leaf, inhale the fumes into our lungs to poison our tissues, and then exhale them in order to pollute everyone else's air space, we would not have the widespread use of marijuana we have today. God did not give us chimneys in our heads; cigarette smoking of any kind is not a natural pattern of behavior. Since there is massive evidence of the harmfulness of tobacco smoking, it behooves anybody who wants to stamp out smoking of anything else to be consistent enough to attempt to crusade against all cigarette smoking, especially if they want to reduce air pollution and be considerate of the nonsmoker.

Great emphasis should be placed on education beginning in elementary school. Nobody knows whether it is best to start at the kindergarten level or first or second grade, but we certainly do know the massive impact of television which even by kindergarten age inculcates pro-drug-taking attitudes.

We also know that in some schools in California children in second grade are jumping rope to the rhyme, "ABC, LSD, marijuana is good for me." Education should take place over a period of time each year. It cannot be done on a crash basis or by an outsider, even a knowledgeable one. It should be done by a specially trained classroom teacher who knows enough about the relevant disciplines to teach about the variety of drugs and, most importantly, who is able to communicate with young people in an atmosphere of mutual trust and respect. It should not be just didactic but should involve extensive student participation and small-group discussions. It should not depend upon films, most of which, like most of the pamphlets, are distorted, using the term drug abuse for any use of most drugs, entirely leaving out alcohol and tobacco, and communicating misinformation such as within 24 hours of smoking marijuana, a person will be a heroin addict prostituting herself on the streets. Drug education has to be entirely reoriented, and each year it should increase in sophistication. It should be given in a broad framework which makes going to school a mind-expanding experience for young people and, in turn, makes it less likely that they will turn to chemicals for alleged psychedelia.

Treatment and rehabilitation programs are another component of the solution. This, like education, has not been tried in our society except for token efforts such as prison hospitals or very inadequate psychiatric clinics. The main rehabilitation needed is long-term out-patient care, blending traditional and innovative techniques in an accessible and human manner. We need clinics that will treat alcoholism, cigarette smoking, barbiturate or amphetamine abuse, bad LSD trips, and heroin addiction—the whole range of drug problems—rather than ignoring some while concentrating on those that will bring money and publicity.

All these things must be done together, or as many of them as possible. It is necessary to stop using just one approach and assume that will take care of the problem. This program would be "hard on drugs" and "soft on people." Most of all, the roots of discontent in our society require our attention—the many alienating properties of education, religion, family life, and our institutions and leaders.

To some extent, there is an inverse relationship between drug use and social change. The more we as a people, young and old, depend upon chemicals to deal with all our tensions, anxieties, frustrations, and despair, the less likely we are to involve ourselves in attacking the roots of these problems. The things that are wrong in our agencies and institutions desperately need to be corrected but will not be corrected if we make a self-fulfilling prophecy by becoming apathetic, hopeless, and preoccupied with "turning on" with alcohol, marijuana, or a variety of other drugs.

T. S. Eliot wrote in "The Rock" of decent people whose monument would be a thousand lost golf balls and asphalt roads. If the drug scene and its origins continue as they are today, his words will easily be paraphrased to communicate that our monuments are roads, golf balls, alcohol, and marijuana. The majority of the young accept and are likely to continue to accept in the 1970s the older generation's preoccupation with drugs as a way of life, the best and quickest source of pleasure, and a key technique for relating (in a generally superficial manner). A major variation on this basic theme exists, with marijuana now running a significant third in popularity (the recent Johns Hopkins survey of 8,000 college students on 48 campuses found that while 31% had used marijuana, 74% had used tobacco, and 89%, alcohol), sought after for pleasure and sometimes introspection, and having great symbolic significance in the war between the young and the Establishment. We can expect more use and abuse of consciousness-changing substances from alcohol to heroin, more evasion of the roots, more destructive overreaction, more careerists and politicians exploiting the drug issue, and more fragmentation and confusion of the institutions dealing with youth. There will be increasing nonenforcement of the drug laws and gradual, incomplete reforms. Many new programs of drug education and treatment will be started, both public and private, but with emphasis on quantity, not quality, a few drugs, and inexperienced personnel.

Within this generally bleak picture, an increasing minority of the young will become involved in more sustained and consistent sources of meaning and pleasure, find drugs boring or insignificant, and turn on to people and the world, tune in to knowledge and feeling, and drop in to improving the society.

10

YOUTH, SEX, AND THE FUTURE

JOHN H. GAGNON
WILLIAM SIMON

During the last quarter-century and especially during the last ten years, there has been a sense in American society of an accelerating change in our sexual practices. While this change has included all age groups, the common focus of attention has been on the young, who appear most vulnerable to change-inducing forces, either because they are less attached to conventional social structures or because they have internalized current norms less well. Whatever the specific explanatory model for change potential among the youthful population, our attention since the fateful days of the Free Speech Movement at Berkeley has been directed to indicators of a revolutionary potential among the young that includes political, familial, chemical, and sexual elements.

AUTHORS' NOTE: *The research on which this paper is based was supported by USPHS grants HD 04157 and HD 02557. The authors' conclusions, however, are their own, and do not necessarily reflect the viewpoint of the agency which funded their research.*

DIFFICULTIES IN ANALYSIS

Our concern with the young is exacerbated because they are the future in its most concrete manifestation. People just under twenty in 1970 will be parents during the late seventies, and grandparents just after the year 2000. The role that sex plays in their lives and the meanings that they attribute to it will be one element in the transmission belt that will shape the role of sex in the lives of their children (adolescent in 1985-1990) and their grandchildren (adolescent in 2015-2020).[1] The degree to which the present cohort of youth is either faithful or unfaithful to the announced sexual standards (already at variance with practice by some 30 to 3,000 years, depending on one's time frame) is the fundamental measure of the mortality or immortality of our present way of life. This mixture of present-day youth, sexual activity, and the idea of the future is a heady one, calculated to make the judgment of the most rational quite unsteady, since we are required to mix not only the pornography of sex, but also the pornography of youth and the pornography of the future.

The current state of confusion about the role of sex in the process of change stems from four main sources. First, we are saddled with, as well as delighted by, an imagery of change—indeed, of revolution—when we talk about sex, youth, or the future. This climate of opinion clouds our ability to judge accurately whether or not there is change and, if there is, what direction it is taking. The demand for novelty even in scientific research distorts the process of data collection, highlighting the dramatic to the detriment of the pedestrian, and forcing the creation of theories that are themselves committed to change. At the same time, the imagery of change becomes a variable not only in scientific activities, but in social life itself. For those who are changing, the experience of change becomes a mark of "being with it"; for those not changing, change becomes both a danger and a measure of being "out of it." The idea of change, differences as experienced, has become as important to the twentieth century as the idea of progress was to the nineteenth (see Bury, 1932).

The second major difficulty which affects any discussion of sexual behavior, perhaps even more than discussions of the future, is our profound lack of information. Not only do we not know very precisely the social bookkeeping of sexuality (how many are doing it, with whom are they doing it, at what ages, and with what frequencies), but, more importantly, there is even less information about the connection between sexual activity and the social and psychological contexts in which such sexual activity occurs. Research efforts are fragmentary and often ill-founded, influenced by fantasy and desire, and, worst of all, are pornotopic in design, seeking to analyze the sexual without reference to the social or psychological circumstances that turn sexual behavior into sexual conduct (for the distinction between these two sexual modes, see Burgess, 1949; Bohannon, 1971).

It was this lack of prior data that made the original interpretation of the volumes *Sexual Behavior in the Human Male* and *Sexual Behavior in the Human Female* such curiosities (Kinsey et al., 1948; 1953). Without prior baseline figures, the cross-sectional data in these volumes were interpreted in any fashion readers wished. Unfortunately, no one interpreted the data conservatively, arguing that there was a great deal more sexual activity in the past and that the Kinsey reports showed that there was decline in sexual activity from a promiscuous and licentious nineteenth century (even though the decline in the rates of purchasing sexual contact with females by males could have been viewed as a humanizing process in the society). Since there were no prior data that anyone was willing to examine, it was presumed that the Kinsey data represented a vast eruption of sexuality, even though the amount and directions of short-run changes were small and muted in the reporting of the data.

The third source of error is perhaps more problematic than a lack of data—it is the flawed interpretive mechanism of theoretical schema or the conceptual apparatus through which sexual phenomena are commonly viewed, analyzed or gathered.[2] This flawed intellectual framework is derived from two sources. The first is experiential: the sexual actor in this culture lives in schizophrenic detachment from his nonsexual life and feels that his sexual impulses are autonomous, even though reflection on most of his experience will show him that his sexual commitments are under extremely good control or are often of little importance to him. Without such reflection, the sexual world appears to be self-starting and self-motivated, as if it exists sui generis in experience. However, it is demonstrable that sexual activity is, in fact, not a very powerful drive, and the word drive itself may be a misnomer. The felt experience during sexual activity is quite disjointed from the importance of sexual activity during the rest of waking or even sleeping life. At the same time, the major theoretical and intellectual apparatus for interpreting the role of sexual behavior in social life sees it as an imperious drive that presses against and must be controlled by the cultural and social matrix. The dominance of this drive-reduction model mediated by cultural and social control is preeminent in the bulk of psychoanalytic, anthropological, and sociological literature.

The explanation of sexual change that flows from this intellectual posture is very simple. The sex drive exists at some constant level in any age cohort of the population and in some rising and then falling level in the individual life cycle. It presses for expression and, in the absence of controls, either existing in the external laws or mores or in appropriate internalized repressions learned in early socialization which channel the sexual fluidity, there will be "outbreaks" of sexual behavior.[3] In its more pristine model, the relationships between the potentiating mechanisms for sex and sin (nearly surrogates) are quite similar. The organism is inherently sexual (sinful), its behavior is controlled by the presence of training, internalized injunctions or the absence of temptations, and, failing these, there will be sexual misconduct. More sophisticated models than this can be found in either functional theory or in psychoanalytic models of behavior, but fundamental to each is a drive model that sees sex as having social consequences as a result of its biological origins. The drive exists, society and culture constrain it, and when constraints are loosed, sexual change occurs.

This control-repression model of sexuality has influenced the majority of discussions of the impact of social change of various kinds of sexual behavior and has yielded rather simple-minded consequences. The introduction of the automobile, teenage dating, going steady, dancing close together, dancing styles related to rock and roll, and short skirts have all been called changes which would result in sexual excess. The discovery of adequate treatment for venereal diseases or the widespread availability of birth control devices were attacked because they would reduce the dangers of sexual activity. The availability of sexually stimulating material (pornography) has been attacked from the time when a nipple was the danger point (1950 or so) to pubic hair (only yesterday). All these reactions are based on variants of the same faulty reasoning: that sexual access among the young will result in unrestrained coitus, that sexual behavior is only constrained by its dangers, or that the sexual beast can be aroused with instant success by the mildest stimuli.

The fourth source of confusion is the self-interest of adult onlookers. There is a certain commitment to finding the world more sexual than it is, more exciting, more porno-graphic. This pastime is to the self-interest of both sexual radicals and sexual conservatives. The sexual radical and the sexual conservative are in disagreement about consequences of lowered controls over the sexual drive, the former believing that there will be a genuine flowering of a more human, more natural way of life, the latter believing that there will be a degeneration of the cultural fabric in all areas of social life. What they agree on is the transcendent power of sexuality when released. The entire older generation which is generally nonideological about sex, is in a sense the ambivalent embodiment of these opposing radical and conservative ideologies and losers if sexual change occurs, whichever is true. If sex is a therapeutic truth which they have hidden from themselves, they will have been cheated of participating in it—if it is a corruption, then all they have worked for will go the way of Rome.[4] Hence, the increased level of cosmetic sexuality in the society, especially on the part of the young, makes the older generation both jealous and angry. They are jealous out of what they feel they missed and angry because the young appear to be having such a good time. It is nearly impossible to live in this society and not to share some of these emotions when watching the selected short subjects of the youth revolution through the mass media.

While corrections can be made for the problems of data, self-interest, sexual ideology, and for the current climate of mandatory change, without changes in the faulty model of sexuality, no serious discussion can be had about the future of sexuality. The theoretical framework is fundamentally in error, and, with the best of data, faulty interpretations would be made. Without an alternative model, our interests will continue to be dominated by the epiphenomenal aspects of sexual change.

AN ALTERNATIVE MODEL OF DEVELOPMENT

In a number of other places, the authors have outlined in some detail a learning and cognitively based model as an alternative explanation for both the individual's existential experience of sexuality and the role of sexuality in the larger sociocultural process (Simon and Gagnon, 1969; Gagnon and Simon, forthcoming). Rather than sex being seen as a drive to be coped with by the system of personality, culture, and social organization, sexuality is seen as a learned capacity. It is a learned capacity all the way down to the level of the identification of the internal sensations that are appropriate to sexual response. The repertoire of learning includes internal bodily states, appropriate anatomic parts on the self and others to respond to or to stimulate, appropriate other persons (by gender, age, familial status, socioeconomic class, race, canons of beauty), situations in which to be aroused, unaroused, to lubricate, to have orgasm, and, in addition, an organizing and sequencing system to put all of this together. Overarching this are the extrasexual meanings and metaphors which infuse the sexual act with passion or constraint, fear or attraction, love or hate, purity or corruption, affirmation or transgression.

It is clear that such processes, values, techniques, and cognitive strategies are not learned all at once, but at the same time the conventional model of psychosexual development which takes as its binding image the organs and orifices of the body in progressive erotization is as faulty as the drive model of sexuality. In large measure, many of the ingredients of the ultimate sexual scenario (and there are a number of such scenarios in most societies) are learned in extrasexual situations and then appropriated to the sexual situation later in life. The attribution of sexuality to the early years of life by the Freudians is an error, though certain forms of attachment, moral commitments, and items of gender identity are formed early in life. The period of life prior to adolescence is remarkable in American and most Western societies for its lack of clearly sexually motivated behavior in most social class situations. There is some sex play, some victimization of children by sex offenders, some early masturbation, but little that conforms to both the objective criteria and subjective experience of adults in sexual activity. The critical learning that relates to sexuality prior to puberty in this society is nonsexual in character. A substratum of nonsexual learning is being formed, composed of a bundle of cultural styles that are a loosely formed gender package (gender differences in aggression, proaction, cleanliness, obedience, conformity), a set of values attached to the body, and the introjection of moral values attached to parental figures. None of these is sexual in character and it only obscures the issue to discern beneath them a mysteriously wise nature working out her wiles through the processes of the object choice and the like.

During early puberty, some overt sexual behavior begins developing rapidly among males into the masturbatory syndrome with social class variation in the ages at which heterosexuality is learned (Gagnon et al., 1970). It is apparent that we know very little about these early years among males and that retrospective data are very tricky to deal with. Among females, there is a continuation of the commitment to romance, love, and marriage which predated menarchy, and the appearance of the menses is rarely experienced as sexual. Too much has been made of the declining age of menarchy which has maintained a far narrower bond in the last fifty years than the changing age of marriage, the average number of children and frequency of church attendance, any one of which is a more powerful impact on female sexual behavior than age at first menses. What does seem to be significant is that there is the emergence during this period of a commitment to certain forms of the sexual and the beginning of an integration of materials that appear to be sexual to adults and earlier nonsexual training. Further, it is with this change in the outward appearance of the bodies of these young people that they begin, at least tentatively, to be treated by adults as sexual creatures and for them to begin to see each other in protosexual roles.

In the middle and late adolescence, these patterns are then put together into the normal processes of dating and mating. The movement here is from a life dominated by homosocial values into a life where there is competition between values based on relations with persons of the same gender to a life in which heterosocial values are either significant or dominant. It is apparent that these dimensions of heterosociality and homosociality are not dependent on or necessarily correlated with the dimensions of heterosexuality-homosexuality. Heterosexual and homosexual acts may occur in various kinds of environments in which the salient referent of the behavior is not the person with whom the act is occurring. Thus, the adolescent boy may have intercourse for the purposes of validation of his masculinity among other males; in like manner, acts of homosexual prostitution can occur among young males who are acting out the needs of a homosocial peer group (Reiss, 1961). In societies (or sub-cultures) where male-male relations are highly valued (high homosocial) and females are viewed only as cooks, mothers, and sex objects, male-male nonsexual relations commonly dominate the societies' interpersonal systems and define the meaning and value of heterosexuality. A situation in which sex occurs primarily within the genders (high homosexuality) and the highest-valued relations occur between males and females (high heterosexuality) is less common, but certainly not an impossible social adaptation.

This is the period during which young people begin to act out and practice the conventional scripts which organize the physiological, psychological, and social elements of conventional sexual responses. Young people with what are defined as deviant or protodeviant feelings or adaptations often find this period extremely confusing, since there is no clear-cut set of definitions of how and in what way their behaviors differ from the behavior of the normal young. Both deviant and conventional sexual carriers are shaped and organized during this period, but the former often delayed in their ultimate organization. Commonly, most young people reach the end of adolescence with an organized set of sexual activities and performances and, depending on class and other factors, have practiced a certain number of the basic sexual physical practices and emotional concomitants that go with them.

The termination of the adolescent period is conventional marriage for most young people, with a certain amount of more extensive sexual experimentation limited to a smaller number of persons who have been defined as appropriate marital partners. Sexual patterns during the rest of the life cycle are largely defined by distinctions between the married and unmarried state. The availability of sexual partners during specific moments in the life cycle is most often determined by whether one is or is not married to the person with whom one is having sex. The concatenation of sexual exclusivity, romantic attachment, child-bearing, and a life-time together shapes the character and meaning of nearly every sexual performance that occurs after the average age when marriage is likely for most people in the society. Even the homosexual has his status as a single person and his lack of children as primary public identifying marks during this period of his life.

During this portion of the life cycle, the bulk of heterosexuals who have married heterosexuals have sex primarily with their marital partners, with varying levels of sexual variation in the specific physical activities that are performed (Kinsey et al., 1948: 571-582; 1953: 346-408). There is a steady decline in sexual activity between spouses in the late thirties and early forties with a major drop in the middle fifties for large portions of the population. Much of this decline is attributable to nonbiological factors, especially up to age 55, in both sexes (Masters and Johnson, 1970). Boredom, declining physical beauty, and alternative social interests, all compete successfully with sexual activity as a major event in the lives of the majority of persons. There is some extramarital coitus, more for men than for women, but few in the population have the endurance, logistical skills, and income necessary to carry on major affairs and a marriage at the same time (Kinsey et al., 1948: 583-594, 1953: 409-445). The steady decline in frequency of coitus is differential by social class, as are the differences in extramarital coitus and variations in types of sexual activity. This decline in sexual activity can be interrupted by divorce and other separations, and there is reversion to a non-married-like pattern during these periods for most, followed by a drift back into marriage. Divorce in later years and widowhood are commonly not accompanied by resurgences in sexual behavior.

While it is not our central concern to develop a stage model of development (following, say, Erikson), since such models tend to become reified and, rather than serving to draw our attention to modal processes, become objects of interest in themselves, it is useful to delineate separate periods in the life cycle during which certain events commonly take place. It should be noted clearly here that these periods are not seen as *necessary,* either within or across cultures, nor *necessary* in some psychodynamic sense. They are roughly what happens in the middle 1960s in a complex Western society, largely to its white working- and middle-class populations and in large measure to those persons of most ethnic and racial minorities who are attached to these model schemes of development or who have not been entirely alienated from them. There can be vast reversals and changes in the design of human sexuality from the feelings it evokes to the kinds of things that are appropriate or included as its performance elements. The age and moment when specific behaviors can be introduced, performed, and lived with vary enormously, so that any biological fixity in the sequence of behavior is most likely to occur in infancy and very little after that.

The rough sequencing that follows is primarily of heuristic

value for examining processes, persons, and institutions that would have to be affected to create change in the outcomes that relate to sexual behavior that are presently observed in any specific life stage. At the present time, certain components of the conventional sexual scenario are learned at various moments in the life cycle through certain socializing agents and institutions. In order to change this, we must either utilize the same agents or institutions and revise their programs (e.g., increasing father's role in infant care or tinkering with mass media presentation of gender role differences on commercials) or substitute other persons or agencies (e.g., mother-mother lesbian parent-caretakers or child care centers). Whether these devices would have any specific sexual outcome is unknown; however, they represent the kinds of changes that would have to occur within the normal life cycle components. Changes in elements that are part of what might be called *the gender identity-sexual identity-family formation-reproduction pattern* in this society are not spontaneous and are commonly dependent on events external to this pattern as the sources of change. As we will note, changes in affluence or bureaucratization have more consequence in changing various parts of this pattern in this society than any change within the cycle itself.

The outline that appears on pages 224 and 225 contains a set of stages with flexible age boundaries, the social components that are significant in either sexual or nonsexual learning that takes place during them, and finally, a rough suggestion of what is being learned or assembled.

This rough outline of a sexual career is the most common heterosexual pattern available and, even with the introduction of divorce and widowhood, the cycle does not vary except in minor ways. Similar modal career patterns with greater or lesser variability could be described for those minorities who operate with deviant sexual patterns in the society. Indeed, this conventional heterosexual process is the model sexual career that all deviant patterns must confront.

The man who desires large numbers of females, the homo-sexual man or woman, and the sexually active women must live with the reality of this pattern, its values, and its links to the past and the future in a day-to-day way. This assembly designates the availability of sexual partners, their ages, their incomes, their point in the economic process, their time commitments, all of which shape their sexual careers far more than the minor influences of sexual desire. If these contentions about the ways in which sexuality is learned and integrated into social life are correct, then the kinds of scenarios that we must develop that will in some tentative way outline the kinds of sexual lives that will be lived in the future must take on a more complex imagery than simply the loosening of libidinal barriers.

For the remainder of the paper, our focus will be on the current processes of change and their effect on the present-day young—that is, roughly that cohort of adolescents aged 14-19 in 1970 and therefore 24-29 in 1980, 34-39 in 1990, and 44-49 in the year 2000. Our concern is with the way in which certain major themes related to sexuality will affect the model cycle of family replacement which is the primary arena for sexual activity in the society. Insofar as is possible, we will attempt to deal with both the sexual bookkeeping aspects of change and changes in the meaning of sexuality to the actors involved.

SOURCES OF CHANGE

Changes in the sexual component of the human condition can possibly arise from the biological, technological, and psychosocial domains of life. It is evident to us that, at the present time, the biological substratum is very nearly a constant in human sexual affairs. Except for specific classes of genetic and hormonal failures, the vast majority of humans are biologically equipped to perform what are conventionally

OUTLINE OF A SEXUAL CAREER

Stage and Ages	Agents	Assemblies
1. Infancy; Ages: 0-2½-3	Mother to Family	Formation of base for conventional gender identity package.
2. Childhood; Ages: 3-11	Family to Peers, Increasing Media	Consolidation of conventional gender identity package; modesty-shame learning; nonsexually motivated "sex" play; learning of sex words without content; learning of sex activities without naming; learning of general moral categories; mass media through commercials and programming content reinforcing conventional gender, sex, and family roles; media also preparing for participation in youth culture.
3. Early adolescence Ages: 11-15	Family, Same-sex Peers, Media	First societal identification as a conventional sexual performer; first overt physical sexual activity with self or others; development of fantasy materials; beginnings of male/female divergence in overt sexual activity; application of gender package to sexual acts; application of moral values to emergent sexual behavior; privatization of sexual activities; same-sex peers reinforce homosocial values; family begins to lose moral control; media reinforces conventional adult content of gender roles; media attaches consumer practices to gender success; basic attachment to youth culture formed.
4. Later adolescence Ages: 15-18	Same-sex Peers, Cross-sex Peers Increasing, Media, Family Reducing	Increased practice of integrating of sexual acts with nonsexual social relations; movement to heterosocial values; increased frequency of sexual activity; declining family controls; continuing media reinforcement of sexual-gender roles, and consumer and youth culture values; sexual experience with wider range of peers; common completion of sexual fantasy content; consolidation of gender differences in sexual roles and activity; good girl/bad girl-maternal/erotic distinctions completed.

Gender Identity (stages 1-2)

Sexual Identity (stages 3-4)

Stage and Ages	Agents	Assemblies
Family Formation		
5. Early adulthood Ages: 18-23	Same-sex and Cross-sex Peers, Media, Minimum Family of Origin	Mate selection, narrowing of mate choice; increased amount of sexual practice; commitment to love by male, sex by female; linkage of passion to love; dyadic regression; insulation from family judgment and peer judgment; increasing pressure to marry; relief from same-sex competition by stabilization of cross-sex contacts; legitimization of sexual activity by peers and romantic code; media reinforces youth culture values of romance and virtues of marriage; experience with falling in and out of love; termination of protected school/student statuses.
6. Final mate selection-Early marriage; Ages: 20-27	Fiancee(s), Spouse, Same-sex Peers, Family of Origin Increases	Regularizes and legitimizes sexual activity; stable rates of sex activity; variation in kinds of sexual behavior; children born in most cases; increasing sexual anxiety about children; family values reinforced by children and family of origin; declining eroticism, increased maternalism; culmination of purchasing/consumer values in wedding gifts or buying new products; routinization of sexual behavior; decreased contact with cross-sex peers unless they are married; interaction in multiple dyads; sexual activities restricted by pregnancy, children, work.
Reproduction		
7. Middle marriage Ages: 28-45	Spouse, Same-sex Peers, Family of Origin, Married Peers	Declining sexual activity in marriage; some extra-marital sexual experimentation; maturing children; conflict of erotic with material; emergence of sexual dissatisfactions; increase in occupational commitments; declines in physical energy and physical beauty; fantasy competition by youth culture; continual multiple dyadic interactions and insulation from cross-sex peers; marriage moving to nonsexual basis for stability and continuity.
8. Post-young children; Ages: 45+	Spouse, Same-sex Peers, Married Peers	Further decline in sexual activity; some extra-marital sexual experimentation; substitution of nonsexual commitments other than children as basis of marriage; further decline in physical strength and beauty; further desexualization of gender identity; movement out of public sexual arena.

[225]

called sexual acts. There is probably a larger proportion with reproductive inadequacy at the biological level than there are those with biological sexual inadequacies. This does not obviate the fact that there are substantial numbers of persons with socially defined performance difficulties in the sexual area, but these are rarely due to biological defects. Even the declining age of menses appears to be essentially trivial in affecting female sexuality.

While technology is the most visible engine of change in Western societies, it affects the sexual aspects of life only through those institutions and persons who link to the gender identity-sexual identity-family formation-reproduction cycle. Developments in medical science with reference to venereal diseases and birth control are the most powerful developments that specifically relate to this cycle and do so by reducing the risks attendant on sexual intercourse in the case of the latter, and all forms of sexual contact in the case of the former. It does not appear that these developments have had widespread impact on illegitimate sexual behavior (though the substitution of the pill for the condom may have increased the spread of venereal disease) and probably have more impact inside marriage, where birth control mechanisms are most frequently used. Other technological developments have not turned out to have impact on sexuality as importantly as they were originally expected. The automobile has not increased sexual activity even among the young, though it has resulted in an increase in privacy for noncoital sexual contacts. It has, however, become another element in the masculinity package resulting in higher rates of car theft and accidents, and it is also part of that successful consumer identity package which makes car ownership both a measure of personal success and a tie to the conventional social structure. In these same ways, other technological developments affect emergent sexuality, but only through the intervention of psychosocial processes.

In the psychosocial arena, the following processes seem to

be most significant impacting the family replacement cycle that we have described previously.

THE ECONOMIC MOVEMENT IN THE SOCIETY FROM SCARCITY TO AFFLUENCE

The movement from scarcity to affluence in the society has clearly been differential in its direct effects, but the sheer existence of long-term affluence in a large sector of the society indirectly affects those who are not affluent. The central consequences of affluence on sexual activity seem to be threefold:

(1) It increases role flexibility throughout the life cycle, especially after age 20.[5]

(2) It changes the attitude of the affluent toward the value of objects and ownership, while not reducing the desire to consume, that is, affluence reduces the value of things, they become more disposable, replaceable, and lose their uniqueness.

(3) It increases the attachment of all members of the society to societal norms primarily through consumption rather than production values.

THE EMERGENCE OF SOCIAL MOVEMENTS WITH SEXUAL SIDE EFFECTS

A large series of social movements has emerged in the society that do not have goals specifically aimed at sexual change, but whose implementation carries with them, as general rhetorical baggage or as a specific commitment to liberalism, a required assent to greater sexual freedom. One of the most significant of these is clearly the generalized youth movement beginning with the hippies and moving through the commune and other current events in youth culture. The political freedom of the young, the eighteen-year-old vote, the experience of Vietnam, or political protest each increase commitments to general anti-adult values.

These oppositions can be expressed through sexual activity during a time when the early experimentation with sexuality is heightened by a reduction in adult controls over the behavior of the young. The second major movement is women's liberation, in which two major elements are intertwined—one, gender politics; the other, sexual politics. It is possible to think of a sexually puritan society, which had equality between the genders in occupational and social domains; however, given the complex intermixture of gender or sexual politics in U.S. society, changes in one will affect the other, so that the women's movement in both its gender and sexual dimensions should have some effects on sexual activity, but clearly not simple ones. A third source of change is the general political revolt of blacks, Chicanos and American Indians, which has created a series of smaller possibilities of sexual change. The sexual relations between ethnic and racial groups can be more generally used by all participants to work out motives representing exploitation, power, guilt reduction, and other forms of normative transgression. Revolutionary romanticism can come to typify members of previously suppressed classes and groups.

THE EMERGENCE OF SPECIFICALLY SEXUAL SOCIAL MOVEMENTS

There are a number of sexual movements in the society whose ends are the legitimization (legalization or normalization) of specific sexual or erotic minorities. The thrust of these changes have come either through "disinterested" legal reformers or through members of erotic minorities seeking legal redress or moving into confrontational politics. The goals of some groups are more radical than those of mere reform and seek not only the legalization of their behavior, but its right to exist as a nonstigmatized public alternative to conventional marital or nonmarital heterosexuality. At the same time, there are other groups which seek to increase the freedom of heterosexual relationships (e.g., kinds and numbers of partners, techniques, feelings). These are often, but not always, related to the encounter and sensitivity group movement. The legal reform movements seek to change the laws with reference to large classes of sexual behavior moving ultimately to a legal situation in which the only offenses are those that offend the public taste, involve great disparities in age (with a fixed lower ceiling), involve force, or close blood relationships. The more radical legal reformers would remove incest from the prohibited list if it did not involve great disparities in age, and there is some serious debate about ages of consent and what is a public nuisance. Indeed, the Sexual Freedom League and other heterosexual groups are working beyond sex law reform toward the celebration of what are currently deviant sexual practices. Gay liberation is the most powerful of the erotic minority groups and seeks both change in the general image of homosexuality and an improved self-image by the homosexual. The slogans "Gay is Good" and "out of the closets and into the streets," suggest the concerns of these groups. Other erotic minorities such as transsexuals and transvestites have done some organizing, but the impact of these groups is unclear. There is no evidence that there has been internal organization among female prostitutes and the various occupational subcategories that are attached to this profession.

THE EROSION OF RIGID GENDER DIFFERENCES

The ritual use of Dr. Spock by the middle classes in child-rearing is an exemplification, along with the involvement of middle-class fathers in family household activities, and the existence of the professional career woman and mother of the processes that have begun to erode some of the aspects of rigid male-female gender difference in early childhood training. This erosion occurs most strikingly in middle-class populations and college going through both the mediation of youth culture and continuing parental commitments and models. Hairstyles, unisex clothing, and non-sexual coeducational living arrangements are outgrowths of this early experience combined with the effects of increasing affluence and role flexibility. Among those with more traditional early gender training, the current more permissive gender atmosphere of adolescence presents alternatives to a more rigid set of role specifications.

THE EROTIZATION OF THE SOCIAL BACKDROP

While more fundamental processes are changing, we are also experiencing a cosmetic sexual shift in the society. The backdrop of daily life and life as experienced in the media has grown more erotic or, at least, what an older generation experiences as erotic. There has been movement in depiction from the Sears Roebuck Catalogue corset ads of the 1940s to fellatio in three dimensions in the 1970s, a larger volume of erotic literature, photography of naked people (mostly women), a literature celebrating sexual athleticism, and in-person, braless, minied, or bikinied females. While there is a heightened sense of the sexual as part of the daily life of the society, at the same time this backdrop only affects behavior indirectly without supplying the social networks for acting out the behavior. While not directly affecting behavior, the shifting of the backdrop does have impact on the way in which people proceed and the generation of sexual expectations in both older and younger generations.

It is apparent that changes in these psychosocial processes will not affect all sectors of the population at the same time or penetrate them at the same rate. Whether individuals or social groups are in the avant garde with reference to change or at the end of the parade will have significance both in terms of structural and psychological consequences. At the psychological and individual level, to be the first to change means dealing with certain kinds of anxieties and ambivalences and being the last poses still another set of problems.

At structural-collective level, if change is occurring within the affluent or central components of the society, it can be defined as valuable; if change is occurring among the disadvantaged and abused, it is the harbinger of revolution. The problems of sequencing, rate of change, and social position are central not only to the character of change, but to the existential experiences of those involved in the process of change.

CHANGES IN GENDER IDENTITY

The pattern of changes in the softening of gender identity lines seems to take most of its force early in life by more strongly curbing aggression among males, increased dressing alike among children, and patterns of child-rearing in which the occupational dimension of male life is nearly totally removed from the life of the child. These patterns are supported by child-rearing experts and make their mark most in middle-class and upper-middle-class families with far less significance in the white working class, among ethnic minorities, and in lower-class populations.

These gender-softening factors have impact on some children early in life, but are more generally felt in early adolescence among a larger proportion of young people if they follow those normal clothing fashions that reduce the differences between the sexes. Here in the world of youth culture, there is far more opportunity for such gender-softening to have cross-class consequences. During this time, conventionally gender-trained young people come into contact with unisex themes and either comply with the styles or resist them. After adolescence, the major attacks on rigid gender difference are being carried out by either the women's liberation movement or in the occupational domain itself, where the content of occupational activity has become unrelated to those activities that were conventionally the goals of male socialization. Occupations no longer require large amounts of aggression, physical strength, or the management of things, and more and more bureaucratic and service occupations require the management and manipulation of other people. Changes in gender difference training and maintenance emerge at three time points and through a number of different processes: Early in life, during gender identity formation, there are differential and changing child-rearing practices; during adolescence there are reductions in the gender differences due to the youth culture; and during adulthood both political and occupational factors work toward the reduction of male or female differences in the world of work both in terms of work content and in terms of access to the positions themselves.

If there is a central theme in gender identity training or definition at these three life-cycle points, it is that, from the point of view of an older set of specifications of the relations between men and women and the content of gender roles, the present convergence between roles will have males moving further toward the female role than females will move toward the male. It is clear that the content of these gender roles have never been fixed, and it is only through using descriptive categories that originate in an older perspective that we can describe changes that will have future men more like current women than future women will be like current men. In one sense, this kind of comparison is partly meaningless and partly obscuring. No future individual of either gender who possesses a new combination of elements that will be then labeled gender specific will experience themselves as a recombination of older elements. There will be no sense of dissonance between culture and self that the present women's liberation participant feels, but the new combination (say, total equality of sexual access) will be experienced as the natural outcome of socialization and the sociocultural situation of that moment.

The decrease in accentuated gender role differences has a

number of potential sexual changes built into it. One of these is the possibility that males whose early rearing is in such a tradition will have lowered commitments to what Evelyn Hooker has called the "male alliance" during early adolescence and will be less exclusively homosocial in their relations during this period. At the same time, they will be able to relate more easily to females, could have lowered rates of early adolescent masturbation, a lowered level of genital focus, and lessened commitments to aggressive fantasies as a part of sexual arousal. For these males the experience of early and later adolescence will contain lowered levels of anxiety about sexual performance from the genital point of view, and a lowered pressure toward premarital coitus as a part of a male achievement syndrome. There may even be slightly elevated rates of coitus as consequence, but partially because such males will be seeking intercourse in much the same terms that females will be.

For those males more conventionally reared, the impact of gender role softening will appear during adolescence through the somatic impact of youth culture. Both stylistically and in the existence of persons of middle-class status who exhibit and voice a different pattern of attitudes toward sex and women, it is possible to generate an interpersonal set of relations among young men which support a change in relations between young men and women. It is important to note that concomitant patterns of gender change do not seem to be occurring among women; that is, there do not seem to be new child-rearing practices emerging early in life, and during adolescence the changes among females seem quite slight. Changes among females are more likely to result from the lack of experienced cross-gender differences that will result from changes in the training of males. It is likely that, in the face of reductions in male sexual assertiveness, women may have to be more self-directive in defining themselves sexually, because the act of defining women as sexual will be less important to men. While many of these early changes are occurring in middle-class populations, it is important to note that they do not seem to be occurring among white working-class males or in large sectors of other racial-ethnic subgroups in the society. It may be possible that there will be a great deal of tension between males in the society as some portion of the male population adopts newer gender role commitments, while other populations, often marked by differences in class and ethnic-racial status, do not. During adulthood, the sexual consequences of the softening of gender boundaries will be unclear. It could make for lower rates of extramarital coitus among some groups of men because of stronger familial attachments, while there could be a counter-movement among women. If there is a most likely outcome, it is that there will be movement toward a less penis-oriented sexual encounter between men and women. There is already some evidence for this in the popularity of the encounter groups movement (experience each other as people, not sex objects), and in the sensualist movement which is moving toward a more total body concern in sexual activity (a definition which again is feminine in an older sense of that word). The water bed is an example of this shift in sexual focus. It changes the kind of physical structure on which coitus can occur, eliminating the fixed surface, and creating a flowing, moving environment that denotes flexibility rather than rigidity in sexual performances.[6] If these movements imply anything about sex, it is to a gourmet pattern with a commitment to a wider variety of sexual activities between sexual partners.

As a process operating independently of all other changes, a decline in gender identity accentuation would produce males with a greater capacity for emotional commitment to females earlier in life, with a lowered pressure for direct sexual gratification and with a wider interest in total bodily commitments. At the same time, they would be more capable of responding positively to changes in women's roles as they occur. There are some indications that those males who make this adaptation historically early in the general process of change will have some problems in maintaining a softened gender identity which will be free from external identifications as being "queer" or "different" (as "hard hat" sexuality views long hair) or even internal doubts and reactions similar to pseudohomosexual adaptation, since there will be continuing pressures toward the conventional definition of masculinity (Ovesey, 1969: 160). Some women will find that their older self-definitions of femininity will not be enhanced in interactions with males who are not as domineering and assertive.

In large measure, there do not seem to be as many kinds of changes occurring to female gender roles at this point as there do to males. It is likely that many changes in women's roles will emerge in reaction to changes in male's roles; hence, the timing of changes for women will be later than that for men. As women move to a more central occupational economic role in the society, the changes in their behavior (sexual and nonsexual) will be less reactive in character.

THE EMERGENCE AND CONFIRMATION OF SEXUAL IDENTITIES

At the present time in American society, a confirmed sense of sexual identity as distinguished from gender identity begins to emerge around puberty, as the surrounding environment begins to treat differently the newly pubescent child. While for some children this emergence into new definition as sexual will be built on the less-restrictive gender identity pattern we noted above, for the most part the integration of new sexual selves will continue to be built on relatively conventional models. The changes that seem most significant for this period appear to be caused by the interpenetration of the mass media with the youth culture and changes in the family produced by increasing role flexibility on the part of adults rather than children.

At the present time, it is apparent that adults are reacting to young people during early and latter adolescence as being sexual—indeed, as being more sexual than they really are. Thus, in the fantasy life of adults, there is a kind of constant eroticism among the young and the overreaction of adults to cosmetic sexuality on the part of youth begins to confirm its acting out. Thus, young women in early puberty dress in what are sexually provocative styles, appearing not as girls, but as women. While this shift in social identity has always been the pattern in adolescence, and the reactions of others have always been the process through which the young of both genders have assembled the sexual role with prior gender commitments, the feedback loop now seems to occur somewhat earlier in development, with adults reacting to young people's dress and styles closer to puberty.[7] This is explicitly true for young girls whose dolls now have breasts, beauty contests, boyfriends, and rock concerts. While the gender role definitions of the children's toy world are conventional, the sexual implications are far more intense and significant. The young are more exposed to a wider range of explicit sexual stimuli in the media than they have previously been in this society, and they are presented with images of their own sexuality characteristic of, at this point, a relative minority of the young.

While the young are becoming cosmetically more eroticized, they nearly all share or reject vicariously other social movements (women's liberation, students' rights, sexual liberation, antiwar activities) which enhance the content of youth culture and deepen the rhetoric of generational differences and the moral inferiority of their elders. Such specific issues, whatever their transience, operate to strengthen the image of rebellion and foster other forms of guerrilla warfare against parents and authority figures. Sexual activity and participation in drug subcultures begin, in part, for most young people as personal vendettas with parents and then become, for a minority, political in character (that is, a testing of the ultimate basis of the parent-child relationships which rest in part on the physical and economic power of the former). As this political rhetoric of the family emerges, it can become, for a few young people, a serious alternative allegiance to familial authority and, for others, each separate cause can become a mixture of justification and rationalization that falls short of ideology.

At the same time these events are occurring, which should enhance the probability of sexual activity on the part of the young, there is not a great deal of evidence that is being acted out at this moment by this generation of high school students. While the temperature of the adolescent hothouse seems to be higher now than ever before, there has not been a concomitant increase in early sexual activity on the part of the young. The earlier and more intense definition of the young as sexual does not seem to be acted out by the young themselves; that is, there is not any direct conversion of a new level of erotic identification into specific forms of behavior. It is likely that this is in part a function of the continued existence of prior conventional gender role commitments on the part of the majority of the young, as well as the continued commitment of both young men and women to the rhetoric of love, interpersonal attachment and ultimately, marriage. At the present time, there is little social or interpersonal payoff for sexual activity of any sort during early adolescence, and minimal payoff for coitus during later adolescence. Outside of the conventional routes to marriage, the payoff for young women in both periods is close to zero, though for males there do exist some rewards of homosocial adulation for sexual success (though these pleasures are not unalloyed). Sexual activity during this period can become symbolic of anti-adult attitudes and performed by either gender, or young women can drift into sexual activity at the behest of young men who are still acting out of an older male sex exploitation ethic, but there is no other specific societal linkage or payoff system that makes the behavior appropriate. Until the ideology of "sex is fun" or that "sex is good in itself" is more widespread, the acting out of sexual commitments does not seem likely in early adolescence. However, when these young people enter later adolescence and especially during the early period of serious mate selection, it is likely that these earlier (in the life cycle sense) definitions may well tend to increase the amount of premarital sexual activity on the part of the young. During the mating period, the definition of sex as a pleasure to which the young have a right can be combined with a payoff system (dating-mating-marriage) that is currently in existence.

A new element that will affect this period of development is the increasing flexibility of parental figures in their role performances. While the youth movement among parents is greeted by the young with derision, it is an amusement often mixed with more than a little anxiety. During the early 1960s, parents who did the twist were figures of fun, but now the serious sexuality of older persons is becoming more apparent to young people. Using the conventional language of psychoanalysis, the central problem of adolescence can be seen as an attempt to solve again the oedipal dilemmas of early childhood, and to come to terms with an independent sexual identity. During this time, parental figures were assumed to be stable objects, if not inside themselves, at least in their representation to children. Indeed, from the Freudian point of view, as the objective correlative of the super ego, parents were to remain parents to their children throughout their lives, evincing a continuity of moral character that could serve as a firm basis for either acceptance or rejection of parental values.[8] The emerging role flexibility supplied to adults by affluence has eroded both the fact and the illusion of this phenomenon, and parents have become increasingly ambiguous figures for their adolescent children. In this struggle, children often revolt in order to coerce their parents to remain the same, and there is in consequence, a mutual identity struggle between parent and child, with the latter often having a more rigid definition of the parent's behavior than the parent has of his child's.

It may well be that the significant sexual changes occurring at present are more apparent in an older generation whose responses to the increasing sexual openness of the society can be acted out with fully formed sexual commitments. The existence of these commitments is more apparent to the young in this generation than previously, and the young are rarely prepared for the dynamic changes that can occur in adults. This does not mean that they will not get used to them, only that in the transition period life for the adolescent will grow more complex. In the long run (one to two generations away), it is likely that there will be a great deal more heterosexual activity in early adolescence and perhaps an increase in eroticism among the young. It is also likely that there will be an increase in sexual activity between persons of a wider range of ages which will serve to introduce sexual activity more widely among the young.

CHANGES IN EARLY ADULTHOOD AND MARRIAGE

In general, it is likely that all the forces we have mentioned will move toward an increase in sexual activity prior to first marriage on the part of the young. At present and for a number of years into the future, the boundary between the sexually active young and those younger will be stable in the middle teens. It appears that there will be a steady increase in the proportion of young people who will have premarital coitus, however, for the present (a decade), there will be no great increase in the number of sexual partners for large numbers of women. While the institution of marriage is in disrepute (more among those who have lived in it than those who have not), the institution of romantic love and its concomitant dyadic regression is not. Intense dyadic attachments are still the norm among the young and still represent the primary situation in which young women engage in heterosexual activity prior to marriage. If these are the main conditions which currently determine whether premarital coitus will occur among young women, then most males would be restricted by them. The current pattern is a steady increase in the proportion of young women who are not virgins at marriage, but who have coitus in the context of love and mate selection. Clearly the increase in the proportion of women who have had intercourse under these conditions will also, as a result of misadventures, result in an increase in the number of women who have had intercourse with more than one male. This proportion should increase somewhat over the next ten years (say, from 15% now to 30% in 1980), but not rapidly. Larger increases in the numbers of sexually active women prior to marriage is probably a generation or two away. Large increases will require that women's economic lives are not tied directly to those of men, as well as a major ideological change in the way in which women view their own bodies as sources of pleasure. In part, such a change can take as its starting ideological points the language of women's liberation (which will become somewhat more meaningful to women just prior to marriage who may be joining the labor force), the increased level of sexual content given to women's identity during early adolescence, and an environment of males who seem less exploitive sexually.[9] These are the elements that are required to produce changes of this type, but for them to be developed will require some time. In this case, it would seem that the more conventional patterns of mate selection will stay the dominant style for the next 15 to 25 years. Most young people will continue to get married after relatively limited premarital sexual careers. This does not mean that there will not be increases in the numbers of nonvirgins, or that the frequency and incidence of premarital coitus will not increase, merely that the emotional and normative content of premarital sexual life will be relatively traditional, at least, for the vast majority of the young. If this is the case, this group of young people will not be the cutting edge of the change for the society.

It is during the periods of early and later marriage that the potential for change is somewhat greater. One factor that may contribute to change during this period is an increasing divorce rate. Much as failure in love relationships can produce females who have an increased sense of their sexual selves, so divorce can, for some women, if it does not erode entirely their sense of self, produce persons who are more available sexually both to themselves and others. An increase in the number of sexually active women in the society can be produced in this manner, as well as from the failure of other nonmarital forms of dyadic sexual relations between men and women. This process will create a larger population of sexually experienced women that will be more open to the language of women's liberation, both occupationally and sexually, and more prepared to act out a newly acquired sexual commitment. With the heightened level of eroticism available in the media as a backdrop, and an increased commitment to a sensualist ethic, it is possible for larger numbers of women to seek out sexual activity than to wait passively for it to come to them. If the number of young (20-23) divorced women is large, they can revert to being part of the never-married population and become personal models for a different pattern of sexual activity for never-married younger women. The difficulty of transmission of behavior models between the divorced woman and the never-married woman in the past has been the stigma of failure attached to the divorcees, since they have failed in the activity to which never-married women were devoting nearly all their time and energy. The divorcee (or the failed affianced) in the past had failed in woman's most precious goal, getting and staying married. However, this pattern has begun to change with larger numbers of divorcees and failed fiancees and with the emergence of a rhetoric to support divorce and the single life as an acceptable alternative to marriage.

The recently observed decline in the number of children per family could also have consequences both directly and indirectly on sexual activity during and between marriages. With fewer children or no children in a marriage, there are fewer economic, social, and moral obligations that will hold the marriage together during periods of stress. Smaller and especially childless families have a higher probability of increasing the pool of divorced men and women. In childless marriages, the absence of children could reduce the conflict between the erotic and the maternal, and males could continue to conceive of their spouses as exclusively erotic creatures rather than having to share them with children. This could increase the rates of sexual activity in marriage and the economic resources to support a more flexible, young adult, life style longer. At the same time, children do increase the emotional and social complexity of marriage, adding to its capital in terms of novel experience for both males and females, for children elaborate the number of roles available to adults, not only in relation to children, but to the surrounding social world as well. Marriages without children, or which have a short child-rearing period as a result of decline in total numbers, will have to find alternative sources of emotional and social novelty in other activities, some of which can lead to more extensive nonmarital contacts for each partner.

It seems that, as part of a general reduction of the economic and social costs of marriage failure and a decline in the number of children, there will be an increase in extramarital activity on the part of both men and women. The general form of extramarital coitus will remain relatively stable—that is, as private adventures on the part of the marital partners, though in some cases there will be mutual extramarital coitus (one of many varients of "swinging").

There will be ideological support for increases in extramarital coitus, both in attitudes expressive of the limitations of conventional marriage and in a rehtoric supportive of sexual expression as a necessary part of human fulfillment. There will probably be an efflorescence of the extramarital coitus behavior sometime in the 1970s (the parents of our 15-year olds) as part of the general crisis among middle-class marriage. Whether or not the efflorescence becomes more general or a normative standard for the society is unclear. Any increase in extramarital intercourse will reinforce the more prominent sexual identity on the part of parents for their adolescent children. In this case, there will be completion of a series of feedback loops between the generations with increasing role flexibility on the part of parents, allowing an increased commitment to nonmarital coitus, followed by a further impact on adolescents of a new set of sexual standards.

ACTIVITY AND AFFECT

If we follow the consequences of these arguments for any cohort of young people, it is our expectation that they will be more sexually active than their parents or any generation over thirty in 1970. Such aggregate changes that will occur among them, however, will be relatively slow in occurrence, and the increases in the proportions sexually active will be smooth rather than eruptive in character. There will be more of a steady increase of premarital sexual activity, mostly after sixteen. The incidence will increase among women and the frequency among both women and men rather continuously over the next 25 years. Toward the end of that period, there will begin to be steady increases in heterosexual activity among young people who are under sixteen, and general increases in erotic behavior during early adolescence. Most of the young will continue to get married, but there will be both a larger number of divorces and a higher frequency of extramarital coitus during marriage, though the two processes are not necessarily related. The cosmetic level of sexuality in the society will probably increase with the increased availability of reproduction technologies that allow private creation of erotic materials, and the general level of the society's erotic character will probably increase a good deal in terms of the availability of commercial erotic materials. What the current availability of erotic material will do to the young person's future appreciation of erotica is unknown, but there will still remain a substantial market for most public forms of erotica among men for at least another generation.

Given these kinds of changes in sexual activity, there is a parallel shift in the affective dimensions of sexuality which is perhaps more important and, indeed, central to shifts that are not merely aggregative in society, but reflect a fundamental difference in consciousness. Along with the increasing role flexibility that has occurred with the increasing affluence of the West, there has been a concurrent, but not necessarily related, drift toward the increasing secularization of the society. Sexuality, which was deeply linked in the minds of most Western Europeans since the rise of Protestantism and the Counterreformation with sin, normative transgression, and the problems of legitimacy, was historically essentially linked to experiences larger than the self and, even though these strictures probably did not descend very far into isolated peasant populations, the posture of the major religious institutions of the West toward sex was, at least, roughly known and observed.

With the emergence of capitalism and the rise of European culture as a worldwide phenomenon, the prior social metaphors linking individuals to collective and cultural forms developed new thematic characteristics. The restraining hand of puritanism was not only set upon the economic world, but upon the sexual in such a way that the emerging metaphors for sexuality in the eighteenth and nineteenth centuries were those of conservation as opposed to excess—metaphors which utilized a merging of a capitalist symbol with psychic and bodily functions and organs and which required the increasing divorce of sexuality from the rest of social life. The economic metaphor of sexuality became dominant and, while the sexual commitment was private in action, it remained social in its meanings. With the emergence of sexual revolutionaries in many forms at the end of the nineteenth century, the battleground for sexual metaphors still remained in the social arena. The rhetoric from Freud to Essalyn, from Lawrence to Mailer, from Comstock to Spiro Agnew is agreed on the social significance of sexuality. When one behaves sexually, one is acting out the metaphor of sex as power, sex as transgression, sex as reinforcing of natural masculine and feminine roles, sex as the apocalypse, sex and the world moves.

While this rhetorical pattern still exists, it has lost a great deal of its power to persuade, for at the same time society was being generally secularized, sex was being secularized as well. The experience of the sexual as being powerful was a natural concomitant of cultural arrangements which carried with them a belief in the dangers of transgression of legitimacy or (in its Enlightenment correlate) the dangers of chaos and disorder. Once these larger sets of cultural meanings had been overthrown or had evaporated, the experience of the sexual that was dependent on them lost its viability as well. It was only those who saw sex as having an autonomous meaning or as giving meaning to the rest of life who could believe that when all other things were changing, sex and the feelings related to it would remain the same.

At this point sex is close to having escaped from the world of the social metaphor. If it does not exemplify health and illness, good and evil, excess and restraint, the essence of the masculine and feminine—if it lies not only in the domain of personal morality, but in the domain of personal choice —then sex can no longer stand for significant social or personal oppositions. The correct modern metaphor has been suggested by Nelson Foote (1954), usefully commenting on Kinsey in the early 1950s, is "sex as play." If sex is merely a form of play, then our concerns with who does it, how old they are, or what their marital status is (unless we are concerned with disease or pregnancy) is misplaced. Sex is fun and subject to the morality of fun. It is entered into by choice of the two or more partners, anyone may do whatever good manners dictate, the rules are made up by autonomous, in the Piagetian sense, partners. We may wish to restrict elders with children, but what objection do we have to older people teaching younger people about games or sport? These are the essential meanings of the phrases, "doing your own thing" and "whatever turns you on." Play is nonconsequential, it is done with low affect, except by professionals whose livelihood depends on the activity. There is an interest in skill, but only to improve the intrinsic content of the game itself.

If one of the present characteristics of sex is that it is experienced as a powerful experience by many people with a great deal of emotional commitment, then the drift of sexuality into the world of play will begin to reduce this emotional intensity. Sex will be experienced like eating, an important, indeed, luxurious experience in stand for fidelity and infidelity, probably its most common social connection today, nor can it any longer be the major gift that a woman gives a man in the form of her virginity. Among the romantics, it cannot stand for passion and constraint or for the tension between ruling and submission. It is perhaps appropriate that *Love Story* should be a major work of the late mid-century which includes both copulation and the flattened emotional effect of the 1930s films, indicating how far we have come from *Romeo and Juliet*.

It should be clear that these cool feelings about sex are not dominant in the social scene today, but increasingly the rhetoric of sex as a matter of personal choice, as being good for one's happiness, or not as being of anyone else's concern, is important in the society. It is embodied in the sex law reform that is stumbling forward. If only force, great disparity in age, and bad manners in public places are reasons for crime, then the remainder of the sexual domain can scarcely stand for the revolutionary impluse. While the young still exhibit romanticism early in adolescence and slightly later, this romanticism is not now linked to sexual exclusivity. While there is still a belief in fidelity in marriage, there is an erosion of it as a fact and as a practice for at least some portions of the population.

The relationship between the intensity of affect attached to conventional sexual behavior and the amount of sexual behavior in any society is difficult to determine. It does seem that there is no necessary connection between them. It is perfectly possible to conceive of a society where there is low affective attachment to sex and yet a great deal of sexual activity, and it is equally possibly to think of a society where there is a lot of affective investment in sex and not domain can scarcely stand for the revolutionary impulse. While the young individuals in it see sexual activity as important and central to their concerns and that sex behavior is normatively linked to larger collective concerns. Figure 1 suggests the varying relation between the amount of sexual activity and the intensity of affect related to heterosexuality in four exemplary cultures, and the arrow suggests the future direction for U.S. society in the relation between these two highly abstract attributes (for descriptions of Inis Beag and Mangaia, see respectively Messenger, 1971, and Marshall, 1971).

What we mean to suggest here is the correlation of two attributes, neither of which will make sexual conservatives or revolutionaries very happy. It seems to us that there will be a general increase in the amount of heterosexual activity in the society over the next 25 years—that will make the liberals happier and the conservatives more unhappy—but that this

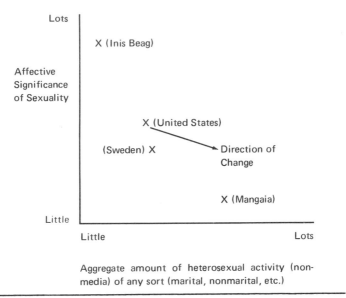

Figure 1: AFFECTIVITY AND AFFECT IN SEXUALITY IN FOUR SOCIETIES

sexual activity will not be experienced as immensely thera-peutic, nor will it be used in revolutionary changes in morality and equity between genders, the classes or the races—for which the liberals will be unhappy and the conservatives will say, "I told you so."

AFTERWORD

What is essential in the creation of a scenario for the future is to recognize that the participants in any future landscape will not experience their present in any way that we can dictate. While the sexual fantasies of men at present may view a future increase in the number of sexually active females with a sense of envy, it is very difficult to predict how the males at that future moment will respond. Cor-relatively, females may feel that women in the future will have a better situation when there are fewer aggressive and exploitive men, and greater equality between the genders, but what the women who are alive at that moment will feel may not be satisfaction. At the same time, we must not submit to the opposite tendency, that is, to degrade change by saying, "they will be doing it more, but enjoying it less." The critical posture to maintain is that the future will not be better or worse, only different.

NOTES

1. Future forecasting is constantly haunted by visions of the apocalypse; if nuclear war occurs, all bets are off.

2. It is not at all clear what the relation of this intellectual attitude or apparatus is to what Thomas Kuhn has referred to as paradigms in science. It might be fruitful to examine the difference between a set of ideas that cohesively structure research and thought and loose overarching metaphors. Any examination of Freud's own work and that of his followers will demonstrate this. In sociology, the best exemplification is Davis (1970).

3. Prescott Lecky described analytic psychodynamics as psychohydraulics; hence, the metaphor.

4. Margaret Mead has remarked that the only thing the modern United States has in common with ancient Rome is good plumbing, but the analogy tends to stick.

5. We emphasize after age twenty since the youthful period has always had a set of larger options in Western societies.

6. Rigidity and flexibility are not value words here; they are descriptions of styles of experience which can be differentially evaluated.

7. This is not the same as the past with early industrial societies. In those situations, reproductive maturity and sexual maturity were coterminous with marriageability and such culturally approved transitions are vastly different from emergent sexual identity without legitimate sexual behavior, marriage, or reproduction.

8. The injunction by psychiatric advice givers not to be permissive is based on the notion that constructive rebellion or rejection requires solid parental figures.

9. Thus Gloria Steinem can be conventionally erotic, which is the usual content of the late normal adolescence, and liberated politically as well. It is the novel joining of these formerly disparate individual themes on a collective level that is significant to social change.

REFERENCES

BOHANNON, P. (1971) Book review of *Human Sexual Behavior* in Science 173 (September 17): 1116-1117.

BURGESS, E. W. (1949) "The sociologic theory of psychosexual behavior," pp. 227-243 in P. H. Hoch and J. Zubin (eds.) Psychosexual Development in Health and Disease. New York: Grune & Stratton.

BURY, J. B. (1932) The Idea of Progress. New York: Dover.

DAVIS, K. (1970) "Sexual behavior," pp. 313-360 in R. K. Merton and R. Nisbet (eds.) Contemporary Social Problems. New York: Harcourt, Brace, Jovanovich.

FOOTE, N. (1954) "Sex as play." Social Problems (April): 159-163.

GAGNON, J. and W. SIMON (1972) The Social Sources of Sexual Conduct. Chicago: Aldine.

——— and A. BERGER (1970) "Some aspects of adjustment in early and late adolescence," pp. 275-295 in J. Zubin and A. M. Freedman (eds.) The Psychopathology of Adolescence. New York: Grune & Stratton.

KINSEY, A. C. et al. (1953) Sexual Behavior in the Human Female. Philadelphia: W. B. Saunders.

——— (1948) Sexual Behavior in the Human Male. Philadelphia: W. B. Saunders.

MARSHALL, D. (1971) "Too much in Mangaia." Psychology Today (February): 43-44, 70, 74-75.

MASTERS, W. and V. JOHNSON (1970) Human Sexual Inadequacy. Boston: Little, Brown.

MESSENGER, J. (1971) "The lack of the Irish." Psychology Today (February): 41-42, 68.

OVESEY, L. (1969) Homosexuality and Pseudohomosexuality. New York: Science House.

REISS, A. J. (1961) "The social organization of peers and queers." Social Problems 9 (Fall): 102-120.

SIMON, W. and J. GAGNON (1969) "On psychosexual development," pp. 733-752 in D. Goslin (ed.) Handbook of Socialization Theory and Research. New York: Rand McNally.

11

ADULT CONTROL IN
FAMILY AND SCHOOL
Public Opinion in Historical and
Comparative Perspective

GLEN ELDER

Historical change in authority relations and socialization presents two faces in American society. From one vantage point, there has been a substantial decline in the prevalence of autocratic ideology and hierarchical relations between adults and youth, providing greater experience for the young in the maturing activities of decision-making and self-direction. The other view interprets this trend as evidence of the continuing abdication of adult authority and as a prime cause of noncompliant, disrespectful behavior among the young. In recent years, adult anxiety over the authority crisis may largely account for what Turner (1970: 353) regards as "a vigorous resurgence of emphasis on discipline and authority in folk concern about child rearing."

Secular trends toward equalitarian relations between adults and children offer some basis for public criticism of excessive permissiveness in family and school. An ideology of personal choice expressed in the belief that youth should have a major role in making decisions relevant to their lives and a correlated decline in hierarchical forms of adult authority are noteworthy aspects of social change in twentieth-century America. The decline in paternal authority is generally regarded as a major change in the family system (Ogburn and Nimkoff, 1955: 18). Comparisons of Americans who were adolescents before 1920 and after 1950 show at least a twofold increase in the percentage reporting involvement in family decision-making, classroom participation through discussion and debates, and the opportunity to discuss conflicts or unfair treatment with teachers (Elder, 1968). While more than two-thirds of the Americans in the younger age group reported such participational experience, this was true of only a third of the older group. Considered together, these trends describe a significant transformation in adult-youth relations which is currently most evident in high-status sectors of urban areas.[1]

It is important to note that a social condition, such as adult control or its absence, only attains prominence as a social problem in the community when it is collectively defined as such (Blumer, 1971), and that definitions of this sort have potentially important consequences. The prevailing belief that discipline is too permissive represents a social construction which may have little basis in fact, although it has far-reaching implications for developmental socialization and innovation, especially in the public arena of schooling. The charge of permissiveness in adult control implies needed steps in disciplinary measures: in relation to the schools, it may promote external controls at the expense of innovative, developmental programs, and, if widespread, would lessen prospects for greater student involvement in the educational process.

Though contemporary concern over matters of adult authority and discipline appears to be greater than in past decades, very little is actually known about its historical dimensions. What conditions are associated with the belief that discipline of the young in family and school is problematic as to firmness, and how are they related to trends in public opinion since World War II, especially since the relatively placid 1950s? Is support for corporal punishment in the schools associated with this perception? This paper reports an investigation of these questions in a series of public opinion surveys, explores possible trends in attitudes toward adult control in the 1970s, and examines the consequences of these attitudes for social innovations that enable greater youth involvement and self-direction in the educational process. The following overview of public opinion during the 1940s and 1950s poses a series of research questions for the analysis of attitude trends and sources up to 1970.

The degree and form of resistance to change in socialization have not been systematically charted, although scattered evidence since World War II shows a high level of dissatisfaction with discipline in most families and schools.[2] Over two-fifths of the adults questioned in a national survey in 1946 felt that teenagers behaved worse than when they themselves were young, while only 9% regarded the young as an improvement over members of their own generation. Approximately 45% of the adults perceived no meaningful behavioral change between the generations. As one might expect, the belief that postwar teenagers were more poorly behaved was associated with conditions supportive of traditional constraints and hierarchical relations between parent and youth, low educational status, and rural residence. The very worst features cited by the respondents were in large part an indictment of adult permissiveness—too much freedom, irresponsibility, and both smoking and drinking. Interestingly, the most commonly cited assets of the postwar generation were qualities that seem to reflect autonomy and criticism of traditional constraints; more intelligent and better educated, frank and open to experience, and more interested in the world about them.

Eight years later, in the McCarthy era, more direct evidence was obtained on the perceived state of adult authority in a nationwide survey of adults. More than four out of five adults criticized discipline in most families for not being strict enough, and two-thirds of the sample voiced similar dissatisfaction with discipline in the schools. These attitudes were highly interrelated and appear to define a generalized stance of opposition to perceived change in authority relations and discipline at a time when youth were relatively apathetic toward social or political issues, and racial strife in the schools was negligible. The repressive climate of the McCarthy era may have increased anxiety over discipline in groups that are normally supportive of independence and participational experience for youth (the well-educated, for instance) since social differences in criticism of the schools and family upbringing were minimal. One might expect even more prevalent dissatisfaction with discipline among contemporary adults, in view of widespread tensions associated with authority and age-group conflicts.

As in socialization theories that emphasize the primacy effect of family upbringing, American adults have generally looked to the family for causes of youth misbehavior. At least through the 1950s, adults seemed to regard the school largely as a mirror reflecting the character of individual families. Most Americans in the mid-fifties who were critical of lax discipline in the schools placed the blame on parents for not permitting school officials to be stricter; two-thirds of the national sample expressed this viewpoint, in comparison to only nine percent who blamed school officials, and a fourth who attributed responsibility to both family and school. This difference in blame attribution is not simply a reflection of uncritical, acquiescent attitudes toward the school, since it was equally large among the most vocal critics and supporters of education, the college-educated. The emergence of parental control as an issue in school decentralization during the 1960s indicates an increasing tendency to blame school officials for student misconduct or failings, especially among the low-income groups in urban areas, but a more general issue in blame attribution involves the clash between universalistic and particularistic policy on school discipline. To the average parent, especially in the middle class, stricter discipline may be overdue for other people's children but not for one's own.

The perception of lax discipline in family and school defines a problem that calls for action, and public discussion regarding corrective proposals has generally considered the wisdom of various control techniques. Corporal punishment is commonly mentioned as an appropriate method for "uncontrollable" students and has recently gained vigorous support from teachers in large metropolitan areas. The concentration of support for such discipline in the rural population, especially within the South and Midwest (1946 and 1954 surveys), suggests that it represents a folk technique, transmitted through familial channels and validated more by belief than by evidence of its effectiveness (Turner, 1970: 348). When undesired consequences occur, they are commonly explained away by reference to external conditions beyond one's control. In nontraditional settings, corporal punishment resembles a crisis approach to socialization, a device used primarily in emergency or extreme situations. Such conditions appear to be widespread in the schools, for disciplinary problems are ranked as a difficult problem by teachers in all parts of the country, but especially in urban areas (see Grade Teacher, 1968).

If demands for greater strictness in discipline are actually on the upswing among Americans, the implications of this trend for educational innovation are not difficult to envision, especially with respect to programs that assign a more active, responsible role to students. Resistance to such programs would directly conflict with the increasing frequency and impact of student petitions for greater involvement in the decision-making process on both academic and social issues. Such involvement has been recommended by a number of recent studies on public secondary education (Chesler and Franklin, 1968; Murphy, 1970). A large-scale evaluation of civic education in relation to the citizenship requirements of the 1970s has proposed modifications in the teacher-student relationship which would facilitate the development of decision-making ability, "the most pressing need of contemporary civic education."

Students must be given the opportunity to make decisions within the classroom. The teacher must spend time as a resource person assisting the student in seeing and analyzing the options and relevant considerations involved in his civic problems. Rather than teaching a specified body of material, the teacher should aim to develop mature, autonomous civic decision-makers [Murphy, 1970: 25].

Findings from the early opinion surveys make forecasts uncertain on the relation between historical trends in attitudes toward adult control and their consequences for student participation in educational process. Traditional attitudes toward discipline appear to be most prevalent in rural areas, as indexed by approval of physical discipline in the schools, yet authority structures should be most problematic in areas of rapid change, such as large cities. If traditionalists are most threatened by the seeming disorder of urban life, concern over lax discipline in the schools would likely be concentrated among urbanites of limited education and rural backgrounds. However, this prediction does not consider educational commitment and involvement, which are generally most prevalent among the college-educated.

The following analysis is organized in three sections. The first part examines historical trends on support for stricter discipline in family and school, the conditions and social contexts associated with these trends, and the extent to which such demands apply to the respondents' own offspring as well as to other children. In the next section, we examine secular trends in the belief that corporal punishment should be used as discipline for recalcitrant students, and explore its meaning as a response to lax discipline in the schools. The implications of these attitudes for adult acceptance of youth involvement and self-direction in decision-making within the family and school are analyzed in the concluding section. Most of the data included in the analysis were obtained from

1946 and 1954 Gallup surveys and from a set of items that was included in a 1970 Gallup survey.[3]

PERMISSIVE DISCIPLINE IN FAMILY AND SCHOOL

Dramatic social and technological changes since World War II might lead one to expect an upward trend in public concern with authority and discipline in the rearing of children and youth. These developments have produced inevitable strains in agencies and structures that regulate conduct, altering the bases of compliance and making authority problematic and vulnerable to criticism. One source of strain is the uneven pace of structural change in authority patterns among families and the public schools. While change toward greater student participation and autonomy has occurred in the schools, these conditions appear to be more prevalent among upper-middle-class families, especially in the social-service sector (see Flacks, 1970), while low-status families tend to be more control-oriented (Kohn, 1969). If families in the lower strata are more discipline oriented than the schools, the problem of disciplinary permissiveness should be a focal concern of parents in these families. Along this line, Michael Young (1967: 140) observes that change in British schools during the last 25 years

> towards more freedom, less rigid discipline, more child-centered study, does not seem to have been matched in the understanding of parents, at any rate of working-class parents. There is a time lag: the schools have moved faster than the parents, and as a result parents are critical of the schools, for not drilling enough sheer information into their children's heads and for being too lax in discipline.

Changes in public schooling since 1940 do provide considerable evidence on the problematic aspects of student control. The most notable change is the striking increase in the proportion of children and youth enrolled in public schools, especially from the lower strata. Change toward a less selective or elitist school system increases the breadth of cultural discontinuity between family and school and enhances the problematic nature of student commitment and the burden of behavior control. The requirements of student socialization and control are inversely related to the degree of selectivity in recruitment. Over the past thirty years, the percentage of nonwhites, ages 25-29, who have at least four years of high school education has increased fivefold, and white high school graduates have nearly doubled (U.S. Bureau of the Census, 1971). This change and its implications are particularly evident in large metropolitan areas that have received a sizable influx of black families from the rural South. These and other conditions in the fluid environment of large cities suggest that adult concern with overly permissive discipline should be greatest in these areas.

Contrary to the expected secular trend, we find that little change has occurred over the past fifteen years in the proportion of Americans who regard family and school discipline as not strict enough. Comparable questions were included in the 1954 and 1970 surveys. Most adults in both surveys believed that discipline was not strict enough, especially in the family. Eighty-three percent, and two-thirds of the adults interviewed in 1954 expressed dissatisfaction with family and school discipline, respectively, and these values remained surprisingly stable until 1970.

These attitudes are highly interrelated; very few adults who were critical of school discipline did not express the same attitude toward discipline in the family. In pretest interviews, using questions included in the 1970 Gallup survey, adult respondents repeatedly drew a connection between lax discipline in the home and behavior problems in the local schools. When adults who were critical of school disipline were asked to suggest corrective adjustments, a majority mentioned changes in the attitude and disciplinary practice of parents. "More discipline in the home" and "greater parental support for school efforts in student discipline" were more common responses to the above question than direct criticism of the schools, including proposals to get rid of certain teachers, administrators, and so on. As in the 1946 survey, the perception of lax discipline in the schools frequently implies "undisciplined parents." As a middle-aged, high school graduate phrased it, behavior problems in the public schools are largely due to parents who "prefer to accept the easy way, avoid confrontation, or do not understand the obligations of being a parent." The connection between family and school on matters of student discipline appeared most frequently in the interviews among adults with more than a high school education, although it was also a common theme in interviews with lower-status white and Negro adults. This causal hypothesis has important implications for school discipline involving the respondents' offspring and students from other families, as we shall see in the subsequent analysis.

When items on strictness of discipline in family and school are combined in a single index, we find that a critical attitude toward discipline in both areas increased only slightly in prevalence between 1954 and 1970 (66 to 71%). Having children at home or in school did not make a difference in this attitude. It is possible that McCarthyism produced an inflated concern with permissive discipline in the early 1950s, although public opinion on school discipline some four years later (1958) had not changed. Unfortunately, we are unable to compare attitudes in the 1940s with those obtained in subsequent years, since no question on the topic was included in earlier surveys.

Social problems and the signs of rapid change are most apparent in metropolitan areas, and there is some evidence that critical attitudes toward discipline have increased among urbanites since the early 1950s, while an opposing trend appears among rural residents. Dissatisfaction with the strictness of discipline is directly associated with size of community in 1954 and 1970, and is most prevalent in the highly urbanized Northeast. Residential variations within

TABLE 1

Percentage of Adults Who Say Discipline is Not Strict Enough in Family and School, by Region and Residence

Region and Residence[a]		Percentage Reporting		
		1954	1970	% Diff.
Northeast	Rural	59 (53)	68 (177)	+ 9
	Urban	66 (74)	75 (173)	+ 9
	Metro	72 (218)	84 (419)	+12
		gamma = .19	gamma = .31	
Midwest	Rural	69 (144)	48 (255)	−21
	Urban	63 (76)	63 (147)	0
	Metro	73 (183)	75 (380)	+ 2
		gamma = .07	gamma = .42	
South	Rural	67 (215)	62 (334)	− 5
	Urban	53 (119)	64 (210)	+11
	Metro	63 (67)	77 (194)	+14
		gamma = −.06	gamma = .20	

a. Rural refers to places of less than 2,500; urban includes places between 2,500 and 100,000; metropolitan refers to places of 100,000 or larger. The Northeastern region includes both New England and the Mid-Atlantic states; the Midwest includes the East and West Central states; the Southern region includes the thirteen states which have been defined as Southern by the U.S. Census.

three regions that differ on urbanization and traditional values are shown in Table 1. The western states vary markedly on urbanization and are much too heterogeneous with respect to traditional values among adult residents to justify inclusion in a single regional category. A desire for stricter discipline has become more of an issue among rural and urban northeasterners over the past twenty years, while trends are in the opposite direction among rural residents of the Midwest and South.

The tendency for urbanites to view lax discipline as a cause of youth problems is not due to age or educational variations. As one might expect, young adults were less inclined to regard discipline as a problem than adults beyond the age of 49 (59 versus 72%) but age variations did not account for residential differences in attitude. Though social tolerance and a preference for self-direction in children are generally related to level of education (see Kohn, 1969), there is no evidence in the total sample that education makes a difference in attitude toward discipline. However, sizable educational differences do appear within social contexts defined by place of residence (Table 2). In the relatively conservative setting of rural America, adults are not as likely as their urban counterparts to regard discipline as a problem, but education is directly related to this perception. By contrast, the college-educated in urban and metropolitan areas are less inclined to view discipline as a problem than adults with a lower level of education. Educational differences are negligible in rural settings and greatest in large cities, with concern over discipline rising most sharply from rural to urban places among adults with less than a high school education.

In the general population, the relatively stable level of concern with lax discipline in family and school over the past twenty years may be due to the conflicting effects of urbanization and the upward trend in educational attainment. Social and economic opportunities attract educated adults to urban communities, and this group, along with rural residents, is least likely to see a need for stricter discipline in family and school. This need is most widely acknowledged by urban residents with limited education and may represent in part a defensive reaction to conflict between cultural roots in conservative, rural America and the perceived threat of city life for parental authority. Rural-born residents of cities tend to be more wedded to traditional values and methods of child-rearing than other urban citizens, and this is especially

TABLE 2
Percentage of Adults Who Say Discipline is Not Strict Enough in Family and School, by Residence and Education (1970)

| | Percentage Reporting | | |
| | Level of Education[b] | | |
Residence[a]	Primary	High School	College
Rural	53 (304)	62 (434)	63 (113)
Urban	81 (132)	68 (354)	60 (147)
Metro	91 (197)	76 (669)	72 (360)

a. Rural refers to places of less than 2,500; urban includes places between 2,500 and 100,000; metropolitan refers to places of 100,000 or larger.

b. Grades one to eight and no education are included in the primary category; high school refers to grades nine through high school and noncollege training in the post-high school years; college includes respondents with some college and those who completed at least four years.

true of persons with limited education and an authoritarian family background (Elder, 1965). Unfortunately, we are unable to verify the defensive reaction thesis since data on place of birth were not obtained in the 1970 survey.

While public support for stricter discipline seems to confirm the belief of some low-income parents that the schools have become more of an agent of social control than a route to social advancement, lower-status urbanites are most likely to perceive a need for more rigorous discipline. The small number of urban, black adults in our sample is equally critical of discipline in the schools. Parents of low status generally rank highest on the tendency to use external forms of punishment such as physical discipline (see Becker, 1964).

When school discipline is described as not strict enough, this may be an indirect way of attributing behavior problems to other people's children. That is, local school officials may be regarded as strict enough with the respondents' children, who are well-behaved, but as too permissive with other students. Considering the widely held view among black parents that school officials employ a double standard in disciplining white and black students, a desire for stricter discipline of other students would be an understandable response to perceived discrimination. This belief may also be found among the college-educated parents who, though concerned with quality education, are prone to ignore behavioral deficiencies in their own offspring.

Using data collected in the 1970 survey, we compared answers to questions which dealt with strictness of discipline for all children in the local schools and for the respondents' own children. These questions were widely separated in the survey schedule. Approximately two-fifths of the adults with children in school reported that discipline was not strict enough for their children *and* for other students, while a third expressed general satisfaction in both respects. As one might expect, very few parents only singled out their child for stricter discipline, while a much larger number excluded their children from the discipline problem (4 versus 27%). The latter view is not associated with low status, rural residence, age, or race. On the contrary, it is most common among college-educated parents and among parents in metropolitan centers. This is shown in Table 3, which divides the parental sample into four groups on residence and education. Forty-one percent of the college-educated urbanites tend to exclude their children from the discipline problem, as compared to only a fifth of the nonurban parents with less than a college education. This contrast is even greater when college-educated parents in metropolitan areas are compared with rural parents who did not enter high school.

Parents who saw other children as the discipline problem at school generally viewed themselves as stricter than other parents in rearing children. A connection is thus drawn between lax discipline in the home and behavior problems in school. The college-educated were more likely to view themselves as stricter than other parents, in comparison to parents with less than a high school education (49 versus 27%) and this difference was greatest in metropolitan areas.

TABLE 3

The Perception of Lax Discipline in the Schools for All Children and Respondents' Offspring, by Residence and Education (1970)

Perception of School Discipline[a]	Percentage Reporting[b]			
	Urban, College	Urban, Noncollege	Nonurban, College	Nonurban, Noncollege
"Not strict enough"				
For my children and others	29	41	41	35
For my children	—	8	3	5
For other children	41	31	25	21
"Strict enough"	30	20	31	39
Total	100	100	100	100
	(173)	(381)	(136)	(602)

a. Two items were used in defining perceptions of school discipline in general and in relation to the respondents' children: "If you think that discipline in the public schools in this community is too strict or not strict enough?", and "Do you think school discipline is too strict or not strict enough for your own child or children?"

b. Urban refers to urban places of 100,000 or more; nonurban refers to all places below 100,000.

The distinction between "my children and theirs" among parents with a college education may accurately reflect the disruptive, alienated behavior of lower-class males in urban schools, but it may also represent a dangerous expectation for preferential or particularistic treatment, a claim with obvious implications for policy on student discipline.

The relatively large percentage of low-status, urban parents who believe that school discipline should be stricter for their own children, even if not for other students, seems to reflect a tendency to rely upon teachers for ensuring that their children are controlled and hard-working. This sentiment might be phrased in the following logic: "If the teachers had been more strict, he would have done more work" (Lindsay, 1970: 43). "Laying the law down" through external measures in the home may foster an expectation of similar control in the school. In our 1970 survey, parents with less than a college education were more likely to report using physical punishment at least sometimes than were the college-educated (a difference of approximately 20% which did not vary by age of child), and corporal punishment in the home is moderately correlated with the belief that school officials should be stricter with the parents' own children (gamma = .36).[4] This mode of discipline was not consistently related to the more general perception that discipline in the local schools is not strict enough.

PUBLIC SUPPORT FOR CORPORAL PUNISHMENT
IN THE SCHOOLS

The large number of Americans who believe that discipline in family and school is not strict enough, the stability of this belief over the past twenty years, and the high level of concern in metropolitan areas identify a problem of considerable importance. This is most clearly evident in large, inner-city schools where student disruptions, assaults on teachers, destruction of school property, and the presence of police officers are commonplace. Various strategies are available for shoring up discipline, and corporal punishment appears to be a leading candidate, especially among grade school teachers in urban centers. There is a parallel between this source of approval and support for "caning" in British schools. Caning remains a legitimate method of discipline in British schools, and, although it has lost favor over the past twenty years, it still remains "firmly entrenched as a 'right' and a 'necessity' " (Wiseman, 1967: 112). Arguments favoring this method come mainly from teachers who are faced with the test of surviving in "problem" schools.

> It is claimed that corporal punishment must be retained as a final and ultimate sanction, particularly in schools drawing their pupils from areas of poverty, crime, and social disorganization. It is implied that without it control would become impossible, and that the behaviour of children, both in and out of school, would become worse [Wiseman, 1967: 112].

While the behavioral consequences of this method vary by context (see Parke, 1970), its costs or disadvantages in British schools (greater cleavage and hostility between staff and students) may outweigh whatever value it has in producing outward compliance (see Wiseman, 1967: 112). If one assumes that school staffs in low-income schools are most strongly in favor of the right to use corporal punishment, their position is likely to receive support from the students' parents, at least as a general principle. This method is most commonly used in low-status families, and may be equally prevalent in the traditional culture of rural families.

Corporal punishment is commonly associated with hierarchical relations in family and school, but attitudes toward this method do not correspond with the postwar trend toward more democratically structured associations. In fact, physical punishment has remained at least as acceptable among Americans during the 1960s as in 1946 when nearly three-fourths of the respondents in a Gallup survey expressed approval. Even more striking evidence of stability is seen in the level of support for physical discipline in the public schools from 1938 to 1970. Adults in five AIPO surveys (1938,[5] 1946, 1954, 1958, and 1970) were asked whether they believed that teachers should or should not have the right to spank or administer other forms of physical punishment to students. In most cases, explicit reference was made to the grade-school level. Of the adults in the prewar survey, 53% thought that teachers should have this right, and this percentage increased to 55 in 1954 and to approximately 63 during 1958-1970. Support in 1946 differed markedly from this trend line, dropping to only 35%. Since this shift occurred in all age groups, it may reflect the liberalizing influence of World War II on social attitudes. Neither the presence of children in the household nor their ages made a substantial difference in receptivity to physical punishment in school.[6]

Now, as in the late thirties and mid-forties, approval of corporal punishment in school is predominantly a rural and regional phenomenon, with only a modest relationship to low education.[7] Americans who favor giving teachers the right to use physical punishment are most likely to be rural, southern or midwestern, and low in education (less than a high school education). The difference between rural and metropolitan residents averages 23% across all five surveys. Corporal punishment is widely used by teachers in the South (see Grade Teacher, 1968; and Reed, 1971), and southerners were consistently more receptive to this method than adults in the Northeast across the five time periods (an average of 31%). Surprisingly, educational variations in attitude were considerably smaller then differences by either residence or region. Adults with less than nine years of education were more supportive of physical punishment over the past thirty years than persons with at least some college education, but the average difference is only nine percent. No consistent trends across time periods occurred within categories of education, residence, region, and age.

Similar to evaluations of school discipline, the relation between educational level and support for corporal punish-

TABLE 4
Percentage of Adults Who Believe Teachers Should Have the
Right to Use Corporal Punishment, by Residence
and Education (1970)

Residence	Total	Percentage Reporting			College %–
		Level of Education			
		Primary	High School	College	Primary %
Rural	76 (921)	66 (359)	75 (470)	84 (134)	18
Urban	64 (722)	72 (162)	59 (425)	55 (166)	−17
Metro	56 (1417)	64 (234)	55 (784)	44 (465)	−20
Total	64 (3060)	71 (710)	65 (1605)	56 (737)	15

ment varies according to residential context (Table 4). Attitudes of the college-educated in 1970 generally resemble the normative climate of their respective setting, whether rural or urban. Corporal punishment is most widely favored in rural America, and rural residents with college educations are most likely to share this attitude. This contrasts with urban support, which is strongest among adults who did not continue their education beyond the eighth grade. Though education effects in rural settings are at variance with usual social correlates of higher education, this might be due to both socialization and recruitment processes, such as the traditional climate of colleges attended by persons who eventually settle in rural areas and the attraction of adults with traditional views to settings with corresponding values. In any case, it is clear that views on school discipline are not uniformly associated with level of education.

Rural-urban differences in the relation between education and attitudes toward corporal punishment in the schools seem to reflect contextual variations in traditional child-rearing values rather than differences in general personality characteristics. Both tolerance of nonconformists (Stouffer, 1955) and support for corporal punishment in the schools increase in prevalence by educational level in rural America. Though dominance structures in the family do appear to be more common in the families of adults who score high on authoritarianism (compare Centers et al., 1971), socially supported norms on traditional child-rearing are likely to be expressed by many rural residents who are nonauthoritarians. This seems most probable among rural adults with a college education.

Rural residents and the college-educated are more inclined to favor corporal punishment in the South and Midwest than in the Northeast, but the interaction effects of residence and education are similar in each region. The greatest variation in attitude is seen in the comparison of college-educated northeasterners who live in metropolitan centers with rural, college-educated adults in the Midwest and South (36 versus 98%). With the exception of respondents below the age of 30, attitudes on corporal punishment do not vary significantly by age; deletion of the younger respondents did not change or alter the above results.

Though rural Americans are more receptive to corporal punishment as student discipline than adults in metropolitan areas, they are less apt to regard lax discipline as a problem in the schools. As a result, physical discipline is not especially popular among adults in the sample who believe that school discipline is not strict enough (gamma = .26). The age and presence of children in the home did not modify this association. In rural areas, one-third of the adults do not regard school discipline as too permissive, although they do favor physical methods as punishment for wayward students, while a similar proportion of large-city residents reject this approach for improving school discipline. Among adults who regard school discipline as too permissive, support for physical punishment is strongest in rural areas among the college-educated and in large cities among persons with less than a ninth-grade education. From these and other results, it is apparent that the secular trend toward higher levels of education does not have common implications for adult attitudes on behavior control in family and school.

Adults who advocated corporal punishment in the schools generally applied this policy to their children as well, regardless of age. Only five percent of the parents did not report identical attitudes on the right of teachers to use physical punishment in general and, if necessary, in disciplining their own children. Forced consistency on the two items was minimized by locating them in different sections of the interview schedule. Attitudinal agreement on a uniform policy may of course not correspond to actual behavior; it is far easier to consent in principle to such policy than to maintain this position when the offending student happens to be one's offspring.

In parental reports, family and school are related on matters involving both strictness and mode of discipline. Parents who regarded most other parents as too permissive were likely to exclude their children from the discipline problem in school and those who reported using corporal punishment at least sometimes were most supportive of the teacher's right to employ this sanction. Regardless of residential area, region, educational level, or age of child, parents who agreed that teachers should have the option of physical punishment were most likely to rely upon this method in rearing their own children (average gamma = .29). The association is strongest among parents in rural and urban areas who were least likely to use physical discipline, those with at least some college education.

The connection between family child-rearing and parental conceptions of acceptable school discipline markedly increases the range of opinion on behavior control, as seen in the boundary between parent and teacher authority on discipline. College-educated parents are most likely to distinguish between the scope of parental and teacher authority, and to give primacy to the former. In pretest interviews with urban respondents, parents with a college education were most inclined to restrict the scope of teacher authority to the establishment of consistent rules and their enforcement to methods characteristic of middle-class upbringing—i.e., reasoning, restriction of privileges, and the like. On serious infractions, a large percentage of these parents felt that school officials should refer the problem to the child's parents.

The strongest resistance to this approach was found among adults with less than a ninth-grade education. An extreme example is provided by a metal worker who roundly criticized local school officials for contacting him about his son's disobedience instead of giving "the boy a whipping" when he deserves it. This sentiment was also expressed in the belief that "parents shouldn't meddle or interfere in school disciplinary problems." While there is clearly some evidence of acquiescence to school authority in these attitudes, the relative absence of a boundary between the rights of parents and those of teachers is a notable contrast to popular sentiment among college-educated parents. A common theme in the latter's responses to the question on corporal punishment is that "such disciplinary action is only the right of parents." This attitude is well-expressed by the wife of a medical doctor: "teachers do not have any business spanking my children or anyone else's. This is the parent's responsibility."

ADULT CONTROL AND YOUTH INVOLVEMENT

Though permissive discipline does not appear to be much more of a problem in the attitudes of Americans now than during the early fifties, it is concentrated in the growing, urban sector of society and may be seen as a manifestation of a crumbling authority structure along with student demands for greater participation in the problem-solving and decision process in the public schools. It is apparent that a belief that discipline should be stricter is not equivalent to support for external control, as indicated by attitudes toward physical punishment. Moreover, we do not know whether favorable attitudes toward corporal punishment in the lower grades reflect sentiment favoring more rigorous control and hierarchical relations between teachers and older students. In our pretest interviews, some adults who were critical of lax discipline in both family and school felt that the problem was due to the exclusion of youth from the responsibilities of decision-making, rather than a matter requiring greater external control. Students who desire a more active role in learning and decision-making are not a majority in high school, but they tend to come from families that offer experience in decision-making (McPartland et al., 1971), a family pattern that has become more prevalent over the past thirty years. This correspondence between family structure and desired school structure parallels our finding on the association between reported strictness and mode of discipline in the home and desired control in the school. In their survey of fourteen urban high schools, McPartland and his associates found that both students and their teachers desired more participation in decision-making for students, especially in nonacademic areas such as social rules, discipline, and political issues. Discipline represented one of three issues that drew the strongest criticism from students; the other two were grades and course assignments. These and other data suggest that the discipline issue mainly involves differences between school staff and parents or between parents, rather than teacher-student disagreement. Some cleavage between school staff and parents on student participation and discipline is perhaps inevitable, given the degree to which parents are isolated from events in school.

Youth participation in decision-making, whether in family or in school, is supported by a majority of the adults who were interviewed in 1970. Four-fifths agreed that children of sixteen should have a great deal or at least some voice in making major family decisions, and a similar proportion thought it was a good idea to encourage students to discuss political and social issues. On family decision-making, the percentage of young adults (aged 20-29) who favor involvement is only slightly lower in 1970 than it was in the late 1950s (84 versus 90; Elder, 1965). A more radical form of student participation than political debate, involvement in administrative decision-making, was approved by a surprisingly large percentage of adults in the 1970 survey (58%). Support for all three forms of youth participation is correlated with age, education, and, to a lesser extent, with residence. Adults who are most inclined to support youth involvement are young, college-educated, and urban.

Since all three items are highly intercorrelated, they were combined to form a single index of youth involvement with scores ranging from zero to five (see Table 5). Scores of four and five were defined as adult support for youth involvement. Only a fourth of the older adults (50 years or older) scored high on the index, as against 70% of the respondents who were in their twenties. This range of variation is comparable on level of education. Supportive attitudes showed much less variation between rural and metropolitan residents (only 10%), while regional location made no difference at all.

TABLE 5
**Percentage of Americans Who Support Youth Involvement
by Age and Education (1970)**

Age Group	Percentage Reporting			Percentage Diff. Between Primary and College
	Primary	High School	College	
20-29	(24)[a]	64 (384)	80 (258)	—
30-49	34 (190)	49 (706)	56 (304)	22
50+	22 (539)	36 (573)	50 (193)	28
Percentage diff. between 20 and 50+	—	28	30	

NOTE: Index of youth involvement is formed by three items (average gamma coefficient for item relationships is .52): "In general, how much voice do you think children of 16 should have in major family decisions"—Great deal = 2, Some = 1, and Little or None = 0; "In some high schools the children are encouraged to discuss and debate political and social issues and to draw their own conclusions. Do you think this is a good idea (scored 1) or a poor idea (this response and "it depends" were scored 0)?"; and "in some high schools the students participate in running the school; in others, teachers and the school administration make all decisions regarding the running of the school. Do you think it is a good idea (scored 2) or a poor idea (scored 0) to let students take some part in running the school?" ("It depends" was assigned a score of 1.) Summation of values on each item produced a scale with values ranging from 0 to 5. Scores of 4 and 5 are defined as support for youth influence.

a. Base too small.

Since educational attainment decreases by age, the effects of these variables are not completely independent; older adults are less in favor of youth involvement than younger respondents, but some of this difference may be due to the lower educational attainment of the older subgroup. Despite this degree of intercorrelation, both variables do have an independent effect on attitudinal support, as shown in Table 5. Within each age group, educational attainment increases support, while younger adults are consistently more likely to favor youth involvement than older Americans. Not surprisingly, the greatest contrast occurs between young, college-educated adults and older respondents with less than an eighth-grade education.

Though residence makes little difference in attitude toward youth involvement, neither age nor education is as predictive of this attitude among rural residents as it is among urbanites, especially those who reside in large cities. Older and younger adults in rural America are more similar in attitude than their counterparts in metropolitan centers (r = −.24 and −.40), a difference which is only partly due to the greater similarity of rural age groups on education. Even with education controlled, the residential difference in age effects remains substantial. Adults at opposite ends of the education continuum differed in relative position on attitudes toward discipline in rural and metropolitan areas, but education is positively correlated with support for youth involvement in both areas and is only slightly stronger among city residents (r = .39 versus .31). The apparent inconsistency in these results is most evident in rural communities; the college-educated are most likely to favor youth involvement in all age groups, yet they are also most supportive of stricter discipline and corporal punishment in the schools. In large cities, the college-educated are least likely to hold these attitudes toward discipline and are most inclined to favor youth participation. These contextual variations reflect differing conceptions of child and youth socialization that are more complex than the usual characterization of traditional and progressive ideas in upbringing.

Only in metropolitan areas are attitudes favoring stricter discipline and corporal punishment meaningfully related in a negative direction to support for youth involvement. The perception of lax discipline in family and school is more indicative of resistance to youth participation in large cities than of attitudes favoring corporal punishment in the schools ($r = -.24$ versus $-.15$). In the rural subgroup, coefficients for thse relationships are less than .06. These results are not influenced by the presence or age of children. Age and education account for approximately 23% of the variance in support for youth involvement among residents of metropolitan areas, in contrast to 12% in the rural subgroup, and attitudes toward discipline add less than 2% to the explained variance in the former subgroup.

These data have implications for public attitudes toward youth involvement during the 1970s if we assume that some of the age effects reflect a continuing secular trend in attitudes favoring democratically structured associations (as against simply a maturational or life-cycle phenomenon); that educational attainment will continue to rise; and that both age and education influence support for youth participation directly as well as indirectly through the belief that discipline should be stricter. Neither age nor education appears to be significantly correlated with concern over lax discipline among metropolitan residents and, in a causal analysis, these factors had only small, indirect effects on support for youth participation through discipline attitudes. Their primary effects are both direct and similar.

The perceived need for stricter discipline has much less impact on attitudes toward youth involvement than age and education. For example, the standardized regression coefficient for the direct effect of education is .29, in contrast to a value of $-.14$ for the direct effect of discipline attitudes. The ambiguous meaning of perceived laxity in discipline is most likely a factor in this result. Unstructured questions in the pretest interviews yielded varied explanations of "not strict enough" in response to the question on school discipline.

To some interviewees, it meant that the schools were too permissive regarding clothing and hairstyles, drugs, disorderly conduct in the classroom, and aggression toward teachers. Such interpretations are more likely to promote repressive action than complaints regarding school officials who are stricter on matters of dress than on serious behavioral problems, or criticism of teachers who do not apply the same rule uniformly to all students.

How adults interpret authority conditions in the schools and how they respond to them are undoubtedly related to knowledge of the situation, among other factors. Presumably a sizable proportion of the adults and parents in our sample had little or no contact with the local schools and may have formed their picture of discipline solely on the basis of news reports and informal communications from children and friends. At the other extreme are adults who actively participate in school affairs through parent associations and volunteer work. Participation may serve to lessen apprehension of student conduct and increase awareness of the underlying cause of problems, as against their surface manifestations. Public interpretation of student unrest, as an expression of some justifiable grievances, increases prospects for settlement by negotiation rather than by coercion (Turner, 1969). If this interpretation is a partial function of acquaintance with the school situation, the typically limited participation of low-status adults may help explain their tendency to perceive discipline as a problem and to support the use of corporal punishment.

The problematic meaning of lax discipline and its implications for the involvement of young people in processes of decision-making should be viewed within the more general process by which adult control, or the lack of it, becomes a social problem. Blumer (1971) has outlined five stages in the natural history of a social problem which identify important deficiencies and unknowns in our analysis. The process by which a condition is collectively recognized as a social problem constitutes the first stage. Owing to data and space limitations, we have not been able to explore the particular circumstances and observations which contributed to the perception of family and school discipline as overly permissive. A more focused, comparative study of stable and changing communities is needed to provide an understanding of the various elements which enter into problem definition, such as student violence, interest groups, opinion leaders, and the mass media. Once a social condition is recognized as a social problem, its survival depends on whether it receives legitimation as a problem worthy of attention in centers of public discussion and action—the church, city hall, school, mass media, and the like. If the problem is legitimated, it enters a stage of active discussion and tactical maneuvers in which competing interests mobilize for action. "Those who seek changes in the area clash with those who endeavor to protect vested interests in the area" (Blumer, 1971: 305). During the late 1960s, the issue of disruptive or violent students in the New York City schools developed into a conflict between teachers and minority groups. Conflicting and cross-cutting interests make the concluding stages of official plan formation and implementation especially problematic.[8]

According to a sizable number of adults in our analysis, problems of student misbehavior or lax school discipline are largely due to parental permissiveness. This folk diagnosis is obviously too simplistic, although it corresponds with some popular beliefs about family change. An example is the belief that the trend toward democratic relations in the family has taken the form of a laissez faire arrangement in many families, a regime in which parents are minimally involved in the responsibilities of child-rearing. Along this line, Bronfenbrenner (1970: 98) suggests that changes in child-rearing since World War II show a progressive decline in "the amount of contact between American parents and their children." Compared to the limited data on child-rearing, this conclusion has stonger support in public opinion as a perception of contemporary parent-child relations, such as the nearly universal belief that family discipline is too permissive. Lack of parental supervision, guidance, and parent-child contact were frequently mentioned by adults in our pretest interviews as causes and examples of permissive discipline. While neither unilateral forms of adult control nor a lassez faire relationship involves the young in the responsibilities of self-direction (Elder, 1971: 44-57), guided opportunities for autonomy establish a developmental context for self-control and mature judgment.

To some extent, student alienation and authority conflicts are related to cultural and structural discontinuities between family and school. The legitimacy of school authority and the meaning of schooling are especially problematic to the young, who are socialized in values and family relationships that conflict with the sociocultural environment of the school. While such conflict is a familiar theme in the school experience of youth from the lower strata and minority groups, it also appears among middle-class youth in the realm of authority relations and values. As noted earlier, there is some evidence which suggests that rejection of unilateral forms of control in the school is most probable among youth who have some influence in family decision-making. In this respect, Flacks (1970: 348) suggests that youth who have experienced democratic relations, humanistic priorities, and encouragement in self-expressive, independent behavior within the family are most likely to find "authority in school to be petty, arbitrary, and repressive." These discontinuities have obvious implications for structural changes in schools, especially in the context of secular trends in family relationships and adolescent maturation. Two arrangements, in particular, seem to have the potential for creating social commitments and responsible independence in the educational process: participation in decision-making on social and academic matters, and involement in the process of teaching other students. Considering present developments, both types of educational structures are likely to become increasingly more common during the 1970s.

We began this analysis by examining public perceptions of adult control from both historical and contemporary perspectives, and have come to the end with an emphasis on forms of youth participation in decision-making and governance. Folk concern with weaknesses in adult authority and discipline has largely forcused on external constraints or punishment, as against experiences that foster social responsibility and self-regulation, and this preoccupation is reflected in the present analysis. The kinds of questions on family and school which the Gallup organization included in its early surveys are indicative of this emphasis. Until recently, no questions were asked about the involvement of young people in decision-making or problem-solving activities, and yet these experiences develop skills and commitments appropriate to adult life.

Age segregation within the larger community, barriers to participation in responsible activities, and exclusion from decision-making have contributed to the "problem" of adult control and age-group conflict by creating the alienating experience of a "functionless" position in postindustrial society. In an age of rapid change, adults have much to learn from the young, for as Erikson (1962: 24) observes, "no longer is it merely for the old to teach the young the meaning of life, whether individual or collective. It is the young who, by their responses and actions, tell the old whether life as represented by the old and as presented to the young has meaning." For young and old, shared meanings and disciplines arise out of shared experience.

NOTES

1. Over this time period, change has also occurred in physical development: "children today are generally taller and heavier than children of the 1930s at the same age, and the increase has been equivalent to four months per decade; thus, children of age 11 in 1930 would be similar in size to children of age 10 today" (Elder, 1971). The implications of this trend for adult control remain to be determined.

2. Two AIPO surveys are the major sources of data on adult control in family and school in the postwar period: No. 377 (1946), a nationwide sample of approximately 3,000 respondents; and No. 538 (1954), a smaller national sample of about 1,600 respondents. More limited data were also obtained from AIPO No. 608 (1958). Three topics included on at least two of these surveys are indicated by the following items: "Do you think discipline in the public schools in this community is too strict or not strict enough?; Too strict, not strict enough, about right"; "Do you think teachers in grade school should have the right to spank children at school, or not?; Should, should not"; and "Do you think discipline in most homes today is too strict, or not strict enough?; Too strict, not strict enough, and about right." We assume the term discipline refers to the matter of behavior control, and was interpreted as such by respondents in these surveys. In relation to the schools, this assumption is problematic since strict discipline could refer to a no-nonsense, subject-matter orientation. Preliminary interviews in a small purposive sample of adults indicated that perceptions of lax discipline in the schools uniformly implied a need for more effective methods of behavior control. Subject-matter concerns were seldom mentioned in this context.

3. In order to explore secular trends and future developments in public opinion on adult control, we included the three items listed in note 1 and additional items on youth involvement in the November 1970, AIPO survey. Completed interviews with 1,609 adults were weighted by a factor of 2 to yield a representative cross-section of the American population. We are grateful to George Gallup, Jr., for his generous assistance on this project. Items included in the 1970 survey were also included in an interview schedule that was used to achieve greater depth on respondent attitudes and interpretations of the questions. Completed interviews in this pretest were obtained from approximately 125 adults from the middle and working classes.

4. Within a historical framework, Musgrove (1966) has explored conditions associated with particular forms of relationship between family and school. Of particular relevance here is the concept of school as an extension of the family. The popularity of this concept among parents is assured by their vested and conditioned interests in the virture of family upbringing.

5. The only question on discipline in the 1938 survey (No. 288) is one on whether teachers should have the right to spank unruly students.

6. Adults who favor corporal punishment in the schools also tend to favor extreme forms of this method in dealing with juvenile delinquents. In the 1958 survey, respondents were presented with two strategies for dealing with delinquents: "In some cities in England, young people who commit minor crimes are required to be whipped by their parents, with a police officer present to see that it is carried out. Would you approve of such a plan in this community?" and "It has been suggested that teenagers who commit serious crimes be whipped in public instead of sending them to reform school or to prison. Would you approve or disapprove of this practice?" Twenty-seven percent of the Americans who approved of "spanking kids" in school also approved of parental whippings for delinquents in the presence of a police officer; the two attitudes were moderately intercorrelated (gamma = .49). Approval of public whippings is also correlated with support for corporal punishment in the schools (gamma = .39).

7. Support for corporal punishment in the schools is also more prevalent among black than among white respondents, among non-Jews than among Jews,

and among men than among women. The racial difference is reduced considerably with education controlled and does not affect the results obtained. The number of Jews in the sample is too small to have any effect on the results, while the sex difference is generally less than five percent.

8. One form of stalemate is implied by a union spokesman (Shanker, 1971) for New York City teachers in comments on student violence. "As on previous occasions when the city was shocked by school violence, a certain ritual followed—a ritual which included newspaper editorials, a denunciation of the violence by the Mayor, and an announcement by the Chancellor (and the Board of Education) that violence would not be tolerated and that specific measures would soon be announced to insure greater security in the schools. The question, after this new round of violence, of whether this time action will replace earlier promises remains unanswered."

REFERENCES

BECKER, W. C. (1964) "Consequences of different kinds of parental discipline," pp. 169-208 in M. L. Hoffman and L. W. Hoffman (eds.) Review of Child Development Research. New York: Russell Sage.

BLUMER, H. (1971) "Social problems as collective behavior." Social Problems 18 (Winter): 298-306.

BRONFENBRENNER, U. (1970) Two Worlds of Childhood. New York: Russell Sage.

CENTERS, R., B. H. RAVEN, and A. RODRIGUES (1971) "Conjugal power structure: a reexamination." Amer. Soc. Rev. 36 (April): 264-278.

CHESLER, M. and J. FRANKLIN (1968) "Interracial and intergenerational conflict in secondary schools." Presented in somewhat different form at the meetings of the American Sociological Association, Boston, August.

ELDER, G. H., Jr. (1971) Adolescent Sociatlization and Personality Development. Chicago: Rand McNally.

——— (1968) "Democratic parent-youth relations in cross-national perspective." Social Sci. Q. 49 (September): 216-228.

——— (1965) "Role relations, sociocultural environments, and autocratic family ideology." Sociometry 28 (June): 173-196.

ERIKSON, E. H. (1962) "Youth; fidelity and diversity." Daedalus 91 (Winter): 5-27.

FLACKS, R. (1970) "Social and cultural meanings of student revolt: some informal comparative observations." Social Problems 17 (Winter): 340-357.

Grade Teacher (1968) "Discipline: not the worst problem . . . but bad." 86 (September): 151-162, 217-218.

LINDSAY, C. (1970) School and Community. London: Pergamon.

KOHN, M. L. (1969) Class and Conformity. Homewood, Ill.: Dorsey.

McPARTLAND, J. et al. (1971) Student participation in High School Decisions. Baltimore: Johns Hopkins Center for Social Organization of Schools.

MURPHY, D. (1970) "Civic education in a crisis age: an alternative to repression and revolution." New York Center for Research and Education in American Liberties. (Summary of a research project to develop objectives for a new civic education curriculum for American secondary schools in the 1970s.)

MUSGROVE, F. (1966) The Family, Education and Society. London: Routledge & Kegan Paul.

OGBURN, W. F. and M. F. NIMKOFF (1955) Technology and the Changing Family. New York: Houghton Mifflin.

PARKE, R. D. (1970) "The role of punishment in the socialization process," pp. 81-108 in R. A. Hoppe et al. (eds.) Early Experiences and Processes of Socialization. New York: Academic Press.

REED, J. S. (1971) "To-live-and-die-in-Dixie: a contribution to the study of Southern violence." Pol. Sci. Q. (Summer).

SHANKER, A. (1971) Statement in the New York Times (April 11): E9.

STOUFFER, S. A. (1955) Communism, Conformity, and Civil Liberties. New York: Doubleday.

TURNER, R. H. (1970) Family Interaction. New York: John Wiley.

――― (1969) "The public perception of protest." Amer. Soc. Rev. 34 (December): 815-831.

U.S. Bureau of the Census (1971) "Characteristics of American youth." Current Population Reports: Special Studies Series P-23, No. 32.

WISEMAN, S. (1967) "Education and environment," pp. 107-122 in M. Craft et al. (eds.) Linking Home and School. London: Longm n, Green.

YOUNG, M. (1967) "Parent-teacher cooperation," pp. 136-142 in M. Craft et al. (eds.) Linking Home and School. London: Longman, Green.

12

THE DRAFT, MILITARY SERVICE, AND NATIONAL UNITY
A Contribution to the Debate

JERALD G. BACHMAN

For more than five years, the United States has been engaged in a vigorous debate concerning the merits of the draft as a source of military manpower. The great urgency of this debate derives from the Vietnam war, but the basic issues transcend this particular war and go to the heart of the role of military forces in a free society.

This paper is intended as a contribution to that debate, as well as a discussion of present and prospective attitudes of youth bearing on military service and national unity. There are several distinctly separate streams of discussion in the paper which converge in the final sections. The first section provides an overview of the national debate concerning the draft versus an all-volunteer force. The second section contains a summary of youth views on national issues, while the third presents data concerning youth attitudes about

AUTHOR'S NOTE: *The author is grateful to Jerome Johnston and Lloyd D. Johnston for many valuable comments and suggestions. For an extended treatment of the topics reported here, see Johnston and Bachman (1972).*

serving in the military. The fourth section contrasts several incentives which might be used to attract enlistees to an all-volunteer force, relating these alternatives to a number of issues raised in the earlier sections. A final section provides summary, conclusions, and projections for the future.[1]

HIGHLIGHTS OF THE DEBATE

The military draft, never very popular during the post-World War II era, came under increasing fire in the 1960s. By 1966, there were widespread student demonstrations against the draft and its inequities. On July 1 of that year, President Johnson appointed a National Advisory Commission on Selective Service (the Marshall Commission) charged to

> consider the past, present, and prospective functioning of selective service and other systems of national service in the light of the following factors: fairness to all citizens, military manpower requirements, the objective of minimizing uncertainty and interference with individual careers and education, social, economic, and employment conditions, and goals and budgetary and administrative considerations.

Shortly before the Marshall Commission was appointed, the University of Chicago began plans for a national conference on the draft. The conference took place in December of 1966, under the chairmanship of Sol Tax. It brought together a wide range of participants including social scientists, legislators, military leaders, and also the executive director of the Marshall Commission, Bradley H. Patterson, Jr. Mr. Patterson attended the conference for the explicit purpose of ensuring that the Marshall Commission had full benefit of the ideas and recommendations generated in the Chicago Conference. A variety of viewpoints was expressed in prepared papers and in several days of careful discussion. Indeed, the great majority of ideas that have been the focus of discussion in more recent years were represented in the

1966 Chicago Conference. No genuine consensus emerged from the conference; nevertheless, there did appear a considerable depth and range of support for an all-volunteer armed force as an alternative to the draft.[2] In March of 1967, President Johnson proposed that Congress enact a four-year extension of the authority to induct men into the Armed Forces. His proposal also included a number of reforms in the Selective Service system intended to make the system more fair and less disruptive to young men; by now most of these reforms have been implemented. The President's message to Congress stated a clear *preference* for a force based entirely on volunteers, but concluded that unfortunately this was not feasible for two reasons: most important, the President felt that an all-volunteer force could not be expanded quickly to meet a sudden challenge; in addition, it would probably be very expensive.

Support for an all-volunteer force continued to grow, however, and, in 1969, President Nixon announced the appointment of an Advisory Commission on an All-Volunteer Armed Force, chaired by former Secretary of Defense Thomas S. Gates, Jr. In 1970 the Gates Commission submitted its report to the President. The following excerpt (President's Commission on an All-Volunteer Armed Force, 1970: 9-10) captures much of the substance and spirit of the report:

> However necessary conscription may have been in World War II, it has revealed many disadvantages in the past generation. It has been a costly, inequitable, and divisive procedure for recruiting men for the armed forces. It has imposed heavy burdens on a small minority of young men while easing slightly the tax burden on the rest of us. It has introduced needless uncertainty into the lives of all our young men. It has burdened draft boards with painful decisions about who shall be compelled to serve and who shall be deferred. It has weakened the political fabric of our society and impaired the delicate web of shared values that alone enables a free society to exist.

These costs of conscription would have to be borne if they were a necessary price for defending our peace and security. They are intolerable when there is an alternative consistent with our basic national values.

The Gates Commission proposed an all-volunteer force as the alternative, and recommended three basic steps as necessary to attain it: raise pay, improve conditions of service and recruiting, and establish a stand-by draft system. The Commission also dealt specifically with many of the questions and objections raised in opposition to an all-volunteer force. We review some of the most important of these issues below, often relying on excerpts from the Commission's report.

FEASIBILITY

Two major questions were raised about the feasibility of an all-volunteer armed force.

(1) Does an all-volunteer force lack the flexibility to expand quickly to meet a sudden challenge? President Johnson stated that this lack of flexibility was his most important reason for not recommending an all-volunteer force. In fact, however, this appears to be a false issue, as Friedman (1967) and later the Gates Commission (President's Commission on an All-Volunteer Armed Force, 1970: 13) pointed out:

> Military preparedness depends on forces in being, not on the ability to draft untrained men. Reserve forces provide immediate support to active forces, while the draft provides only inexperienced civilians who must be organized, trained, and equipped before they can become effective soldiers and sailors—a process which takes many months.

The argument seems compelling—a draft would be far too cumbersome to provide genuine flexibility to meet a sudden challenge. Thus it cannot be said that national security requires the continuing presence of the draft. (But just for good measure, the Gates Commission developed machinery for a "standby draft" which could go into effect immediately, provided the Congress gave its approval.)

(2) Can the nation afford the cost of an all-volunteer force? This was the second reason President Johnson gave for not recommending an all-volunteer force. But later the Gates Commission pointed out that the real issue boils down to *who* should bear the costs of the armed forces. The present system, because it pays draftees (and draft-induced volunteers) less than would be required to induce truly voluntary service, involves what has been termed a "conscription tax."[3]

Men who are forced to serve in the military at artificially low pay are actually paying a form of tax which subsidizes those in the society who do not serve. . . . This cost does not show up in the budget. Neither does the loss in output resulting from the disruption in the lives of young men who do not serve, but who rearrange their lives in response to the possibility of being drafted. Taking these hidden and neglected costs into account, the actual cost to the nation of an all-volunteer force will be lower than the cost of the present force [President's Commission on an All-Volunteer Armed Force, 1970: 9].

This distinction between real costs and those which show up in a budget was not originated by the Gates Commission; the point had been made sharply and clearly at the 1966 University of Chicago Conference on the Draft by a number of participants, particularly economists Milton Friedman (1967) and Walter Oi (1967). It is thus a matter of no small interest that President Johnson, in his 1967 message urging the extension of the draft, chose not to acknowledge that the reason an all-volunteer force would involve a higher military budget is primarily because it would eliminate the unfair (and hidden) conscription tax.

Summarizing our discussion thus far, we see that the two

major questions which President Johnson raised about the *feasibility* of an all-volunteer force were anticipated in the 1966 Chicago Conference and were again answered very effectively in the report of the Gates Commission.

(1) The flexibility to meet a sudden challenge depends upon the forces presently under arms, rather than forces which could be called up by means of a draft.

(2) An all-volunteer force would actually have a lower real cost to the nation; moreover, the cost would be visible rather than hidden, and would be equitably shared among all taxpayers.

There are other, perhaps more fundamental, issues in the debate over whether we should have a draft or an all-volunteer force. Many of these issues were raised in the 1966 Chicago Conference and then treated also by the Gates Commission.

(3) Would an all-volunteer force attract disproportionate numbers of the poor and blacks? Would it fail to attract a sufficient number of skilled and highly qualified men? These several issues hinge on some labor-market assumptions about how a volunteer force would be recruited. The main assumption is that pay would be raised just enough to ensure a sufficient number of volunteers. It is further assumed that this would make military service most attractive to those whose civilian opportunities are most limited—particularly those disadvantaged by a background of poverty or racial discrimination.

The Gates Commission countered this argument in several ways. First, it argued that if we continue to have a mixed force of conscripts and volunteers, the majority of service-men are likely to be "true volunteers" (i.e., volunteers not motivated by the draft). Thus a conversion to a fully volunteer force would not drastically alter the manpower composition of the armed services.

Second, the commission argued that military pay is already relatively attractive to those who have the poorest civilian alternatives. Raising pay levels "will increase the attractiveness of military service more to those who have higher civilian earnings potential than to those who have lower civilian potential" (President's Commission on an All-Volunteer Armed Force, 1970: 16-17).

(4) Would an all-volunteer force encourage a separate military ethos, and thus constitute a political threat? It is often maintained that the presence of draftees—civilians who serve only temporarily and do not really consider themselves a permanent part of the military establishment—provide a form of insurance against a further growth of military power, autonomy, and adventurism.

The Gates Commission again took the position that an all-volunteer force would not really be very different from a *largely* volunteer force, especially since the present officer corps is overwhelmingly staffed by true volunteers. Milton Friedman (1967: 206-207) made the same basic point in the Chicago Conference, but in a less sanguine tone. His statement is worth quoting at length:

> There is little question that large Armed Forces plus the industrial complex required to support them constitute an ever-present threat to political freedom. Our free institutions would certainly be safer if the conditions of the world permitted us to maintain far smaller armed forces.
>
> The valid fear has been converted into an invalid argument against voluntary armed forces. They would constitute a professional army, it is said, that would lack contact with the populace and become an independent political force, whereas a conscripted army remains basically a citizen army. The fallacy in this argument is that the danger comes primarily from the officers, who are now and always have been a professional corps of volunteers.
>
> However we recruit enlisted men, it is essential that we adopt practices that will guard against the political danger of creating a

military corps with loyalties of its own and out of contact with the broader body politic.

For the future, we need to follow policies that will foster lateral recruitment into the officer corps from civilian activities—rather than primarily promotion from within. The military services no less than the civil service need and will benefit from in-and-outers. For the political gain, we should be willing to bear the higher financial costs involved in fairly high turnover and rather short average terms of service for officers. We should follow personnel policies that will continue to make at least a period of military service as an officer attractive to young men from many walks of life.

One theme in Friedman's statement needs special emphasis here. It need not necessarily follow that an all-volunteer force will be staffed by career men with long-range commitments to the military establishment. On the contrary, we can (and in Friedman's view, we should) design policies that will encourage greater turnover, especially in the officer corps —provided, of course, that we are willing to pay the financial costs in an open and aboveboard system of accounting.

To summarize the discussion about the nature of an all-volunteer force, it has been argued fairly effectively by the Gates Commission that the volunteer force it proposed would not differ greatly from the mixed force of volunteers and draftees we have today—especially since our present force is directed by a professional officer corps, with upper levels staffed entirely by career men. This conclusion may be accurate in large measure, but it is not entirely satisfactory. Recent disclosures of widespread corruption, deception, and atrocities involving our present military force are not likely to put its critics at ease about the prospects of continuing "business as usual" if we convert to an all-volunteer force. Friedman's argument in favor of greater turnover remains very persuasive. The nature of an all-volunteer force may depend heavily upon whether we are willing to spend the money and effort necessary to develop incentives that bring to officer as well as enlisted ranks a wide cross-section of citizens for relatively short tours of military duty.

SOME WORKING ASSUMPTIONS GROWING OUT OF THE DEBATE

The debate over the draft versus an all-volunteer force has been summarized here for two reasons. First, it provides an important background for understanding the changing attitudes of youth toward the draft and military service. More important, it provides the context in which the research reported here must be considered.

An underlying assumption of this paper is that the United States is presently in the process of moving toward an all-volunteer armed force. Available data (summarized below) indicate that young people are rapidly coming to favor this alternative, and are growing less willing to tolerate the draft no matter how much it is reformed. As more and more young people, teachers, and parents come to realize that our present draft system imposes an unfair conscription tax on a fraction of our young, able-bodied males, it seems inevitable that we will finally rise above the problem of a larger budget. The question is not whether we can afford an all-volunteer force, for we surely can. The fundamental question is what *kind* of voluntary force we want, and what kinds of incentives will be most likely to produce it.

A further assumption of this paper is that the nation will be best served by a military force with the following manpower characteristics:

(1) There should be wide variety of abilities and socioeconomic backgrounds. We will not be served best by a "one-class" armed force.

(2) A broad range of political views should be represented, including some who are willing to make independent judgments about our military actions. If we have an armed force manned only by those who uncritically follow the call, "My country, right or wrong," we increase the risk that our country will indeed be wrong.

(3) We need a substantial proportion of *non*-career men at all levels—men who see themselves as essentially civilians spending a few useful years in military service before returning to civilian life.

A final assumption is that all these manpower objectives are attainable within a voluntary framework, provided we choose and implement an appropriate system of incentives. We will consider some specific examples of incentives in a later section of this paper. But first it will be useful to consider some data bearing on the way young people, especially young men, feel about national issues in general, and about the draft and military service in particular.

YOUTH VIEWS ON NATIONAL ISSUES[4]

The findings in this section and the following ones come primarily from a longitudinal study called "Youth in Transition." The study began in 1966 with a representative sample of 2,213 tenth-grade boys located in 87 public high schools throughout the United States. Follow-up data collections took place in 1968 (n=1,890), 1969 (n=1,800), and 1970 (n=1,620); thus, the study followed the young men in the initial sample through high school (most graduated just after the 1969 data collection) and into the several worlds of higher education, jobs, and military service.[5]

VIEWS ON VIETNAM

Attitudes about the draft and military service exist within a broader context of attitudes about the nation and its policies. No doubt the single most important national issue, so far as young people are concerned, is U.S. involvement in the Vietnam war.

As early as 1966, when they were starting tenth grade, a few of the respondents in the Youth in Transition study (7%) mentioned the draft or the Vietnam war in response to the open-ended interview question, "Can you tell me some of the problems young men your age worry about most?" The 7% figure in 1966 grew to 38% in 1968, and 75% in 1970. The

1970 data collection included an item used in several Gallup Polls, which gave respondents a choice among four plans for dealing with the war; 25% favored "immediate" withdrawal, 34% favored withdrawal "by the end of 18 months" (i.e., by the end of 1971), 25% favored withdrawal taking as long as needed to turn the war over to the South Vietnamese, and 12% favored a step-up in the fighting. The attitudes of the young men in the Youth in Transition sample were slightly more "dovish" than those of males in the Gallup Polls, but the differences were by no means large; moreover, there is evidence that the percentage of adults favoring rapid withdrawal is growing (Bachman and VanDuinen, 1971).

The data collections in 1969 and 1970 included a "Vietnam Dissent Index" based on six questionnaire items. In the spring of 1969, there seemed to be more support for the war than dissent, although a large group gave a mixed picture of some support and some dissent. A clear shift was evident by the late spring and early summer of 1970; the number of dissenters increased, while the supporters decreased. Closer inspection of the data revealed that the changes occurred largely among those who spent the year in college. Just before high school graduation in 1969, those bound for college differed little from their classmates in Vietnam dissent; after their first year of college, they were on the average noticeably more critical of U.S. policy in Vietnam (Bachman and VanDuinen, 1971).

Additional data are available to indicate that there was a sharp increase in Vietnam-related dissent among college students from spring in 1969 to spring of 1970. Yankelovich (1971) reports that strong agreement to the statement "The war in Vietnam is pure imperialism" increased from 16% in 1969 to 41% in 1970, based on two cross-sectional studies of college students in the United States. These and other results led Yankelovich to conclude that the continuation of the war has increased alienation of college students and reinforced their doubts about the system. Some findings based on

Youth in Transition data lend further support to this conclusion, as we shall note a bit later.

TRUST IN GOVERNMENT AND "THE SYSTEM."

All four data collections of the Youth in Transition project included a series of questionnaire items dealing with trust in the government and political leaders. Responses to these items show a steady decline in trust from 1966 through 1970, with the largest shifts occurring between 1969 and 1970. For example, those feeling that the government wastes "a lot" or "nearly all" of the money paid in taxes increased from 30% in 1966 to 56% in 1970. When asked how much they could "trust the government in Washington to do what is right," 72% of the respondents in 1966 answered "often" or "almost always," but by 1970 only 53% showed that same level of trust. Further evidence indicates that this drop in trust cannot be written off as something limited to those going through the high school years, nor is it evidence of a generation gap between youth and their elders. Voter studies conducted by the Political Behavior Program at the Institute for Social Research found that the same questions showed a sharp decline in trust among adults between 1964 and 1970; moreover, the overall level of dissatisfaction among adults in 1970 equalled or exceeded that shown by the Youth in Transition sample of young men (Bachman and VanDuinen, 1971).

These findings are by no means unique, as our earlier report indicated (Bachman and VanDuinen, 1971: 25-28):

> Our findings of dissatisfaction with government are corroborated by findings from other studies. Thirty-nine percent of Ohio high school students agree that the government does a "bad job" of representing the views and desires of the people. Even more striking are the responses to this statement, "The form of government in this country needs no major changes." Forty-eight percent disagreed, whereas only 31 percent agreed [Bryant, 1970]. The Harris Poll in *Life* (1971) found similar results to the

question, "How much confidence do you have in the government to solve the problems of the 70's?" Twenty-two percent said "hardly any"; 54 percent said "some but not a lot"; and only 20 percent said "a great deal." Similar results were found in the Purdue study of high school students. Forty-eight percent of the sample of twelfth-graders felt that "There are serious flaws in our society today, but the system is flexible enough to solve them"; the remainder were divided equally between complete endorsement of the present American way of life, calls for radical change, and undecided [Erlick, 1970].

THE ROLE OF THE MILITARY IN NATIONAL AFFAIRS

Two questions in the 1969 Youth in Transition data collection dealt with the role the military plays in the United States. The first question asked, "Do you think military personnel have too much or too little influence on the way the country is run?" Twenty-five percent answered "too much" or "far too much," 17% checked "too little" or "far too little," while 56% considered the influence "about right." The second question asked, "Do you think the U.S. spends too much or too little on the military?" Those who indicated we spend "too much" or "far too much" totaled 42%, while 18% felt we spend "too little," and 39% considered the level of military spending to be "about right."

These questions were not included in the 1970 data collection; had they been repeated, they probably would have shown an increased inclination to limit the role of the military, especially among college students. Yankelovich (1971) reports that college students urging "fundamental reform" in the military increased from 50% in 1969 to 56% in 1970, while those taking the more radical view that the military should be "done away with" increased from 5 to 10%.

THREAT OF NUCLEAR WAR

Certainly the Vietnam war is a basic cause of discontent with the role of the military in our society, but perhaps another reason that some would be willing to limit military influence and spending is that there is less perceived threat of all-out war than might have been expected among youth raised in the "nuclear era." When the 1970 Youth in Transition interview asked respondents to rate the importance of a number of problems facing the nation, the "chance of nuclear war" was rated as "very important" by a much smaller number than were problems of population, pollution, race relations, crime and violence, and hunger and poverty. Many young men stated explicitly their view that a nuclear stalemate had been reached and, as one respondent put it, "no one is stupid enough to kill everyone." When asked what they thought should be done to avoid nuclear war, 8% said they didn't think it was much of a problem or threat, and 9% said nothing more could (or should) be done. About 5% proposed relatively "hard-line" solutions such as strengthening our arms, anti-ballistic missiles, bomb shelters, or civil defense measures. In contrast, a total of 35% urged banning nuclear weapons, negotiations with other countries, improving foreign relations, and simply "making peace." (The remaining respondents gave vague, uncodeable answers, or could offer no opinion on how to avoid nuclear war.) Our earlier report summarized these findings in the following terms:

> The present generation of young men have strong concerns, and express growing opposition, when it comes to the war in Vietnam. The larger threat of nuclear war, however, does not alarm them nearly as much as may have been expected. Perhaps this is simply a contrast effect; Vietnam is a clear and present danger, especially for young men, whereas the danger of a nuclear holocaust is more abstract and remote. On the other hand, it may be the demise of the foreign policy of "brinkmanship" which is responsible for this feeling that nations can and will avoid the use of nuclear weapons. These young men have seen the bomb shelters come and go; since 1962 (the time of the Cuban missile crisis) there has been a more-or-less steady movement away from nuclear threat and counter-threat. In short, the overall trend of

experience for young men (in contrast to that of their parents) has been gradual reduction in emphasis on nuclear war.

Whatever the reasons may be, the dominant attitude among young men seems clearly to be that a stalemate has been reached. They feel that the major powers are sufficiently aware of the potential for total destruction in a nuclear war that they will not start one [Bachman and VanDuinen, 1971: 80-82].

INTERRELATIONS AMONG VIEWS

The views on national issues outlined above do not exist in isolation from each other. In particular, the Vietnam war has often been cited as a major cause of eroded trust in government and the military. This assertion is supported by the correlational data presented in Table 1. Vietnam dissent is negatively related to trust in government, and positively related to statements that military influence and spending are excessive.

Since Vietnam dissent and trust in government were measured in 1969 and again in 1970, we can note their stability across time. The stabilities are fairly high (.56 for Vietnam dissent and .48 for trust in government), especially

TABLE 1

CORRELATIONS AMONG VIEWS ON NATIONAL ISSUES[a]

	1	2	3	4	5
1. Vietnam dissent, 1969	—	—	—	—	—
2. Vietnam dissent, 1970	.56	—	—	—	—
3. Trust in government, 1969	−.29	−.22	—	—	—
4. Trust in government, 1970	−.35	−.46	.48	—	—
5. Military has too much influence in U.S., 1969	.30	.27	−.11	−.17	—
6. U.S. spends too much on military, 1969	.36	.33	−.14	−.20	.42

a. Table entries are product-moment correlations based on approximately 1600 to 1800 cases. All are statistically significant beyond the .001 level. The data were obtained in the Youth in Transition study in 1969 and 1970. All scales and items shown here are discussed above in the text. More extensive descriptions of the Vietnam Dissent and Trust in Government scales are provided by Bachman and VanDuinen (1971).

when we consider that the scales are very brief (six items and three items, respectively). Many young men shifted their views on these dimensions between 1969 and 1970, but the overall ordering remained pretty much the same—those dissenting in 1969 were likely to be among the most dissenting in 1970.

The cross-time data may be used in another way to provide further clues about the causal relationship between Vietnam dissent and trust in government. Figure 1 presents the necessary data in schematic form using a technique which Campbell and Stanley (1963) have termed "cross-lagged panel correlation." We should note first that the negative correlation between Vietnam dissent and trust in government increased from −.29 in 1969 to −.46 in 1970, suggesting that the two dimensions became more closely interrelated during the intervening year. More important, we can see that the two "causal" arrows are unequal in strength: it appears that 1969 Vietnam dissent "caused" a decrease in 1970 trust in government (r = −.35) to a distinctly greater degree than 1969 trust in government influenced 1970 Vietnam dissent (r = −.22). In short, our cross-time data provide some empirical support for the widespread view that dissatisfaction

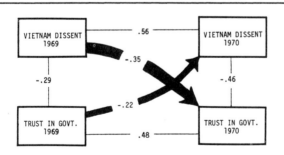

*The values displayed in this figure are product-moment correlations taken from Table 1.

Figure 1: CROSS-LAGGED PANEL CORRELATION BETWEEN VIETNAM DISSENT AND TRUST IN GOVERNMENT*

with the Vietnam war is among the basic factors eroding confidence in government among youth.

YOUTH VIEWS ON NATIONAL ISSUES—AN APPRAISAL

The evidence cited above clearly indicates that young people are dissatisfied with their government and its policies in a number of areas. The level of dissatisfaction increased considerably between 1969 and 1970, especially among college students. But this does not necessarily indicate a generation gap, since adults are also increasingly dissatisfied with government.

The feeling is widespread among youth that there must be major changes in the system in order for it to deal effectively with the needs of the nation; however, additional data suggest that most feel such changes can be accommodated within the present system of government. Indeed, it is encouraging to note that youth support for the eighteen-year-old vote increased sharply from 1965 to 1969, and was especially strong among those dissenting from U.S. policy in Vietnam (Bachman and VanDuinen, 1971).

There is growing dissatisfaction, then, but a feeling on the part of most that the system can still be made to accommodate the necessary changes. But do young people think it *will* change, and do they expect to be able to make a genuine contribution to that change? Here we can do little more than speculate, except to note some chilling new evidence about feelings of powerlessness among college students. Rotter (1971: 59), summarizing more than a decade of research on feelings of "internal control" or "personal efficacy," concluded that

> there is little doubt that, overall, college students feel more powerless to change the world and control their own destinies now than they did 10 years ago.... If feelings of external control, alienation and powerlessness continue to grow, we may be heading for a society of dropouts—each person sitting back, watching the world go by.

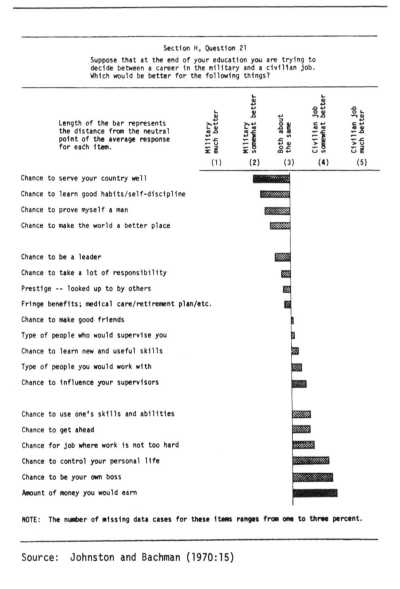

Section H, Question 21

Suppose that at the end of your education you are trying to decide between a career in the military and a civilian job. Which would be better for the following things?

Length of the bar represents the distance from the neutral point of the average response for each item.

	Military much better (1)	Military somewhat better (2)	Both about the same (3)	Civilian job somewhat better (4)	Civilian job much better (5)

Chance to serve your country well

Chance to learn good habits/self-discipline

Chance to prove myself a man

Chance to make the world a better place

Chance to be a leader

Chance to take a lot of responsibility

Prestige -- looked up to by others

Fringe benefits; medical care/retirement plan/etc.

Chance to make good friends

Type of people who would supervise you

Chance to learn new and useful skills

Type of people you would work with

Chance to influence your supervisors

Chance to use one's skills and abilities

Chance to get ahead

Chance for job where work is not too hard

Chance to control your personal life

Chance to be your own boss

Amount of money you would earn

NOTE: The number of missing data cases for these items ranges from one to three percent.

Source: Johnston and Bachman (1970:15)

Figure 2: COMPARISON OF MILITARY AND CIVILIAN CAREERS

In sum, it is a mixed picture. Youth are more dissatisfied these days; but, given current conditions, that dissatisfaction could be a sign of health—at least in the short run. Most young people still have faith in the system's potential (if not its present performance), and they want some part in improving it. But they have not thus far seen much evidence that their efforts have been effective, and feelings of impotence in the face of a massive and unyielding system continue to grow.

PERCEPTIONS OF MILITARY SERVICE[6]

In the preceding section we examined youth attitudes on a range of important national issues. Now we focus more specifically on the perceptions of young men when asked to consider military service as a short-term or long-term occupation. The data for this section come from portions of the Youth in Transition study, primarily from the data collected in 1969 and secondarily from the measurement in 1970.[7]

MILITARY VERSUS CIVILIAN CAREER OPPORTUNITIES

In the spring of 1969, when most Youth in Transition respondents were about to graduate from high school and many were looking forward to entering the world of work, they were asked to compare military and civilian career opportunities along a number of dimensions. The mean responses to those questions are summarized in Figure 2. At the top of the figure appear those opportunities which most respondents associated primarily with military service. Some of the perceived advantages of military service fit the traditional stereotype of military life—good habits and self-discipline, a chance to prove oneself a man and become a leader. Perhaps less expected, in light of the findings in the previous section, is the fact that a majority felt that a military career offered a superior opportunity for making the world a better place to live and serving one's country well. These data were collected in 1969, and current high school seniors might show a somewhat less idealized conception of military service. Nevertheless, these data suggest that there has been a good deal of positive feeling about military service, and that the armed forces do not have a totally negative image in the eyes of young men.

Of course, there are a number of areas in which a civilian career is generally viewed as superior to military service, as shown in the lower portion of Figure 2. Advancement, income, and utilization of skills and abilities are thought by most to be better on the civilian side. And when it comes to independence—being one's own boss and controlling one's personal life—a civilian career is considered superior by the overwhelming majority of respondents.

Some additional evidence that young men underrate the more tangible rewards of military service came from the direction of wrong answers to a test of "military knowledge." Relatively few high school seniors in 1969 had accurate knowledge of military pay and benefits; most of their wrong answers were underestimates. Similarly, perceptions of military working conditions, hours, and vacation allowances tended to err on the unfavorable side (Johnston, 1970).

On the other hand, several other questionnaire items reveal that most respondents felt that the armed services provide relatively good opportunities for the poor and blacks.

In sum, military service was perceived by high school seniors (and dropouts) in 1969 as providing relatively fewer personal rewards and less freedom than civilian jobs. On the other hand, the military was viewed as a good place for the disadvantaged to succeed, and a place for one to develop manhood and leadership and to serve one's country.

It was not possible to repeat the above items in the 1970 Youth in Transition questionnaire, but a few new questions were asked, focused on justice and fair treatment in military and civilian life. When asked what proportion of people in civilian life who are accused of something get a fair trial, 73% of the respondents checked "all" or "most." Only 58% felt that all or most accused persons in the military get a fair trial. Another question asked "how likely is it that a person in a civilian job can get things changed and set right if he is being treated unjustly by a superior?" Only 3% of the respondents considered it "not at all likely" and 22% rated it "a little likely"; the rest considered it somewhat likely, quite likely, or very likely. When asked how likely a person in the military would be to get things set right if mistreated by a superior, 22% rated it "not at all likely," and another 35% considered it only "a little likely." A final question asked each respondent about his own prospective treatment: "Do you personally feel that *you* would receive more just and fair treatment as a civilian or as a member of the military?" Thirty-two percent felt treatment would be about the same as a civilian or in the military, 14% felt treatment would be fairer in the military, and 54% felt it would be fairer as a civilian. Clearly the majority view in mid-1970 was that military justice fell short of that available to civilians.

FEELINGS ABOUT THE DRAFT

The Youth in Transition questionnaire in 1969 asked respondents, "If you were drafted, which of the following would be most true of you?" Twenty-two percent checked the statement, "I'd serve if I had to, but I wouldn't like it," while another 4% took the more extreme alternative, "I'd refuse to serve; go to jail or leave the country instead." Thus about one-quarter of the respondents took a clearly negative view of the prospect of being drafted. The response "I'd be happy to serve," was checked by 13%. (And it should be noted that another 11% were not asked the question because they had earlier indicated their plans to enter the service within a few months.) The remaining half of the respondents selected the neutral answer to the question about being drafted, saying simply "I'd serve." As would be expected, scores on the Vietnam dissent scale tended to be high among those individuals who said they would resent or resist being drafted.

Some additional data concerning attitudes about the draft come from a recent report on the attitudes of entering college freshmen. Based on three large national surveys, the American Council on Education found the following trend:

> there was a steady increase in the proportion of freshmen who favored an all-volunteer army: from 37 percent in 1968, to 53 percent in 1969, to 65 percent in 1970. This trend may be attributable in part to growing disdain for the Vietnam war and for the military in general and in part to an optimism engendered by recent changes in the draft system and by statements from the Federal government indicating that an all-volunteer army is a workable alternative [Bayer et al., 1971: 56-57].

This dramatic shift in support of an all-volunteer force represents a great deal of change in a span of only two years. But a change of similar magnitude occurred in attitudes toward the eighteen-year-old vote just a few years earlier —support among (male) high school seniors rose from about 50% in 1965 to 80% in 1969 (Bachman and VanDuinen, 1971). The change in views about the younger voting age corresponded to an increased national discussion about its appropriateness and feasibility. It seems likely that the same process is at work in the changing attitudes about an all-volunteer force. College freshmen are likely to keep themselves up to date on any major discussions of the draft and military service, and this would surely include an awareness of the President's support of the concept of an all-volunteer force, his appointment of the Gates Commission in 1969, and the Commission's report early in 1970 supporting the feasibility of such a volunteer force.

INCENTIVES TO ATTRACT AN ALL-VOLUNTEER
ARMED FORCE

In this section we return to the major issues raised in the first section. In many respects, these issues boil down to the question of what kinds of men would enlist in an all-volunteer force. However, no single answer to that question is possible (even if adequate data were available), until we decide upon the nature of the incentives used to attract volunteers. It is often assumed that the paramount incentive is increased pay, but there is no reason to limit our consideration to that rather obvious approach. Instead, we will consider a number of alternatives, and ask what sort of young men each incentive is likely to attract.

WHICH INCENTIVES DO YOUNG MEN FIND ATTRACTIVE?

We made two efforts to measure young men's responses to various incentives designed to make military service more appealing. Our first attempt took place in 1969, when most respondents were about to graduate from high school. In a fairly extensive questionnaire segment (the 1969 data collection did not include interviews), respondents were asked how attractive they would find each of eleven different incentives, assuming that the Vietnam war had ended and the draft had been eliminated. Our preliminary report of these data expressed a number of reservations about some aspects of the findings.

Nevertheless, we were singularly impressed by one finding. Considering the first choice of the respondents, one incentive stands out above all others: "The government agrees to pay for up to four years of college . . . in return for four years of active duty." This was selected by a margin of 4-to-1 over the second-ranked incentive, military pay comparable to civilian pay. Each of the remaining incentives was selected as first choice by less than ten percent of those who completed this section. If we look at their top three choices combined, the schooling incentives remain on top. More than three-quarters include government payment for college, technical or vocational school among their top three choices [Johnston and Bachman, 1970: 40].

In 1970, we had another opportunity to explore incentives to enlist, this time using an interview segment rather than items in a paper-and-pencil questionnaire. Most respondents were one year out of high school, and had spent the last year in higher education or on a job. (Those who were already in military service were not asked the questions on enlistment incentives.) We concentrated on just four incentives which were among the most important in the 1969 data: higher pay, guaranteed assignment, paid schooling, and a shorter enlistment period. The four incentives are shown in Figure 3, using exactly the same wording as was presented to the respondents.

There is one other crucial difference between the 1969 and 1970 questions about incentives. In 1969, we asked respondents to imagine that the Vietnam war and the draft had both

---

A. **Higher Pay** - Military pay starting at $5,000 per year and reaching $7,200 for the fourth and last year. You would pay for your own food and lodging.

B. **Guaranteed Assignment** - *Before you enlist,* you are given a guaranteed job assignment, including necessary training, in the military specialty of *your choice.* Before enlisting you would be tested to see if you could meet the requirements of your specialty choice. Here are some examples of specialties: draftsman, electronic technician, bulldozer driver, paratrooper, auto or aircraft mechanic, foreign language expert, pilot.

C. **Paid Schooling** - The government agrees to assume the cost, including living expenses, for up to four years of schooling at a college or technical/vocational school to which you can get accepted. In return, you serve on active duty for four years. You must *enlist first,* but the schooling could come either before or after you serve.

D. **Shorter Enlistment Period** - An enlistment period of only two years.

Figure 3: **INCENTIVES TO ENLIST**

ended; in other words, we asked them to conceive of the kind of situation in which a volunteer armed force seemed most feasible. By 1970, we decided to omit these conditions for two reasons. First, we found the highly hypothetical questions difficult to interpret and were frankly concerned about their validity. Second, and even more important, it seemed clear by early 1970 that the nation is most likely to move *gradually* toward an all-volunteer force, testing incentives during a transitional period while the draft is still in force.

The 1970 questions about incentives were asked of 1,273 respondents (representing all participants except those already serving in the military and those who felt sure they were permanently disqualified from military service). Respondents were asked to examine the incentives shown in Figure 3 and select the one change which would make military service most attractive to them. Then they were asked this question: "Taking into account other things that you are involved in, and given only this change, how likely is it that you would enlist?" Responses ranged on a scale from "definitely enlist in the next six months" to "definitely not enlist in the next 5 years." The first-choice responses to the incentives and the likelihood of enlisting are summarized in Table 2. Note that the higher pay incentive was attractive to the smallest number (14.7%), while guaranteed assignment was the most frequently chosen (37.3%). On the other hand, when we consider whether incentives are attractive enough so that respondents say they would definitely enlist, then the paid schooling seems to be the most effective.

The data in Table 2 are presented primarily to indicate the relative attractiveness of different incentives under present conditions; it is not suggested that the responses are an appropriate basis for projecting *how many* would actually volunteer given one or another incentive. Furthermore, the effectiveness of any incentive will depend heavily upon the context in which it is offered. A shorter enlistment period may be attractive as an incentive only when there is a threat

TABLE 2
RESPONSES TO INCENTIVES

Incentive Chosen as Most Attractive	Definitely Enlist in the Next 6 Months	Definitely Enlist in the Next 5 Years	Probably Enlist in the Next 5 Years	Probably Not Enlist in the Next 5 Years	Definitely Not Enlist in the Next 5 Years	Total
	Likelihood of Enlisting Given First-Choice Incentive					
	1.	2.	3.	4.	5.	Total
A. Higher pay	0.8[a]	0.9	3.5	3.9	5.5	14.7
B. Guaranteed assignment	1.0	2.1	9.6	12.8	11.8	37.3
C. Paid schooling	2.2	2.4	6.2	8.0	5.5	24.5
D. Shorter enlistment period	1.0	1.2	4.7	7.3	9.4	23.6
Total	5.1	6.6	24.1	32.0	32.2	100%

a. Cell entries are percentages based on a total of 1,273 young men from the Youth in Transition study (summer 1970).

of being drafted; it is difficult to imagine that offering a shorter enlistment period is likely to be a very positive attraction to an all-volunteer armed force. Similarly, it may be the case that the guaranteed assignment incentive would be most appealing to young men who are draft-motivated; a guaranteed assignment no doubt has a special appeal when contrasted with an uncertain (but almost surely less attractive) assignment under the draft. But if the draft were removed the guaranteed assignment might not, taken by itself, prove to be a very effective incentive. Of course, this discussion is necessarily rather speculative; nevertheless, of the four incentives we have examined, it seems reasonable to suppose that two are most likely to retain their attractiveness after the draft is removed—higher pay and paid schooling. Accordingly, we will focus much of our attention on these two alternatives as we examine the differences among young men who are attracted to different incentives.

TO WHOM DO THE INCENTIVES APPEAL?

Early in this paper, we noted that some fear an all-volunteer force based on higher pay will appeal mostly to the disadvantaged, the less skilled, and perhaps the less ambitious. We can now ask whether those who respond positively and negatively to different incentives really do differ along these and other dimensions; moreover, we can compare them with other respondents in the Youth in Transition study who had already entered military service by the summer of 1970. For each of the four incentives, we will distinguish between "positive respondents"– those who said they probably or definitely would enlist (in the next five years or earlier) given their first-choice incentive–and "negative responders"–those who said they probably or definitely would not enlist even if they were given their first-choice incentive.

Would an all-volunteer force appeal primarily to the poor? The data in Figure 4 suggest that there may be some truth to that assertion, if the volunteer force is to be attracted primarily on the basis of increased pay. Those who say they would probably or certainly volunteer given the incentive of higher pay are appreciably lower in socioeconomic level than others. On the other hand, their family socioeconomic level is not much lower on the average than that of young men already in military service.

Looking at the other data displayed in Figure 4, we find no appreciable socioeconomic differences between those attracted by guaranteed assignment, paid schooling, or shorter enlistment period; however, in each case it is true that those who respond positively to the incentive average a bit lower than those who think they would not serve.

Test scores of intelligence and verbal skills (measured in tenth grade) follow a pattern fairly similar to that shown in Figure 4. For each of the four incentives, those who think they would respond positively average somewhat lower in test scores than those who would not expect to volunteer.

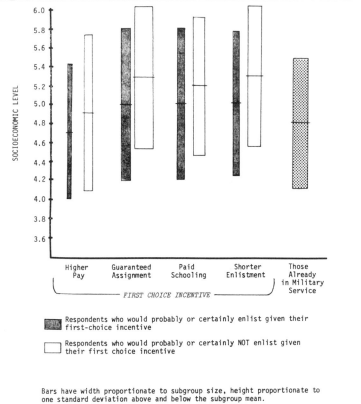

Bars have width proportionate to subgroup size, height proportionate to one standard deviation above and below the subgroup mean.

Figure 4: FAMILY SOCIOECONOMIC LEVEL RELATED TO PREFERENCE FOR INCENTIVES

More important, those attracted by the higher pay incentive are lowest in average intelligence, while those choosing the paid schooling are highest. The test-score differences between those responding positively to higher pay and those responding positively to paid schooling are about two-thirds of a standard deviation (a difference statistically significant beyond the .01 level).[8]

Several personal characteristics also distinguish between those attracted by higher pay and those attracted by paid schooling. On measures of ambitious job attitudes and status of aspired occupation, those attracted by paid schooling average one-half standard deviation higher than those drawn by higher pay (p<.01). When asked what they expected to be earning twenty years later (in the civilian occupation to which they aspired), the average response for those attracted by higher military pay was about $10,000, whereas for those attracted by paid schooling the average response was about $15,000. (The expected pay question used a series of dollar ranges rather than exact amounts; thus the figures given here can only be approximations.)

Some further distinctions may be drawn between those attracted by higher pay versus paid schooling. Self-esteem, needs for self-development, and needs for self-utilization are all about one-third standard deviation higher for those who favor paid schooling (p<.05). Another difference which falls slightly short of statistical significance is nonetheless interesting; those who are attracted by the higher pay incentive are a bit below average in their feelings of internal control or personal efficacy.

In sum, we find that background, ability, and personality differences do exist among those attracted by different incentives. In particular, those who say they would probably enlist given their first-choice incentive of higher pay are a bit lower on the average than those attracted by paid schooling, along the following dimensions: family socioeconomic level, test scores, occupational ambition, self-esteem, and needs for self-development and self-utilization.

For each of the dimensions noted above, the mean scores of those respondents already in military service lie between the means for the two contrasting incentive groups. This suggests that the use of a higher pay incentive might tend to attract those slightly lower in ability and aspirations than the men presently serving, while the use of the paid schooling incentive might lead to average increases along these dimensions. Our data do not suggest large differences; nevertheless, the direction of the differences is consistent with concerns raised by critics of a volunteer force recruited primarily by the incentive of higher pay. The incentive of paid schooling, on the other hand, might lead to an all-volunteer force with higher levels of ability and ambition than is found in our current force.

IS RESPONSE TO INCENTIVES RELATED TO "POLITICAL" ATTITUDES?

One of the major concerns about an all-volunteer force is that it might encourage a separate military ethos and thus constitute a political threat. Accordingly, it is of some considerable interest to know whether those responding positively and negatively to different incentives show some difference in attitudes about national issues—particularly along dimensions which might indicate a willingness to make critical, independent judgments about our military actions. Certainly one such dimension is the Vietnam dissent index discussed in a previous section. Figure 5 relates responses on that index (in 1970) to preferences for different incentives.

Several conclusions can be drawn from the data in Figure 5:

(1) There are only small and rather unimportant differences among those who respond positively to each of the four incentives.

(2) Vietnam dissent is much stronger among those who respond negatively to the incentives; moreover, it is particularly strong among those who list paid schooling as their first-choice incentive but say that they still would not enlist.

(3) Vietnam dissent is, as we might have anticipated, lowest among those already serving in the armed forces.

The differences in Vietnam dissent as of 1969 were not so strong as the 1970 differences shown in Figure 5; nevertheless, the 1969 data pattern is essentially the same way. It

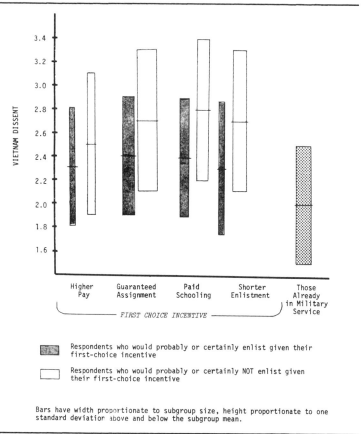

Figure 5: VIETNAM DISSENT (1970) RELATED TO PREFERENCE
FOR INCENTIVES

is of interest to note that while Vietnam dissent increased somewhat from 1969 to 1970 for the sample taken as a whole, it remained consistently low for those who were in the military service as of 1970. Since most of these respondents entered the service between the 1969 and 1970 data collections, this suggests that the military has been tending to attract those who are least skeptical about U.S. policies in Vietnam.

A number of other dimensions are related to Vietnam

dissent, as indicated earlier in Table 1, and they also relate to responses to incentives. As might have been expected, those who (in 1969) considered military spending and influence too high were more likely (in 1970) to say that they would not respond positively to incentives. The measure of trust in government also was related to response to incentives, but in a more complex way. The "positive" and "negative" responders showed little overall difference in trust back in 1969 when most were about to graduate from high school. But by 1970 those who were the "negative" responders had experienced a relatively sharp drop on the trust in government scale. The largest drop (.6 of a standard deviation) occurred among those who picked paid schooling as their first-choice incentive but said that they still would not be likely to enlist. This shift suggests that growing dissatisfaction with the government, caused in large measure by the Vietnam war, may be a major deterrent to enlistment for these young men. Perhaps in a climate of less dissent and dissatisfaction, a good many of these young men would react more positively to the incentive of paid schooling.

HIGHER PAY VERSUS PAID SCHOOLING—CONTRASTING INCENTIVES

Of the four incentives considered here—higher pay, paid schooling, guaranteed assignment, and a shorter enlistment period—the first two seemed most likely to retain their attractiveness in a voluntary system in which no one would enlist to avoid the draft.

It appears that paid schooling would be attractive to a higher percentage of young men than the alternative of higher pay (Table 2). Perhaps more important are the differences in the kinds of young men attracted by the two incentives. Those attracted by paid schooling averaged higher in intelligence, verbal skills, occupational ambitions, and self-esteem.

If we are willing to speculate about the sort of young men

who *might* be attracted by incentives, given a different and less negative climate of national opinion concerning the military and its activities, it seems likely that paid schooling would have less appeal to the "My country, right or wrong" individuals, and more appeal to those willing to make independent judgments.

In short, our examination of incentives suggests that it may be unwise to make higher pay our primary incentive for enlistment in an all-volunteer force. The paid schooling incentive, or others like it, may come closer to meeting many of our national needs in an all-volunteer force.

SUMMARY AND CONCLUSIONS

The data summarized in this paper document the widespread view that youth are becoming more dissatisfied, distrusting, indeed, alienated, when it comes to their government and "the system." But our findings also suggest that this is not evidence of a generation gap, since the growing dissatisfaction is not limited to youth. Undoubtedly the Vietnam war is responsible for much of this negative climate; and for young men in particular, the military draft has "weakened the political fabric of our society and impaired the delicate web of shared values that alone enables a free society to exist" (President's Commission on an All-Volunteer Armed Force, 1970: 10).

Any system involving compulsory service is likely to conflict with the principles of freedom, but in the case of the draft this problem has been exacerbated by further and unnecessary inequities. An unduly heavy financial burden has been borne by draftees and draft-motivated enlistees; until recently, the government has refused to acknowledge this "conscriptive tax" and has argued that the nation cannot afford the cost of an all-volunteer armed force. To the more perceptive among our young people, this argument and many of the others which have been used to extend the draft must seem shallow, if not cynical. A nation which can afford vast expenditures for military material can surely afford to pay its military manpower costs fairly and above-board.

An all-volunteer force is feasible, but is it desirable? Critics have argued that a strictly voluntary system might appeal primarily to the poor and the less able, and perhaps those susceptible to a sort of "military mentality" which could eventually pose a political threat. A report of the Gates Commission has argued that an all-volunteer force attracted primarily by higher pay would not really be very different from the present mixed force of volunteers and conscripts, especially given the fact that we already have a professional officer corps staffed largely with career military men. That argument is not entirely convincing. It may be that even a small minority of conscripted civilians provide a corrective against military excesses. It requires a few individuals to "blow the whistle" on corruption or atrocities, as we have recently been reminded. It can be argued that an all-volunteer force would not include such individuals, and thus make a bad situation worse. We should think twice before adopting a military manpower system which does not include at least some individuals who see themselves as civilians whose military service is only temporary. Perhaps instead we should be searching for mechanisms to ensure some greater degree of turnover, especially in the officer corps.[9]

The desirability of an all-volunteer force cannot be considered in the abstract, apart from the question of what changes will be required to make military service attractive to volunteers. It is generally agreed that enlistment may be encouraged by less emphasis on "spit and polish," more attractive living conditions, and fewer unnecessary restrictions on personal freedom. Such changes seem desirable in any case. But these alone would be unlikely to attract sufficient volunteers to staff the armed forces. Greater financial incentives will surely be necessary if we are to have an all-volunteer force. It has often been assumed without question that such financial incentives should take the form of higher pay. This paper has taken the view that alternative incentives may better serve the nation's needs.

PAID SCHOOLING IN RETURN FOR MILITARY SERVICE

An incentive which offers up to four years of paid schooling in return for four years of military service (before or after the schooling) has a number of attractive features:

(1) It appeals to the more able and ambitious of our young men.

(2) It has the *potential* of appealing to those young men who are by disposition most willing and able to exercise independent and sometimes critical judgment about military activities, those best equipped to act as "watchdogs" against excessive militarism in a "professional army."

Apart from the question of *whom* it would attract, the paid schooling incentive has some built-in advantages:

(3) Those electing to serve first for four years and go to school afterward would help ensure a healthy rate of military turnover and a supply of young servicemen who see their primary, long-term commitments as being outside the military.

(4) Those going to college first and then entering the service would help meet military needs for skilled and educated manpower, especially in the junior officer ranks. Moreover, the broadening and liberalizing effects of college, plus the maturity of additional years, would make these men less malleable, more confident and self-reliant than those recruited at an earlier stage of education and maturity.

(5) Finally, the by-products of an educational incentive for military service would be almost entirely positive throughout the society.

It is not the contention of this paper that the educational incentive discussed here is ideal in its present form. Obviously the nature of the "contract" needs far greater specificity than that provided by the statement reproduced in Figure 3, and there is no reason to suppose that the years of schooling and service should both be set at four.

Nor is it contended that an educational incentive should completely replace the proposed incentive of increased pay—there is probably room for both types of incentives, and perhaps others as well.

If this paper makes any contribution to the debate, it should be the broadening of our thinking about the possible nature of an all-volunteer force and the incentives and policies we use to attain such a force. If, as a nation, we decide that we want our military service to continue to include a large proportion of men whose basic identity is as civilians, we should not jump to the conclusion that this can be accomplished only by the coercive mechanism of the draft. Systems of incentives can be developed to accomplish this objective within a voluntary framework.

IMPLICATIONS FOR THE FUTURE

The present administration has pledged to end the Vietnam war and has made a commitment to phase out the draft and return to an all-volunteer force. Any estimates about how youth relate to the larger society in the seventies must make some assumptions about the way in which these objectives are reached.

The lessons of Vietnam have been incredibly costly. To a considerable degree, trust in government has been one of the casualties of the war. It is likely to take a long time to rebuild. A conversion to an all-volunteer armed force can play a positive role in such a rebuilding of trust, especially among young people. One of the first steps should be a national commitment to pay a fair price for military manpower; an end to the inequitable and deceptive conscription tax is long overdue. Another step should be a searching examination of the role of the military in a free society, with emphasis on ensuring a broad base of civilian control. Then we can proceed to establish a system of incentives that will meet our military manpower needs and serve other national needs as well, within a voluntary framework.

NOTES

1. It should be noted that an all-volunteer force is not the only alternative which has been proposed to take the place of the present draft system. Other possibilities include Universal Military Training, or mandatory National Service (which provides both military and nonmilitary alternatives for serving the national needs). Such alternatives have not been examined here because they seem much less feasible, and thus less likely to become a reality, compared with an all-volunteer armed force.

2. The products of the University of Chicago Conference on the Draft, both position papers and transcripts of the discussions, are contained in a volume edited by Tax (1967).

3. Indeed, the Commission estimated that the conscription tax paid by draftees amounts to a tax burden more than three times that paid by comparable civilians. A Commission staff report on the conscription tax put the matter succinctly: "As a tax, conscription under Selective Service is brutally inefficient —virtually in a class by itself" (Sjaastad and Hansen, 1970: IV-1-34).

4. Much of the data and discussion in this section are adopted from earlier reports by Johnston and Bachman (1970) and Bachman and VanDuinen (1971).

5. For detailed descriptions of study design, sampling procedures, and response rates, see Bachman et al. (1967) and Bachman (1970); see also Bachman and VanDuinen (1971).

6. Many of the findings in this section are summarized from earlier reports by Johnston and Bachman (1970) and Johnston (1970).

7. These portions of the Youth in Transition project were conducted under contract with the U.S. Department of Defense. The Department of Defense contributed constructively to the development of measures, including those dealing with incentives; however, the analyses and conclusions presented here are solely the responsibility of the author.

8. A much more detailed reporting of these findings than is possible here will be included in a forthcoming volume of the Youth in Transition monograph series. Most of the dimensions mentioned in this section are described extensively in Bachman et al. (1967) and Bachman (1970).

9. It should be noted that the Gates Commission report supported a change in the system of retirement benefits for military men. The present system requires almost twenty years of service before any benefits can be realized. An alternative system of providing both officers and enlisted men with the same retirement arrangements as civil service employees would do away with this unnecessary emphasis on twenty years of service and might encourage higher rates of turnover.

REFERENCES

BACHMAN, J. G. (1970) Youth in Transition. Volume II: The Impact of Family Background and Intelligence on Tenth-Grade Boys. Ann Arbor, Mich.: Institute for Social Research Survey Research Center.

––– and E. VanDUINEN (1971) Youth Look at National Problems: A Special Report from the Youth in Transition Project. Ann Arbor, Mich.: Institute for Social Research Survey Research Center.

BACHMAN, J. G., R. L. KAHN, M. T. MEDNICK, T. N. DAVIDSON, and L. D. JOHNSTON (1967) Youth in Transition. Volume I: Blueprint for a Longitudinal Study of Adolescent Boys. Ann Arbor, Mich.: Institute for Social Research Survey Research Center.

BAYER, A. E., A. W. ASTIN, and R. F. BORUCH (1971) "College students' attitudes toward social issues: 1967-70." Educational Rev. (Winter): 52-59.

BRYANT, B. E. (1970) High School Students Look at Their World. Columbus, Ohio: R. H. Goettler.

CAMPBELL, D. T. and J. C. STANLEY (1963) "Experimental and quasi-experimental designs for research on teaching," in N. L. Gage (ed.) Handbook of Research on Teaching. Chicago: Rand McNally.

ERLICK, A. C. (1970) "People problems: population, pollution, prejudice, poverty, peace." Report of Poll 89%, the Purdue Opinion Panel, June.

FRIEDMAN, M. (1967) "Why not a volunteer army?," pp. 200-207 in S. Tax (ed.) The Draft: A Handbook of Facts and Alternatives. Chicago: Univ. of Chicago Press.

JOHNSTON, J. (1970) "The future soldier: a profile of today's youth." Presented at the conference on Current Trends in Army Social Work, Denver.

––– and J. G. BACHMAN (1972) Youth in Transition. Volume V: Young Men and Military Service. Ann Arbor, Mich.: Institute for Social Research Survey Research Center.

––– (1970) Young Men Look at Military Service: A Preliminary Report. Ann Arbor, Mich.: Institute for Social Research Survey Research Center.

Life (1971) "A new youth poll: change, yes–upheaval, no." Volume 70 (January 8): 22-30.

OI, W. Y. (1967) "Costs and implications of an all-volunteer force," pp. 221-251 in S. Tax (ed.) The Draft: A Handbook of Facts and Alternatives. Chicago: Univ. of Chicago Press.

President's Commission on an All-Volunteer Armed Force (1970) Report. Washington, D.C.: Government Printing Office.

ROTTER, J. B. (1971) "External control and internal control." Psychology Today 5 (June): 37-42+.

SJAASTAD, L. A. and R. W. HANSEN (1970) "The conscription tax: an empirical analysis," pp. IV-1-1 - IV-1-61 in President's Commission on an All-Volunteer Armed Force. Washington, D.C.: Government Printing Office.

TAX, S. (1967) The Draft: A Handbook of Facts and Alternatives. Chicago: Univ. of Chicago Press.

Yankelovich, D., Inc. (1971) Youth and the Establishment: A Report on Research for John D. Rockefeller III and the Task Force on Youth.

13

RURAL YOUTH
Current Status and Prognosis

WILLIAM P. KUVLESKY

Much has been said and written about the rebellious youth of today, about how their values, attitudes, and style of life are diverging from those of their parents' generation. Yet many of the scholars who have written about research findings on these matters have questioned the cleavage in cultural continuity implied by the term *youth culture* (Bealer and Willits, 1961; Reiss, 1961; and Dansereau, 1961). Keniston (1965) provides a picture of contemporary youth drifting "toward a world of private and personal satisfactions" and who find their parents "increasingly irrelevant as models" —but he explicitly presents this under a subtitle, "Outlooks of Elite Youth." In a very excellent analysis of divergent youth patterns, Matza (1961) explicitly develops the case that dramatic extremist versions of "youth rebelliousness" are more or less institutionalized modes of adaptation selected by a minority of youth. Feuer (1969: 15), in a recent book on student movements, supports this view and goes on to say that most of the noise is made by young people of the middle class. Bealer and Willits (1967) present a comprehensive review of research to demonstrate that most youth accept conventional normative standards and still rely on the family as a primary reference group for behavior in general. American youth are likely to reflect the heterogeneity of their parents, churches, and schools in their values, attitudes, and behavior. And, if we observe general changes of significance in youth, it is likely that similar changes have also taken place among adults.

If our society is undergoing the bloodless, youth-led revolution described by Reich (1970), America is not being "greened" in a smooth and even manner. Reality is painted somewhat differently, perhaps with a more ragged brush, than he would have us believe.

Rural youth are not chafing at the bit to enter the value configurations and behavioral patterns labeled by Reich as "Consciousness III." My interpretation of existing research findings and my experiences with rural youth lead me to the conclusion that the vast majority of rural youth, for better or worse, are still much imbued with the success ethic: they still desire to achieve higher social rank, more material amenities, and to improve their life chances as compared with their parents. While they struggle with the transition from adolescence to adult status, as have all youth of all time, most do not reject the prime values and life goals of their parents (Bealer et al., 1965). The remainder of this paper will be concerned with describing the present circumstances of rural youth and evaluating prospects for change in these during the next decade.

RURAL YOUTH AND THE RURAL SCENE

According to Beegle and Rice (1965: 8-10), in a recent demographic overview of rural youth, there were about 7.5 million rural youth between the ages of 15 and 25 in the United States in 1960, of whom about 5.7 million were nonfarm residents.[1] This constituted approximately one-third of the total U.S. population of that age. Beegle indicates that most of these youth are concentrated in two regions, the South and North Central; much smaller numbers were to be found in the economically more favored and more industrialized regions of the Northeast and West.

The term "rural" has lost much of its descriptive utility as the several highly correlated dimensions of life once defined it—farming as a job, low density and physical isolation in reference to residence, and a conservative culture—have come unraveled (Bealer et al., 1965). Because of the various ways the term is used, it is important to specify the referent I intend here. By rural youth, I mean those people between the ages of 15 and 25 residing in nonmetropolitan areas, in places of 25,000 or less. It is important to note that *I am not referring to only farm-reared youth* by the term rural, which is one common usage (Haller, 1969: 8).

Most of the assessments of contemporary rural life indicate that place of residence is becoming less significant as a basis for differentiation of social behavior in our society (Taylor and Jones, 1964: 44-45). In a recent collection of essays edited by Copp (1964), a number of prominent rural sociologists provide evidence that rural-urban differences are decreasing in reference to levels of education, fertility, complexity of social organization, and family structures and marital relations. These authors and others still report rural-urban differentials. Glenn and Alston (1967), using national survey data, note a continuation of a conservative set of orientations on the part of rural (farm) people as compared with urban, and Willits and Bealer (1963) report findings that indicate that rural youth in Pennsylvania are still slightly more conservative than urban youth in reference to moral norms. It is my judgment that, while these valid, statistically significant differences do exist, they tend to play down the existence of substantial variation in both population types and ignore the fact that a sizeable, perhaps increasing, proportion of rural young people are very much like their metropolitan counterparts in their values, attitudes, and behavioral patterns. Some small indication that this homogenizing of population attributes might be taking place faster than most authorities think is evidence of an apparent reversal of the long-standing generalization that farm-reared youth have lower educational goals and plans than other youth, as indicated by evidence from recent studies in Washington (Slocum, 1968) and Texas (Kuvlesky, 1969: appdx. E).

THE CURRENT STATUS OF RURAL YOUTH

One should be wary of easy generalizations that are cast broadly over the vast array of different subcultures, social categories, and populations that fall under the gross category of rural youth. Certainly, the life conditions and behaviors of a boy expected to inherit his father's large commercial farm in Iowa differ dramatically from that of a son of a migrant farm worker in South Texas. Region, ethnicity, social class, and, yes, even sex status have been found to make a difference in patterns of behavior among rural youth (Kuvlesky and Pelham, 1966; Kuvlesky and Jacob, 1968).

At the same time, there are many common attributes of circumstances, values, aspirations, needs, and prospects that cut across the majority of these diverse groups—those that are most disadvantaged (i.e., Chicanos, blacks, hill-country whites, Cajuns, American Indians, and open-country poor in the Northeast, Midwest, and West). Most are at a relative disadvantage to compete with metropolites (Taylor, 1968). Yet most rural youth have high mobility aspirations, while lacking social facilitation to accomplish their goals (McClurkin, 1970), although they apparently do not realize this (Griessman and Densley, 1969: 62). In addition, like all other youth, the rural young are bugged by the age-old problem of transition into adult status (i.e., sex relations, drinking or drug usage, and intermittent conflict with the older generation). It is my intention next to describe the common attributes of these diverse groupings that might be appropriately labeled "the rural disadvantaged" in reference to their ambitions and hopes, their values and norms, and their social circumstances.

Most of the recent research and writings on rural youth by sociologists have centered on their orientations toward social mobility. Much less attention has been given to seeking an understanding of their broader values and conceptions of morality, and even less attention has been directed toward the description and explanation of actual patterns of overt behavior (i.e., dating, interaction with adults in nonschool roles, delinquency, political action, leisure time activities, and so on). The quality of the following appraisal of rural youth's present status will undoubtedly reflect these research biases.

ASPIRATIONS AND EXPECTATIONS

It is a common notion that rural youth lack the ambition and the inclination to suffer deferred gratification necessary to climb the social ladder in our society. A great deal of research has been accumulated on the aspirations and expectations of rural youth during the past two decades that provide a basis for rather rigorous evaluation of these notions (Kuvlesky and Pelham, 1966; Kuvlesky and Jacob, 1968).

Researchers have had the tendency to view aspirations and expectations for attainment along a single dimension. Even though almost two decades have passed since Merton (1957: 132), a prominent sociologist, asserted that, in reality, youth maintained aspirations in more or less integrated sets, which may vary in the types of goals included as well as in the valuation of these goals. Several very recent research analyses have demonstrated that youth do, in fact, maintain more or less integrated systems of aspirations and expectations and that they do differentially evaluate the particular status goals involved in a hierarchy of importance (Kuvlesky and Upham, 1967; Pelham, 1968). Consequently, it is important to keep in mind that the various kinds of status goals and expectations to be reviewed separately here are, in fact, part of a more or less integrated, holistic conception of the future held by youth, which provides a cognitive map for anticipatory socialization into future adult roles (Turner, 1964: 15-18). In the remainder of this section, I will try to sketch the picture that evolves from current research of the kind of life rural youth are projecting for themselves.

The accumulated evidence clearly indicates that most rural youth *do not* have low-level job and educational aspirations and expectations at present. Recent analyses of regional data collected in the South on black and white youth clearly support this generalization (Lever and Kuvlesky, 1969; Thomas, 1970; Pelham, 1969; Picou and Cosby, 1971). Rural youth predominantly prefer and, to a large extent, expect employment in professional or semi-professional and technical types of jobs. Few rural youth expect to hold unskilled types of work, and evidence from both the South and the Northwest indicate that few rural youth currently either desire or expect to farm (Youmans et al., 1965; Kuvlesky and Ohlendorf, 1968; Slocum, 1968). In reference to educational attainment, the vast majority of rural youth desire college degrees, and almost all desire at least formal vocational training or junior college after high school. A tendency exists for deflection from college goals toward anticipation of post-high-school vocational training. The evidence is abundantly clear that few rural youth of any type desire to terminate their education before completing high school.

It is also abundantly clear that the rural/urban differentials that have been repeatedly observed in reference to mobility orientations of youth are much less important than the similarly high aspirations and expectations held by most youth (Kuvlesky and Pelham, 1966; Kuvlesky and Jacob,

1968). Certainly class, race, and ethnic differentials exist—the disadvantaged youth tend to hold lower-level goals and anticipated attainments. Still, the majority of even the most disadvantaged youth, the rural Negro in the South and the Mexican American rural youth of the Southwest, predominantly desire high-prestige job attainments and college-level education (Kuvlesky et al., 1971). Additional support is provided for this assertion from a recent comparative study of Mexican American dropouts and in-school age peers living in rural South Texas (Wages et al., 1969). Even these doubly disadvantaged youth generally maintained high-level aspirations—almost all wanted to complete high school, and most desired even more training. Obviously, their actual expectations were lower in general.

In conclusion, most rural youth, regardless of class or race, are like most urban youth in having high ambitions for social advancement. At the same time, it should not be overlooked that sizeable minorities of disadvantaged rural youth have relatively low-level aspirations and expectations (Kuvlesky et al., 1971; Picou and Cosby, 1971). Certainly, any program of guidance or vocational training established to help these youth will have to take these differences into account—the same programs are not likely to work effectively for both the very ambitious and the unambitious.

Most rural youth do not want to stay in the country and even fewer expect to. At least, this is what the scant evidence on the subject indicates. Studies done in Florida (Youmans et al., 1965: 16), Louisiana (Hernandez and Picou, 1969: 13-14), and Texas (Kuvlesky and Pelham, 1970) indicate that almost all black children and most of the white (more of the girls than boys) living in the nonmetropolitan areas studied desired and expected to live in or near cities. A statewide study by Boyd (1970: 38-41) of high school students in South Carolina produced similar findings. Additional support from evidence of other studies done in Kentucky (Schwarzweller, 1960: 13) and Michigan (Cowhig et al., 1960: 19) support the contention that this is a general pattern.

The place of residence projections of rural youth represent a rational alignment with their high job and educational goals and the limited opportunities for vertical mobility available in the hinterland. It seems clear that, unless the orientations of today's rural youth can be changed, there is little utility in attempting to sell them so-called "rural values" and to prepare them for local, rural labor markets. A recent comparative analysis of metropolitan and rural black youth in a southern state provided evidence that rural blacks are very much like their city cousins in desiring to live in or near a large city (Kuvlesky and Thomas, 1971). As an interesting aside, this report also indicated that a very small percentage of metropolitan black youth desire to live in rural areas.

Very little research has been done on rural youth's orientations toward the development of a family (Kuvlesky and Reynolds, 1970). The rural-urban differences in age of marriage and procreation, although decreasing, are still so marked and persistent (Bogue and Beale, 1964), that one might presume differences in valuation of the family and, derivatively, differences in aspirations for such things. Yet, evidence from several studies of rural girls' projections for age of marriage and size of family apparently contradicts these notions. An investigation of East Texas rural girls indicates that most desire to wed relatively late (21 for the white and 22.5 for the black)—considerably after the age of normal high school completion—and want small families (3 children; Kuvlesky and Obordo, 1972). A similar investigation on comparable populations by Hernandez and Picou (1969: 15-16) produced similar results. The fact that similar findings have also been reported for samples including urban youth indicates a lack of substantial rural-urban difference in relation to current youth projections for family (Backman and VanDuinen, 1971: 65; Boyd, 1970: 24-26). Again, this evidence appears to be in rational alignment with other status projections of rural youth and is indicative of a willingness to tolerate deferred gratification in reference to entering marriage and having children. The configuration of aspirations begins to look like a portrait of contemporary middle-class, urban life. This is apparently the style of life most of our rural youth, even the most disadvantaged, want, and which many expect to obtain. Recent research in Texas has indicated that rural youth do place a higher valuation on goals linked to achieving social mobility (i.e., education, job, income) than they do to goals related to family and place of residence (Kuvlesky and Upham, 1967). An investigation of black metropolitan youth produced similar findings (Kuvlesky and Thomas, 1971). These research findings, however, are compatible with those described above and add to the evidence indicating that rural youth are, in fact, strongly oriented toward the American "success ethic" and are not too different from their urban counterparts in this regard. The stereotyped notion of rural youth being predominantly oriented toward short-run gratifications related to family, procreation, and rural living to the detriment of their ambitions for mobility stands seriously questioned. Their difficulty in competing on equal terms with metropolitan youth is more likely a result of their lack of adequate preparation and facilitation for the contest.

BEHAVIORAL PATTERNS

Relatively little has been done in terms of reliable statistical studies that permit easy generalization on the subject of rural youth's everyday behavior, and the best accounts are descriptions of particular populations. I strongly suspect that overt behavioral patterns of rural youth vary more than aspirations (or even values and attitudes) by regional and ethnic delineations (Preston, 1968, 1969). Descriptions of these types of patterns have been recorded for Mexican Americans (Moore, 1970; 99-136; Grebler et al., 1970: 420-441; Heller, 1966), Negroes (Broom and Glenn, 1965; Proctor, 1966; Stapler, 1971), American Indians

(Henderson, 1971: 61-70), and Appalachian youth (Weller, 1965).

In general, rural youth do not have access to the variety of cultural depositories and events as compared with other youth (Allen, 1968). Their alternatives for use of leisure time and peer associations are often centered around high school activities and events, outdoor activities, watching TV, and parking along back roads. Perhaps one of the most frequently heard complaints of rural young people about their communities is that "there's nothing to do around here." For many of the large proportion of rural youth who are disadvantaged relative to income, the isolation they experience—without access to mass literature in the home, frequently without access to a car, and sometimes without a TV set—and the monotony of the everyday life they endure must present problems of adjustment (Nelsen and Storey, 1969).

What does the extant research have to say about general behavioral patterns of rural youth? There is no doubt that rural youth spend less time in school (legitimately or otherwise) and drop out of school more often than others —this problem is particularly acute for ethnic minorities (Cervantes, 1966; Burchinal, 1965: 113-148). On the other hand, particularly among the most economically poor, they spend more time in working at jobs, both during the normal school year and during vacations (Amos, 1965). A good summary of medical and health conditions and practices of rural people by Wallace (1965) indicates that rural youth in general have less contact with medical professionals and spend more time at home disabled with sickness or injury than most of their urban counterparts. The fact that these kinds of patterns of rural-urban differences are linked with class position is demonstrated by a recent New York study reported by Ellenbogen and Lowe (1968). Their results demonstrate that rural-urban differences in acceptance of modern health practices observed generally did not exist for the high-income portion of their sample. Not surprisingly, it has been reported that rural youth spend more time in face-to-face contacts with "kin" (Straus, 1969), but that this does not necessarily mean they have a better family life (Haer, 1952) or are better adjusted (Nelsen and Storey, 1969). Perhaps the most widely researched aspect of rural youth's behavior has been in the area of delinquency. In a recent overview of the literature on this subject, Polk (1965) has concluded that there are rural-urban differences in the nature of delinquent activity, organization of delinquency ("the delinquent subculture"), community definitions of delinquency, and in the way deviance is handled. According to the descriptions he gives of rural youth as compared to urban, they are more often guilty of "general misconduct" and less often of "serious offenses." Furthermore, rural youth are not as "sophisticated" as their urban counterparts and are rarely organized into gangs. Findings Polk reviews indicate that rural communities are more lenient toward youth raising hell (i.e., drinking, fighting, gambling, picking up girls, trespassing on and destruction of property) and treat them more · leniently when they are apprehended. This last point is supported by the fact that a much higher proportion of rural youth offenses than urban are resolved "by closing the case at intake." However, although fewer rural youth than urban are kept in detention, when they are, they are more likely to be in jail and less likely to receive special care or consideration apart from adult criminals (Downey, 1965).

VALUES, ATTITUDES, AND PERSONALITY

Unfortunately, little has been done in recent times to check the validity of the common, stereotyped images commonly held about rural people, many of which received legitimation from widely quoted polar-type constructs of well-known sociologists. Glenn (and Alston, 1967: 381), in discussing this problem, writes that "the literature on rural-urban attitudinal differences still consist [sic] more of impressions and speculation than of reliable data." Glenn then goes on to report a host of rural (farmer)-urban comparisons, utilizing data from national polls, which lead him to conclude that the stereotypes are generally correct: in his own words: "The leveling of traditional rural-urban differences, if there has been such a trend, has not progressed as far as some observers seem to think." While I personally do not agree with this sweeping implication derived from his findings (Kuvlesky and Lever, 1967), a more recent study by Nelsen and Yokley (1970) has produced evidence to indicate that rural adults, at least, are more conservative in attitudes toward civil rights. Regardless of whether or not rural-urban differences in values and attitudes still prevail, there is little doubt that rural people in general are becoming less traditional in their outlook and less conservative in the political, religious, and moral values and attitudes (Willits and Bealer, 1963).[2] Recent descriptions of the rural South (Bertrand, 1966) and of Mexican Americans in the Southwest (Grebler et al., 1970; Moore, 1970) indicate that even the most resistant, tradition-oriented subcultures are giving way to change.

Studies specifically focusing on values and attitudes of rural youth—excluding those on mobility orientations—are few. Nelsen and Storey (1969) provide a thorough overview of relevant studies that show mixed results. Their own findings from a comparative investigation of personality adjustment problems among rural and urban youth indicate that rural youth much more frequently indicate "worry" than city youth. Other studies they review provide contrary results on rural-urban differences relative to religious attitudes and behavior (Burchinal, 1961), conservatism-radicalism (Haer, 1952), and a general scale measure of social traditionalism (Bealer and Willits, 1963).

The study of Willits and Bealer (1963) mentioned above involved Pennsylvania rural adolescents at two points in time—separated by thirteen years. At both times, they found statistically significant but minor rural-urban differences in social conservatism. In addition, they concluded that "rural adolescents in Pennsylvania today can be generally characterized as less conservative than their counterparts of thirteen years ago."

Haller (1969), in attempting to synthesize the current state of knowledge on the attributes of rural youth related to education, indicates that, in general, rural youth start school with about the same level of capabilities and aptitudes (i.e., nonverbal ability, reading comprehension, and mathematics achievement) but tend to fall behind as they move through the grade sequence.

A number of other studies have shown that rural youth differ, in a negative sense, when compared with urban youth on self-image, self-assurance, and social adjustment (Kuvlesky and Pelham, 1966).

In summary, it looks as if rural youth are similar to urban youth in values (such as conservatism-liberalism), which fits logically with the findings reviewed previously relative to aspirations and expectations for social mobility. On the other hand, present knowledge also appears to clearly indicate that rural youth suffer general disadvantages as compared with their urban counterparts in reference to personality adjustment, anxiety, and development of cognitive skills. It would appear then, that their greatest problems relative to advancing their prime goals are not attributable to a lack of acculturation into the ways of the highly urbanized, larger society, but, rather, rest in their disadvantaged circumstances and resulting maladjustments of personality, social relations, and underdeveloped abilities (Burchinal, 1965: 257-354).

PROGNOSIS

It is generally difficult to read the future, and most of us are reluctant to project trends, as pure extrapolations, too far. Yet I see no reason to be overly cautious in making a judgment that the trends previously described in the conditions, attributes, and behavioral patterns of rural youth are not likely to change much. In other words, rural youth are becoming more like metropolitan youth in their values, aspirations, attitudes, and probably behavioral patterns, too. I invited several respected colleagues having particular expertise on rural youth or rural-urban differentials to share their speculative judgments with me to assist in weighing the objectivity of my own assessment, and this is the one point upon which they all agreed.[3] Most rural youth, regardless of region, ethnicity, or class, want and will continue to want the following:

(1) a richer material and social life than their parents; they desire the middle-class life style represented in TV commercials and family comedies;

(2) quality education beyond high school, and in most cases, through a college degree;

(3) prestige, white-collar jobs or at least a skilled trade;

(4) more money than their parents could produce and more income security;

(5) to move to or near the metropolitan centers for the services and cultural diversity offered there;

(6) a better chance to realize their aspirations and expectations for social mobility than their counterparts have had in the past.

While much of this article has been focused on rural youth's orientations and prospects for social mobility, I am certain that most rural adolescents of high school age still rank highest in their primacy of concerns the problems of boy-girl relations, parental and generational conflict, ego security, and such deviant behavior (for the young) as drinking and grass. Yet they apparently find difficulty in seeking useful advice and guidance on these matters. They express a strong need for this kind of guidance. This felt need is likely to go largely unmet for most of these youth through the seventies unless adaptive structures are created in their communities. I do not pretend that the same kind of problems do not exist for many, if not most, metropolitan youth living outside the more affluent suburban areas. But much more attention (experimental efforts) are being directed toward resolving these problems for the youth of metropolitan America. At the same time that rural youth have become attuned to the urbanization of our country in their values and orientations, their chances for fully joining the society on equal terms have probably not kept the same pace. Many concerned people are pessimistic about the possibility of bringing about the kind of difficult changes in institutionalized patterns and current priorities that will be required to improve the life chances of hinterland youth. My attention will now turn to the exploration of some of these important needs.

MEETING THE NEEDS OF RURAL YOUTH

In all probability, if any effective, broad program of action is going to be developed to assist rural youth, it will have to come through their schools. It would be economically prohibitive to attempt individual or family treatment intended to have broad impact under the conditions inherently present in most rural places. In addition, the school represents the principal focus of community cohesion and identity in most rural communities, provides a ready nexus of interpenetrating ties among local, state, and federal political units, and usually represents the largest single collection of well-educated, relatively progressive professionals available. Consequently, it is the school that should receive the prime focus as a vehicle for change in assisting rural youth in improving their life chances and to meet adjustment problems.

The plight of the disadvantaged rural youth in our society has stimulated a number of publications over the last ten years that provide a wealth of ideas on changes needed in rural educational structures and schools to assist young people (Burchinal, 1965; Nash, 1965; Griessman and Densley, 1969; Haller, 1969; Wilson, 1970; McClurkin, 1970; Henderson, 1971). There would be little utility in my attempting to offer specific suggestions for needed structures and techniques of education and guidance already covered in greater depth by people with more technical expertise than myself. The reports cited above cover quite well a broad range of ideas directed toward such things as curricula, school consolidation (including development of specialized area and regional schools), mobile vocational units, advisory councils, work experience programs, counseling programs, and needs in teacher education. I strongly recommend these reports to anyone interested in exploring ways to further the interests of rural youth. What I intend to do is to view this problem from a broad sociological perspective and offer general implications at two levels: suggestions for needs in collaboration and cooperation between certain subsystems of the larger society, and high-priority needs for broadly reorganizing certain structures of rural education to better serve the needs of rural young people.

A more advantageous time for seeking broad support for amelioration of problems faced by rural youth has probably never existed. We are dealing with a problem that has broad ramifications for all the people and areas of our society and that is finally becoming recognized by the public at large (President's National Advisory Commission on Rural Poverty, 1967). Rural people are not happy with the progressive depopulation their communities have experienced, nor are urban dwellers pleased with either the magnitude or quality of the rural migrants. Obviously, the flow of the disadvantaged from rural areas into major metropolitan centers has contributed greatly to the general critical stresses our nation faces today (Hansen, 1971). The touchstone of the solution to many of these problems lies with the quality and effectiveness of rural education structures. This would seem to be the case regardless of whether or not the bulk of the rural poor continue to migrate to large urban centers. In either case, it is to the advantage of rural areas, the metropolitan centers, the nation as a whole, and certainly to the individuals involved to improve the prospects of social mobility for the rural disadvantaged.

As others have pointed out, probably the first requisite is the need for a national policy on rural education with a special emphasis on the disadvantaged. I concur with Haller's (1969) judgment that

> we need a single overall educational policy for rural regions, rural ethnic groups, and rural peripheries of urban areas—a long-range program for improving rural education with special but coordinated emphasis for different regions and ethnic groups.

The enactment of such a national policy would bring about a widespread awareness of the magnitude of this problem and its diverse implications, which would provide legitimation for giving it top priority for action and resources. This is not just a problem of local or county units; it is a national and state problem. Consequently, massive federal and state assistance should be sought to provide the heavy investments of resources needed to materially effect this problem (President's National Advisory Commission on Rural Poverty, 1967: 41-57). Strong, well-organized cooperation among federal, state, and local governments is a requisite for implementation of a policy that will have any kind of impact on this situation. Conant's (1964) ideas for stronger state agencies of education and a "nationwide educational policy" can serve as a guide for moving in this direction.

In addition, we need to creatively orient ourselves toward

breaking down the provincial community orientations that tend to prevail in rural areas, particularly in the South and Southwest, so that innovative, cooperative structures might be established between and among rural schools within counties, areas, and regions to better utilize scarce resources in developing the potential of rural youth. This would also facilitate the development of cooperative programs of job placement and social adjustment that need to be built between rural and urban political units.

Another form of cooperation that might facilitate the accomplishment of these ends and is very often overlooked in statements of needs pertaining to rural education, involves the relationships existing between social scientists, on one hand, and policy makers and educators on the other. There is a need for more effective and continuous communication and collaboration among these groupings of professionals in order to realize a commonly held objective of improving the prospects for self-realization and social development of disadvantaged rural people. Social and political power could be marshalled through cooperative associations of these professionals relative to influencing the development and implementation of a comprehensive national policy on rural education and rural youth. These groups need a systematic and intensive effort to begin sharing ideas—first at the national level and then at progressively less-complex levels of organization (i.e., regional, state, and local). Also, they need to work toward establishing more effective ties in their day-to-day working relationships as well—both within universities and colleges and between these systems and the rural school systems.

A sensitive problem involving cooperation of a different order, between racial and ethnic groupings of the populations involved, is present in the rural South and Southwest (Henderson, 1971; Moore, 1970). We need to face up to this problem in a direct and honest way, to examine its dimensions closely, and to develop programs and organizational structures that will overcome local and regional prejudices and discriminatory practices in both education and employment without producing mutual distrust and disaffection. This is a large order, but one that will not wait.

In considering the needs for changes in educational structures in particular rural areas, there is a need to recognize the complexity of the problem and resist the notion that there is an easy or simple solution (i.e., generally raising aspirations, better facilities, or better teachers; Haller, 1969: 19-20). We must work simultaneously across a number of fronts to have any hope of success. In looking at particulars, there are a number of general institutionalized structures impeding the possibility of innovative changes in counseling, training, and occupational placement of rural youth. Some of the more important structures that need to be altered are as follows:

(1) the sanctity of the concept of the local community school and total local domination of the ends and programs of education that tend to put local community interests ahead of the felt needs of rural youth (Conant, 1964; McClurkin, 1970: 38-40; Wilson, 1970: 3-7);

(2) the tendency to maintain vocation agriculture as the most important vocational program for adolescent boys in rural, particularly agricultural, areas (Cowhig and Beale, 1967; McClurkin, 1970: 22-23);

(3) the tendency to neglect or give low priority to the need for comprehensive and intensive guidance programs (including career counseling and job placement) and the almost total lack of a systematic broad counseling service for youth in rural areas outside the vocationally oriented structures in the school; problems of sex, drugs, and other anxieties go unresolved for most rural young (Nash, 1965: 146-163; President's National Advisory Commission on Rural Poverty, 1967: 46-47);

(4) the tendency to make do with teachers who can be recruited at low salaries and the utilization of locally available, partially or poorly trained individuals as teachers (McClurkin, 1970: 1-6; President's National Advisory Commission on Rural Poverty, 1967);

(5) the lack of concern for the development of a broad, continuous educational program beyond adolescence geared to adult needs and desires (Burchinal, 1965: 91-95; Nash, 1965: 145-146; President's National Advisory Commission on Rural Poverty, 1967: 50).

(6) the lack of concern with and involvement of the new generation in planning curricula (President's National Advisory Commission on Rural Poverty, 1967: 47).

In a report by the President's National Advisory Commission on Rural Poverty (1967: 41-58), 33 recommendations (including most of those singled out above) were offered to improve rural education. This document could be used as a start toward formulating a national policy for improving the life chances of rural youth through more adequate education and guidance. Without such a policy or broad public support for it, the future is certainly grim for improved life chances of rural youth, particularly for the blacks, Chicanos, and American Indians.

NOTES

1. Although the detailed age breakdowns of youth by residence type from the recent 1970 U.S. census are not yet available, the gross, preliminary figures cited in a U.S. Department of Commerce report (U.S. Bureau of the Census, 1971) lead me to believe that the absolute number of rural youth probably has not changed too much from 1960.

2. In a recent letter to me, Norval Glenn supports the proposition that rural youth are probably becoming more like their urban counterparts. However, in his judgment, it is the more progressive youth that are likely to migrate to the city, thus maintaining the pattern of rural-urban differences among the adult populations.

3. In order to provide some basis for judging the objectivity of my ideas about the future trends relative to rural youth, I invited several colleagues with particular expertise about rural youth or rural-urban differentials to share their judgments with me. Those listed below responded and deserve recognition: Walter Slocum (Washington State University), Eli Ginzberg (Columbia University), George Ohlendorf (University of Wisconsin), Lee Coleman (University of

Kentucky), Norval Glenn (University of Texas), Steve Picou (Ohio State University). While the responses from these exceptionally generous men influenced my thinking, the responsibility for the judgments offered is solely mine.

REFERENCES

ALLEN, I. L. (1968) "Community size, population composition, and cultural activity." Rural Sociology 33 (September): 328-338.

AMOS, W. E. (1965) "Child labor standards and school attendance laws as related to rural youth," pp. 335-342 in L. G. Burchinal (ed.) Rural Youth in Crisis: Facts, Myths, and Social Change. Washington, D.C.: U.S. Department of Health, Education and Welfare.

BACKMAN, J. H. and E. VanDUINEN (1971) Youth Look at National Problems. Ann Arbor, Mich.: University of Michigan Institute for Social Research.

BEALER, R. C. and F. K. WILLITS (1967) "The religious interests of American high school youth: a survey of current research." Religious Education 62 (September/October): 435-444.

––– (1961) "Rural youth: a case study in the rebelliousness of adolescents." Annals of Amer. Academy of Pol. and Social Sci. (November): 63-69.

––– and W. P. KUVLESKY (1965) "The meaning of 'rurality' in American society: some implications of alternative definitions." Rural Sociology 30 (September): 255-266.

BEALER, R. C., F. K. WILLITS, and P. R. MAIDA (1965) "The myth of a rebellious adolescent subculture: its detrimental effects for understanding rural youth," pp. 45-61 in L. G. Burchinal (ed.) Rural Youth in Crisis: Facts, Myths, and Social Change. Washington, D.C.: U.S. Department of Health, Education and Welfare.

BEEGLE, J. A. and R. RICE (1965) "Some demographic characteristics of rural youth," pp. 3-17 in L. G. Burchinal (ed.) Rural Youth in Crisis: Facts, Myths, and Social Change. Washington, D.C.: U.S. Department of Health, Education and Welfare.

BERNARD, J. (1961) "Teen-age culture: an overview." Annals of Amer. Academy of Pol. and Social Sci. (November): 1-12.

BERTRAND, A. (1966) "The rural south: under confrontation by mass society." Rural Sociology 31 (December): 447-457.

BOGUE, D. J. and C. L. BEALE (1964) "Recent population trends in the United States and their causes," ch. 3 in J. H. Copp (ed.) Our Changing Rural Society: Perspectives and Trends. Ames: Iowa State Univ. Press.

BOYD, V. A. (1970) Aspirations, Expectations, and Attitudes of South Carolina High School Students. Clemson: South Carolina Agricultural Experiment Station.

BROOM, L. and N. D. GLENN (1965) Transformation of the Negro American. New York: Harper & Row.

BURCHINAL, L. G. [ed.] (1965) Rural Youth in Crisis: Facts, Myths, and Social Change. Washington, D.C.: U.S. Department of Health, Education and Welfare.

――― (1961) "Farm-nonfarm differences in religious beliefs and practices." Rural Sociology 26 (September): 256-269.

CERVANTES, L. F. (1966) The Dropout: Causes and Cures. Ann Arbor: Univ. of Michigan Press.

CONANT, J. B. (1964) Shaping Educational Policy. New York: McGraw-Hill.

COPP, J. H. [ed.] (1964) Our Changing Rural Society: Perspectives and Trends. Ames: Iowa State Univ. Press.

COWHIG, J. D. and C. L. BEALE (1967) "Vocational agriculture enrollment and farm employment opportunities." Southwestern Social Sci. Q. 47 (March): 413-423.

COWHIG, J. D., J. ARTIS, J. A. BEEGLE, and H. GOLDSMITH (1960) "Orientations toward occupation and residence: a study of high school seniors in four rural counties of Michigan." Agricultural Experiment Station Special Bull. 428, East Lansing.

DANSEREAU, H. K. (1961) "Work and the teen-ager." Annals of Amer. Academy of Pol. and Social Sci. (November): 44-52.

DOWNEY, J. J. (1965) "Detention care in rural areas," pp. 241-253 in L. Burchinal (ed.) Rural Youth in Crisis: Facts, Myths, and Social Change. Washington, D.C.: U.S. Department of Health, Education and Welfare.

ELLENBOGEN, B. L. and G. D. LOWE (1968) "Health care 'styles' in rural and urban areas." Rural Sociology 33 (September): 301-312.

FEUER, L. S. (1969) The Conflict of Generations: The Character and Significance of Student Movements. New York: Basic Books.

GLENN, N. D. and J. P. ALSTON (1967) "Rural-urban differences in reported attitudes and behavior." Southwestern Social Sci. Q. 47 (March): 381-400.

GREBLER, L., J. W. MOORE, and R. C. GUZMAN (1970) The Mexican-American People: The Nation's Second Largest Minority. New York: Free Press.

GRIESSMAN, B. E. and K. G. DENSLEY (1969) Vocational Education in Rural Areas. Las Cruces: ERIC-CRESS New Mexico State University.

HAER, J. L. (1952) "Sociological variation in contemporary rural life." Rural Sociology 13 (September): 256-269.

HALLER, A. O. (1969) Rural Education and the Educational and Occupational Attainments of Youth. Las Cruces: ERIC-CRESS New Mexico State University.

HANSEN, N. M. (1971) Rural Poverty and the Urban Crisis: A Strategy for Regional Development. Bloomington: Indiana Univ. Press.

HELLER, C. S. (1966) Mexican American Youth: Forgotten Youth at the Crossroads. New York: Random House.

HENDERSON, G. (1971) America's Other Children: Public Schools Outside Suburbia. Norman: Univ. of Oklahoma Press.

HERNANDEZ, P. F. and J. S. PICOU (1969) "Rural youth plan ahead: a study of occupational, educational, residential, and marital expectations of rural youth in Louisiana." Louisiana Agricultural Experiment Station Bulletin 640, Baton Rouge, August.

KENISTON, K. (1965) "Social change and youth in America," pp. 191-222 in E. H. Erikson (ed.) The Challenge of Youth. Garden City, N.Y.: Doubleday.

KUVLESKY, W. P. (1970) "Dynamics of occupational and educational status projections: a theoretical perspective." Presented to the annual meeting of the Rural Sociological Society Research Committee on Educational and Occupational Behavior, Washington, D.C.

——— (1969) "A synthetic overview of research on rural youth's projections for occupational and educational attainments: a progress report." Presented at the annual meetings of the Rural Sociological Society, San Francisco.

——— and N. L. JACOB (1968) "Educational status orientations of rural youth: structured annotations of the research literature." Texas A&M University Department of Agricultural Economics and Sociology, DTR 68-3, October.

KUVLESKY, W. P. and M. LEVER (1967) "Rural-urban differences." Southwestern Social Sci. Q. 48 (September): 211-213.

KUVLESKY, W. P. and A. S. OBORDO (1972) "A racial comparison of teen-age girls' projections for marriage and procreation." J. of Marriage and the Family.

KUVLESKY, W. P. and G. W. OHLENDORF (1968) "Rural-urban comparison of occupational orientations of Negro boys." Rural Sociology (June): 141-152.

KUVLESKY, W. P. and J. T. PELHAM (1970) "Place of residence projections of rural youth." Social Sci. Q. 50 (June): 166-176.

——— (1966) "Occupational status orientations of rural youth: structured annotations and evaluations of the research literature." Texas A&M University Department of Agricultural Economics and Sociology DTR 66-3, September.

KUVLESKY, W. P. and D. H. REYNOLDS (1970) "Youth's projections for residence, income, and family status: a bibliography of research." III. Departmental Information Report 70-6. Texas A&M University Department of Agricultural Economics and Rural Sociology.

KUVLESKY, W. P. and K. A. THOMAS (1971) "Social ambitions of Negro boys and girls from a metropolitan ghetto." J. of Vocational Behavior 1 (April): 177-187.

KUVLESKY, W. P. and W. K. UPHAM (1967) "Social ambitions of teen-age boys living in an economically depressed area of the South: a racial comparison." Presented at the annual meetings of the Southern Sociological Society, Atlanta.

KUVLESKY, W. P., D. E. WRIGHT, and R. Z. JUAREZ (1971) "Status projections and ethnicity: a comparison of Mexican American, Negro, and Anglo youth." J. of Vocational Behavior 1 (April): 137-151.

LEVER, M. F. and W. P. KUVLESKY (1969) "Socio-economic status projections of rural southern youth." Presented at the annual meetings of the Rural Sociological Society, San Francisco.

McCLURKIN, W. D. (1970) Rural Education in the United States. Las Cruces: ERIC-CRESS New Mexico State University.

MATZA, D. (1961) "Subterranean tradition of youth." Annals of Amer. Academy of Pol. and Social Sci. (November): 102-118.

MERTON, R. K. (1957) Social Theory and Social Structure. New York: Free Press.

MOORE, J. W. (1970) Mexican Americans. Englewood Cliffs, N.J.: Prentice-Hall.

NASH, R. C. [ed.] (1965) Rural Youth in a Changing Environment. Washington, D.C.: National Committee for Children and Youth.

NELSEN, H. M. and S. E. STOREY (1969) "Personality adjustment of rural and urban youth: the formation of a rural disadvantaged subculture." Rural Sociology 34 (March): 43-55.

NELSEN, H. M. and R. L. YOKLEY (1970) "Civil rights attitudes of rural and urban Presbyterians." Rural Sociology 35 (June): 161-174.

NYE, I. (1950) "Adolescent-parent adjustment: rurality as a variable." Rural Sociology 15 (December): 334-359.

PELHAM, J. (1968) "Inter-state differences in educational, occupational, and income status aspirations of southern rural males." Presented at the annual meetings of the Association of Southern Agricultural Workers, Mobile.

PICOU, J. S. and A. G. COSBY (1971) "Social origins, occupational goals, and southern youth." Youth and Society (March): 307-322.

POLK, K. (1965) "An exploration of rural juvenile delinquency," pp. 221-232 in L. Burchinal (ed.) Rural Youth in Crisis: Facts, Myths, and Social Change. Washington, D.C.: Department of Health, Education and Welfare.

President's National Advisory Commission on Rural Poverty (1967) The People Left Behind. Washington, D.C.: Government Printing Office.

PRESTON, J. D. (1969) "Religiosity and adolescent drinking behavior." Soc. Q. (Summer): 372-383.

——— (1968) "Community norms and adolescent drinking behavior: a comparative study." Social Sci. Q. 49 (September): 350-359.

PROCTOR, S. D. (1966) The Young Negro in America: 1960-1980. New York: Random House.

REICH, C. A. (1970) The Greening of America. New York: Random House.

REIS, I. L. (1961) "Sexual codes in teen-age culture." Annals of Amer. Academy of Pol. and Social Sci. (November): 53-62.

SCHWARZWELLER, H. K. (1960) Sociocultural Factors and the Career Aspirations and Plans of Rural Kentucky High School Seniors. Lexington: Kentucky Agricultural Experiment Station.

SILBERMAN, C. E. (1970) Crisis in the Classroom: The Remaking of American Education. New York: Random House.

SLOCUM, W. L. (1968) "Educational aspirations and expectations of students in rural Washington schools." Washington State University Agricultural Experiment Station Bulletin 690.

——— (1966) Occupational Careers: A Sociological Perspective. Chicago: Aldine.

STAPLER, R. (1971) The Black Family: Essays and Studies. Belmont, Calif.: Wadsworth.

STRAUS, M. A. (1969) "Social class and farm-city differences in interaction with kin in relation to societal modernization." Rural Sociology 34 (December): 476-495.

TAYLOR, L. (1968) Occupational Sociology. New York: Oxford Univ. Press.

——— and A. R. JONES, Jr. (1964) Rural Life and Urbanized Society. New York: Oxford Univ. Press.

THOMAS, K. A. (1970) "Educational orientations of southern rural youth: an analysis of socio-economic status and racial differences." M.A. theses. University of Kentucky.

TURNER, R. (1964) The Social Context of Ambition: A Study of High-School Seniors in Los Angeles. San Francisco: Chandler.

U.S. Bureau of the Census (1971) Current Population Reports. Series P-23, Number 34. Washington, D.C.: Government Printing Office.

WAGES, S., K. THOMAS, and W. P. KUVLESKY (1969) "Mexican American teen-age school dropouts: reasons for leaving school and orientations toward subsequent educational attainment." Presented at the annual meetings of the Southwestern Sociological Association, Houston.

WALLACE, H. M. (1965) "The health of children and youth in rural areas," pp. 173-185 in L. Burchinal (ed.) Rural Youth in Crisis: Facts, Myths, and Social Change. Washington, D.C.: U.S. Department of Health, Education and Welfare.

WELLER, J. E. (1965) Yesterday's People: Life in Contemporary Appalachia. Lexington: Univ. of Kentucky Press.

WILLITS, F. K. and R. C. BEALER (1963) "The utility of residence for differentiating social conservation in youth." Rural Sociology 28 (March): 70-80.

WILSON, A. P. (1970) Educational Innovations in Rural America. Las Cruces: ERIC-CRESS New Mexico State University.

YOUMANS, E. G., S. E. GRIGSBY, and H. C. KING (1965) After High School What: Highlights of a Study of Negro and White Rural Youth in Three Florida Counties. Gainesville: University of Florida Cooperative Extension Service.

14

THE REAL GENERATION GAP
A Speculation on the Meaning and Implications of the Generation Gap

LUIZ R. SIMMONS

Dig it or not, American youth is not in rebellion against its parents, their values, or the authority of their culture (Nisbet, 1969). The protagonists of an arching "generation gap" (Mead, 1970; Kenniston, 1969; Feuer, 1969) conceived the fulcrum of student activism to be the logical consequence of cultural time dimensions, the hypocrisy of the parents' muted idealism,[1] or the "deauthorization of the elders." These interpretations of youth activism had been supplemented by the popularization of an exiguous "counterculture" (Rozak, 1969; President's Commission on Campus Unrest, n.d.), whose mythological juggernaut has greatly exceeded its numbers (Nisbet, 1970).

In fact, the cumulative effect of empirical research has revealed disconcertingly little foundation of a fierce "conflict of generations" (Lipset and Raab, 1970; Yankelovich, n.d.)

AUTHOR'S NOTE: *This paper was delivered at the American Association of Public Opinion Research, in the section on "Transitions in the Youth Culture: A Framework for Speculation," Luiz R. Simmons, Chairman.*

and has spawned little faith in the framework of previous diagnoses. Since then, it has become more than evident that one must do more than "dig the music" to "dig the youngsters" (Friedenberg, 1969) or scour the society for incongruous moral practices in need of rehabilitation to begin to invent plausible explanations for the distemper of the previous decade.

And if it should become necessary to revive a few sociological anachronisms from the thralldom of eschatology, one feels the unrequited confidence of a new decade where fear of irrelevance is no longer the final arbiter in and of human behavior.

At any time in American history, there have probably been more sons like their fathers than unlike them (Lane, 1959).

The young are no longer teenagers (Gottlieb, 1970a), but neither is there empirical evidence to suggest that they are passing into a new stage of psychocultural moratorium called "youth" (Kenniston, 1970)—in fact, there is some evidence to suggest the contrary (Wilensky; 1961).

Adolescence *is* a time of transition between childhood and manhood which has been lengthened by the social policies of advanced industrial nations.

Adolescence *is not* a magical mystery tour (Reich, 1970) of cultural inventiveness for the majority of young Americans whose primary preoccupations remain defined by marriage, family, and work (Gottlieb, 1970b).

Further, the public dialogue which has surrounded the "youth question" has created a monolithic image of American youth unprecedented since the American preoccupation with Communism. Youth was represented as a kind of cultural high, nearly a state of the mystical,[2] a cabal of Stürm und Drang, who, in conjunction with young blacks, would "save" America (Chisolm, 1969). It is not unfair to recommend that we have tended to emphasize the psychology of youth (a state of mind) at the expense of a scrupulous understanding that youth interacts with the historical processes in a strange and subtle madrigal[3] and that, more often than not, student movements have been an extension of the historical mood, not a radical reinterpretation of it (Laquer, 1969).

What sense can we make of this historical conjunction, which would anticipate an explanation of the meaning of this generation?

Both the hip and the nonhip analysts have adopted the habit of estimating the significance of this generation by scrutinizing the behavior, demands, concerns, and ideological flights of elite or "forerunner" student formations (Yankelovich, n.d.b). This approach to interpreting the meaning of a generation in the historical continuum can be worthwhile in periods of historical transaction, where the student movement is a protagonist of the central passions of the age and the other actors in the system are characterized by inertia. But in times of historical and cultural transition, the valve of evaluating elites or "forerunners" must produce only the limited understanding of a particular class or interest group (see Kahn and Wiener, 1967: 42). Historical transitions are irreducible phenomena, and the essence of their interpretation is not easily distilled into what must be only artificial theories regarding a particular class, constituency, or group behavior.

As a historical transition, the Reformation summoned Western man from the cosmological recesses of the Church and stimulated a realignment of perceptions which issued forth in religious diversity, national forms of development, and economic competition.

The message of the Reformation was a psychocultural liberation (Feuer, 1963) which assumed a variety of forms among a variety of classes and constituencies.

The theme of current student movements in the United States and Western Europe suggests a similar renewal of psychocultural liberation (Flacks, 1967).

The message of this historical transition has little to do with the specific manifestations of a sensate class (see Kahn and Wiener, 1967) unless we decide to recommit the error of analyzing the expressions of an elite constituency following the path of the preponderance of research and diagnoses. It is of little importance whether these young are imputed to be the best-educated, best-motivated (Heard, 1970)[4] national merit scholar finalists (Kenniston and Lerer, 1970)[5] or whatever, because in an age of historical transition, the significance of a generation and its peculiar interaction with history can be best explained by accepting a synoptic view of the actors, for the action is clearly not taking place at any one game.

Youth, not only funky student youth, have been actively involved in antagonizing the sensibilities of this period of history and national consciousness. This antagonism cannot be adequately understood or explained by theories of value differentation because, clearly, many youth share their parents' values, attitudes, and norms.

What, in fact, they do not share, and on occasion have confronted, are their parents' sensibilities regarding modern institutions, personal identity, and the conundrum of alienation in postindustrial society. Instead, many different kinds of youth are affirming a variety of alternatives to what they perceive to be the rootless institutions of their parents.

A politics of neoethnicism is investing itself in the styles, politics, and folkways of American youth, which will impact widely on theories of national development and integration. Neoethnicism is a transition from the national consciousness of the nation-state to more communal forms of identity and organization, cultural patriotism, and a revolt against anxiety. A primary agent of this transformation is the primacy of communication in a process of mobilizing unassimilated minorities and subcultures (Deutsch, 1966: 129),[6] the growth of particularistic and minority nationalism (Wirth, 1936),[7] in a redefinition of national consciousness. It has been described at its farthest points by a process of retribalization, the philosophical concession to the communal imperatives of the "interdependence of fate" (Lewin, 1948), and a proliferation of related life styles. In its paramount

expression, it is the apostasy of the nation-state, an exhaustion with the cumulative preoccupations of national and world institutions and the preference for the pursuit and study of personal and parochial problems.

It is expressed in a variety of ideologies, among a variety of classes and has become a relevant preoccupation of not only the "forerunner" but, sui generis, the young. It touches not only the hip rich kid, but a broad panoply of youth. It has assumed both subtle and overt expressions and is stimulated in both passive and political repartees.

Neoethnicism is not an exercise in the apocalyptic. It is an articulation of the crisis in expectation and promise of national institutions. It confutes the viability of a national ethic. It is a disenchantment with the incapacity of national institutions to respond to the needs of social utility and community, and it has found its expression in themes and motifs as seemingly diverse as civil disobedience, the fiery chants of La Raza, ethnic consciousness, the "psychological" burdens of foreign policy (Kissinger, 1968: 599),[8] youth ghettos (Lofland, 1968), subcultures (Toffler, 1970), the behavior of new social interest groups (Goldman, 1969: 16-17), privatism,[9] decentralization, community control, rural communes, and the growth of the modern university. It is defiant to a single ideology and value orientation.

The legitimacy of the modern state is struggling to overcome a national challenge to its supremacy as profound in its implications as were the transitions in communal psychology from the household to polis, the rise of the territorial state, and the loss of faith of the thirties.[10]

It has been incongruous to hear the incessant clamor for community *and* community control (which preoccupation I believe fair to associate with a broad spectrum of American youth) when we contemplate the original purposes of the nation-state. It was to be the "terminal community" (Emerson, 1960), the "remnants of former types of ethnicity" (Gordon, 1964), the source "of all cultural energy and economic well being" (Kohn, 1951), a "community in behavior" (Pillsbury, 1919), the consummation of strange and diverse loyalties.

But what sense are theorists to make of a generation of youth engaged in a redefinition of the "terminal community," which has convoked a renaissance of what Paul Goodman (1960) has called the "smaller patriotisms?"

The restoration and creation of new entreposts of authority and sources of competing patriotism are salient characteristics in youth protest behavior in which college and high school activism, ethnic resurgence, preoccupations with the occult, young "hard hats," and the emergence of mass movements share a common theme: the transition to new phases in communal psychology.

This revolt against the discontinuities of modern American life found its expression in rich popular sociology of the fifties. The alienation of today is perhaps more pronounced among the young, but not confined to them (Kenniston, 1960).

The decline of the terminal community as the focal point for diverse loyalties has produced a sense of "powerlessness" among those who continue to wrestle the contradiction of national institutions and neoethnic, communal aspiration, while shaping original and smaller, personal and social, institutions. This contradiction is an especially poignant preoccupation of this generation which has suffused the politics of neoethnicism and community with a spectacular vigor.

Was this an unexpected phenomenon? The dialogue of the moderns has placed extraordinary emphasis upon political strategies, relying on a diffusion of state power through decentralization, revenue-sharing, freedom of choice, school designs, the philosophical limitation of statism inherent in "benign neglect," and a political agenda which parodies the nostalgic "power to the people" slogan of the Port Huron statement. Is it so strange that the young would demand in their universities, high schools, industries (Gans, 1970),[11] and personal ideologies a passion for reexamination?

However, the "sickness of government" (Drucker, 1970) is only a political symptom of the disenchantment with the disutility of the modern state, otherwise described by a regression into currents "which are rooted in a return to instinctual modes" (Bell, 1970: 73).[1][2] Inquiries into the foundations of the nation-state and nationality tend to agree with the proposition that nationalism is a conscious choice where a nationality "seeks to find its expression in what it regards as the highest form of organized activity, a sovereign state" (Kohn, 1951: 17-23).

However, the "impermeability" of the nation-state, its significance as the custodian of "territoriality," has declined with the advent of nuclear weaponry (Herz, 1957). The significance of this transformation was not wasted on the young Beats for whom the cold war and new weapons had ushered in an age where "you have a sense of utter helplessness in the face of forces apparently beyond the control of man" (Podhoretz, 1958).

The intensity of neoethnic politics among the young reflects the changing sensibilities in an age of maximum weaponry where the utility of the state as a territorial instrument for preservation has lost its cogency, and where security has become a function of technology, not of geopolitics (see Steel, 1963).

This reorganization of security has acted as a catalyst in the reexamination of other national institutions and functions and has revealed an extraordinary degree of weariness with the institutions of the nation-state.[1][3] In such a system, where the nation-state is no longer regarded as the "highest" form of organization, interest groups—cultural and racial minorities—not receiving satisfaction from the processes of the state, are easily mobilized to pursue nonnational alternatives.

The real generation gap of legendary parlance lies in a generation of American youth which does not demonstrate radically different values from those of its parents, but which is developing a variety of nonnational institutions to enact them.

It is curious to note that expressions of tribalism and "peoplehood" among the young are found not only in the extended families of hippies, but among young blue-collar workers in Corpus Christi, Texas:

Everybody says "Naw, man, I don't need *anybody.*" There comes a time when you've got, you need somebody bad. And like with your outlaw groups, especially with the Bandits, there's just something about it that, you're brothers. Anything your brother's got you've got. And, there's no, nobody turns anybody down. Or nobody messes over anybody. You don't hurt a brother. And if, if a brother thought that it would save your life for him to die for you, he'd do it. Some people say, "Well, this is crazy. You don't do stuff like that." That's real love and freedom, also. You're doin' your own thing and you've got somebody that, you can fall back on, somebody that can fall back on you, but you're doin' something [Simmons, n.d.].

The prologue of youth activism and the themes of community and protest suggest the imminence of new social forms and associations and the relocation and creation of "smaller" and original patriotisms. While legitimacy and authority have suffered the vicissitudes of neoethnicism, the transitory phases of mass movements, social unrest, the proliferation of radical journals, emergence of temporary and exotic fringe cultures (happenings, identified with the youth culture) in sum, the rush to alternative forms of community, prefigure the rise of an alternative organic social order. The decline in the legitimacy of the nation-state has sponsored a revival in alternative image systems, initially described in the "forerunner" groups by the rage for the occult, mysticism, the nonrational with its implications for the sociology of religion (Greely, 1970). It is important to recognize that, historically, mysticism has corresponded with the romantic stage of religion and a certain communal way of living and believing (Scholem, 1961).

It may be the "privatism" of college students, the contrameritocratic revolt of hippies (Pitts, 1969), the efforts of ethnic groups in "upbuilding their neighborhood and communal institutions sensitivity training for young workers" (Shrank, 1970), or the significance of draft evasion for the legitimacy of the state (Boulding, 1967), but these expressions must be seriously contemplated as rising forms of protest to the raison d'etre of the nation-state.

It is no longer adequate to explain black nationalism as a fantasy (Draper, 1970) or ethnicism as a folly (Boorstin, 1970), with a rising sense of community and purpose among young blacks. Exhortations to adopt a "black ideology in toto, a path itself to blackness and nationhood" (Jones, 1969: 59), and the decision in some communities to create a "greater sense of identity, unity and spirit of nationalism" (Cohen, 1967) augurs the rise and prominence of minority nationalism.

A speculative essay in forecasting the future of ethnic groups (Greely, n.d.) has observed that "cultural shock" precedes the formation, organization, and emergence of immigrant self-consciousness. If this "culture shock" can be compared analytically to the disfigurations of continuity for which we are told we must prepare (Toffler, 1970), then it is worthwhile to make several observations regarding the current invigoration of ethnic politics in the United States.

Since ethnicism was hardly studied in the last decade, it is difficult to speculate on the depth and future of ethnic feelings or whether the ethnic group can still provide the communal satisfaction which the explosions of smaller and lesser communities and subcultures are providing for the young. During the sixties, an ethnic reformation may have been much in evidence, however much neglected. One need only study the confused faces of white college students to observe that many did not conceal their envy of the black students' "peoplehood." Jewish activists, too, have acquired valuable lessons from the tactics of black ethnic politics. As one commentary insists, "The establishment has not comprehended what the radical Jews are saying. The radicals have taken important positions on Jewish issues. They are radical about being Jewish" (Newsweek, 1970). These lessons have not been wasted on older ethnic groups in New York or Chicago, whose rumblings can no longer be regarded as innocuous effusions.

Ethnicism may be emerging as yet another private response to the decline of national consciousness and the growth of neoethnicism. The explanation for its vitality can be found in the explanation for the burgeoning lesser communities and subculture of the young: identity and communal satisfaction.

The fulcrum of current youth movements in the United States has been the university, and it is here that the broad scope of the politics of neoethnicism may finally be attenuated and emerge as a national body of political doctrine, not as the manifestation of a peculiar youth group.

The university occupies a prominent role with regard to the articulation of neoethnicism. What we have tended not to realize is that it is but one impressive focus of advocacy.

It is not only the rich hip kids who have articulated their fascination with new centers of political and social authority and expression. If we scrutinize the themes of the past decade, we see this motif among bikers and Ivy League students and "in the suburbs and the academy—two bastions of that faith which would state that a man would be allowed to lead a modest and reasonable life without interference by large forces" (Mailer, 1968: 91). These expressions have assumed a specific and peculiar form at the university level for obvious considerations of cultural and class perspectives. Thus, reflecting upon the university focus, Professor Huntington cites James Kurth's reference to the "counterculture" and continues that "it is also in a more fundamental sense a counterculture because it is opposed to social or intellectual structures, to hierarchy and specialization in either learning or institutions."

A distinguishing characteristic of neoethnic life is the emergence of the university life style as an alternative life style to the rationalization of the "technetronic" society.[14] Analysts have become of late overly romantic about the role of hippies, yippies, left-wing radicals, and activists in the turmoil of the university. This but represents the fringes of a deeper and more pervasive movement. Increasing numbers of young people are expressing interests in university graduate and postgraduate instruction and administration (Horowitz and Friedlaired, 1970: 22).[15] In fact, most reliable analysts of student protest tend to deemphasize the role of the extremist and concentrate on the role of the graduate students, young instructors, and a high incidence of participation by older students (see the Cox Commission Report, 1968: 7; Smith et al., 1970). The events of the past decade are an extension of the politics of community and life style, where a relatively homogeneous grouping of young men and women came to recognize through the medium and catalyst of the Vietnam war that they shared a certain inarticulate but tenable set of interests. In the sense of the Western experience, these communities began the arduous and often violent process of redistributing power and privilege, and the creations of roles and functions.

Thus privatism, ethnicism, the occult, community-oriented protest, consumer unionism, and communes testify to the decline of the national ethic and the absence of the subscription of diverse national, ethnic, minority, and individual preferences to the creation of national initiatives and ideology. The deauthorization of the symbols and the ideology of the nation-state is not a temporary phenomenon, nor is it primarily a casualty of the Vietnam war. It is bound up in, although not necessarily intrinsic to, the neoethnic rage. But public temperament is in transition, as well; decentralization, revenue-sharing, and community control are manifestations of this postponement of national gratification and a commitment to the development of smaller, more manageable administrative units. The young have been among the first to grasp the signficance of the transition and shape of themes which accommodate their perspective "youth cultures." As such, these themes prefigure issues as seemingly diverse as revenue-sharing and freedom of choice school designs, "youth ghettos," a new sex consciousness of young women, and the unmanageability of social conflict and disorder.[16] One senses in the ugly sinews of distrust which gripped the United States in the past decade a crisis of expectation. No longer convinced that national or state administrative bodies were prepared or capable of developing efficient responses to local and individual conflicts, a countenancing of distinct local, regional, and ethnic problems as prime foci of concern has eroded the foundations of the theories of national integration.

Thus, what was essentially perceived as a phenomenon of upper-middle-class students has erupted into the Western American democracy in a host of guises and expressions, much like the fabled centaurs. One articulate expositer of this body of political doctrine has been the university. Once again we must not confuse the expression as the only expression; it is but one highly defined manifestation of peculiar class and social preoccupation.

For too long, we have only been listening to one kind of kid. It is not that he has not had something to say; it is simply that there are more kids on the way—the poor, the black, the blue-collar—and although they, too, are both progenitor and heir to this species of political stylism, they will be asking and demanding different things from their government and different kinds of institutions where they perceive a national incapacity to respond. They will seek new ones relevant to being poor, black, blue-collar, Appalachian, a Californian, a rural Tennesseean, or a constituent of the Texas panhandle. But it would be a triumphant mistake to assume that these young people will excite and adopt radically different values. Their cultural values will remain for the immediate future essentially circumscribed by traditional consideration of economic, yet increasingly nonnational political participation. What they will be seeking now is more effective nonnational institutions to realize them. Thus, this new activism will have to reconcile the occasional articulation of national goals and aspirations with a preference for ethnic, regional, or community institutions. Why this transition in collective behavior has occurred now must be a subject for further definitive inquiry, but therein lies the emphasis of the real generation gap. What this will augur for the formulation of national priorities, for theories of national development, when youth is clearly soliciting and pushing for answers in a variety of personal, community, ethnic, and even state and national institutions, is difficult to assess now. The action has moved to another game insofar as the nation-state is concerned.

A politics of neoethnicism is emerging within the United States, and the dilemma is that for too long we have been searching for its explanation in the ideology, rhetoric, and occasional good sense which gushes from the modern university. This is understandable, because most of the historians and political scientists were understandably concerned with what their kids were saying.

But they were not the only ones on the block.

NOTES

1. When a demographic sample of American youth (ages 15-21) were asked "Have parents lived up to [your] ideals," eighty percent responded affirmatively (see Harris et al., 1970).

2. Upon the occasion of Woodstock, *Time* magazine noted, "More important, Bethel demonstrated the unique sense of comments that seems to exist among the young, their mystical feeling for themselves as a special group and 'us' in contrast to 'them.' "

3. Still relevant to the dialogue regarding the role of psychological and cultural interpretations of behavior is Whyte (1947).

4. "One senses that from the best of our young comes the worst of despair."

5. "A freshman class that has a high percentage of students who mark 'none' for religion on questionnaires, many National Merit Award winners, and many students who seek competence in a performing art, tends to have large anti-war demonstrations" (Kenniston and Lerer, 1970: 78).

6. "There are those persons who are mobilized but differentiated: they have been mobilized for intensive communication but have not been assimilated to the predominant language and culture. These persons have remained culturally or linguistically different from the members of group N, and they are frequently and acutely reminded of this difference by the intensity of social communication in which they must take part. These persons therefore are more likely than any

others to experience national conflict, and they are the persons who first take part in it" (Deutsch, 1966).

7. "Particularistic nationalism is based upon the 'secessionist demand for national autonomy and . . .' cultural autonomy."

8. Kissinger (1968: 599) observes that "If the United States remains the trustee of every non-communist area, it will exhaust its psychological resources." But the issue extends much farther than Kissinger's limited description. The "psychological" burden of American foreign policy is a consequence of the fact that security is more a function of technology than of geopolitics. Under such conditions, the conventional role of the trustee or guardian of others (for the purpose of protecting yourself) is increasingly irrelevant to the new security arrangement.

9. Privatism is putatively the "thing" on the college campus today. But the larger theme inherent in this upward turning suggests a weariness with the complexities of social change and an interest in the affairs of the community.

10. I tend to regard the eruption of World War II as the ideological substitute for community and purpose which were absent in the decade prior to its advent. On this point, see Stillman and Pfaff (1970).

11. "From the limited journalistic and sociological research so far available, it would appear that a yet unknown number of blue collar workers, particularly on the assembly line, complain like the students, that their work is unauthentic, and their workplace dehumaning" (Gans, 1970).

12. "The characteristic style of an industrial society is based on the principles of economics and economizing on efficiency, least cost, maximization, optimization, and functional rationality, yet it is at this point that it comes into sharpest conflict with the cultural trends of the day, for the culture emphasizes anti-cognitive and anti-intellectual currents which are rooted in a return to instinctual modes" (Bell, 1970: 73).

13. I am much in agreement with Lifton (1970), who notes that "nuclear weapons alter and blur the boundaries of our psychological lives, of our symbolic space, and in ways crucial to our thought, feelings and action."

14. It would be foolish and tautological to insist that all forms of youth protest are rebellions against the assumptions of nationality and state. Yet the rebellion against technique is not isolated from considerations of the influence of the state. "The state and technique—increasingly interrelated—are becoming the most important forces in the modern world; they buttress and reinforce each other in their aim to produce an apparently indestructible, total civilization" (Ellul, 1964: 318).

15. One of many writers on this point, he notes, "Student orientations to university life once were colored by the view that the university was only a transitional and brief phase of each student's existence. . . . However, many students now plan to enter graduate study and, even though graduate work may be contemplated in a different institution from undergraduate study, students still recognize that they will be spending many more years at the university than they once did" (Horowitz and Friedlaired, 1970: 22).

16. "What is deeply troubling is that we seem simultaneously to be intensifying conflict to be weakening our powers of reconciliation. Unless this spiral is broken, we risk being torn apart as a nation, with catastrophic consequences for the whole world" (Lubell, 1970).

REFERENCES

BELL, D. (1970) "The cultural contradiction of capitalism." Public Interest (Fall).

BOORSTIN, D. (1970) Sociology of the Absurd. New York: Simon & Schuster.

BOULDING, K. (1967) "The impact of the draft on the legitimacy of the state," in S. Tax (ed.) The Draft: A Handbook of Facts and Attentives. Chicago: Univ. of Chicago Press.

CHISOLM, S. (1969) Article in the Washington Post (April 17): B-11.

COHEN, N. E. (1967) The Los Angeles Riot Study. Los Angeles: UCLA Office of Public Information.

Cox Commission (1968) Crisis at Columbia: Report of the Fact Finding Commission. New York: Vintage.

DEUTSCH, K. W. (1966) Nationalism and Social Communication. Cambridge, Mass.: MIT Press.

DRAPER, T. (1970) The Rediscovery of Black Nationalism. New York: Viking.

DRUCKER, P. (1970) The Age of Discontinuity: Guidelines to our Changing Society. New York: Harper & Row.

ELLUL, J. (1964) The Technological Society. New York: Vintage.

EMERSON, R. (1960) From Empire to Nation—The Rise of Self-Assertion of Asian and African Peoples. Cambridge, Mass.: Harvard Univ. Press.

FEUER, L. S. (1969) The Conflict of Generations. New York: Basic Books.

——— (1963) The Scientific Intellectual. New York: Basic Books.

FLACKS, R. (1967) "The liberated generation: an exploration of the roots of student protest." J. of Social Issues 23, 3.

FRIEDENBERG, E. Z. (1969) "Current patterns of a generation conflict." J. of Social Issues 25 (April).

GANS, H. J. (1970) "The protest of young workers." New Generation (Fall).

GOLDMAN, E. (1969) The Tragedy of LBJ. New York: Alfred A. Knopf.

GOODMAN, P. (1960) Growing Up Absurd. New York: Random House.

GORDON, M. M. (1964) "Assimilation in American life," in The Role of Race, Religon and Natural Origins. New York: Oxford Univ. Press.

GOTTLIEB, D. (1970a) "The rise and fall of the American teenager: a more personal view of the sociology of American youths." Youth and Society 1 (June).

——— (1970b) National Youth Survey, conducted by Gilbert Youth Research for the White Conference on Children, August.

GREELY, A. (1970) "Implication for the sociology of religion of occult behavior in the youth culture." Youth and Society 2 (December).

——— (n.d.) "Why can't they be like us?"Facts and Fallacies About Ethnic Differences and Group Conflicts in America. Institute of Human Relations.

HARRIS, L. et al. (1970) Youth Attitudes for Life Magazine Year End Issue. Study 2047, November.

HEARD, A. (1970) Statement upon completion of his mission as special adviser to the President, July 23.

HERZ, J. H. (1957) "The rise and demise of the territorial state."World Politics 9.

HOROWITZ, I. L. and W. H. FRIEDLAIRED (1970) The Knowledge Factory: Student Power and Academic Politics in America. Chicago: Aldine.

JONES, L. (1969) "A black value system." Black Scholar 1.

KAHN, H. and J. A. WIENER (1967) The Year 2000, A Framework for Speculation on the Next Thirty-Three Years. New York: Macmillan.

KENNISTON, K. (1970) "Youth: a 'new' stage of life." Amer. Scholar 39 (Autumn).

——— (1969) The Young Radicals. New York: Harcourt, Brace & World.

——— (1960) "Alienation and the decline of Utopia." Amer. Scholar 29 (Spring).

——— and M. LERER (1970) "The unholy alliance against the campus." New York Times Magazine (November 8): section B.

KISSINGER, H. (1968) "Central issues of American foreign policy," in K. Gordon (ed.) Agenda for the Nation. Washington, D.C.: Brookings Institution.

KOHN, H. (1951) The Idea of Nationalism: A Study in its Origin and Background. New York: Macmillan.

LANE, R. (1959) "Fathers and sons: foundations of political belief." Amer. Soc. Rev. 24, 4.

LAQUER, W. (1969) "Reflections on youth movements." Commentary 47 (June).

LEWIN, K. (1948) Resolving Social Conflicts. New York: Harper.

LIFTON, R. J. (1970) Boundaries: Psychological Man in Revolution. New York: Vintage.

LIPSET, S. M. and E. RAAB (1970) "The non-generation gap." Commentary 50 (August).

LOFLAND, J. (1968) "The youth ghetto." J. of Higher Education (March).

LUBELL, S. (1970) The Hidden Crisis in American Politics. New York: W. W. Norton.

MAILER, N. (1968) Miami and the Siege of Chicago: An Informal History of the Republican and Democratic Conventions of 1968. New York: World.

MEAD, M. (1970) Culture and Commitment. New York: Doubleday.

Newsweek (1970) "The American Jew today." (March 1).

NISBET, R. A. (1970) "An epistle to the Americans." Commentary 50 (December).

——— (1969) "The twilight of authority." Public Interest 15 (Spring).

PILLSBURY, W. B. (1919) The Psychology of Nationality and Internationalism. New York: Appleton.

PITTS, J. (1969) "The hippies as contra-meritocracy." Dissent 16 (July/August).

PODHORETZ, N. (1958) "Where is the beat generation going?" Esquire (December).

President's Commission on Campus Unrest (n.d.) Report. Washington, D.C.: Government Printing Office.

REICH, C. (1970) The Greening of America. New York: Random House.

ROZAK, T. (1969) The Making of a Counter-Culture: Reflections on the Technocratic Society and Its Youthful Opposition. New York: Doubleday Anchor.

SCHOLEM, G. (1961) Major Trends in Jewish Mysticism. New York: Schocken.

SHRANK, R. (1970) "It makes no difference now." New Generation (Fall).

SIMMONS, L. (n.d.) "Reflections of a blue collar youth." Interview with a biker club in Corpus Christi, Texas, for the White House Conference on Children and Youth. (unpublished)

SMITH, M. B., N. HAAN, and J. BLOCK (1970) "Social psychological aspects of student activism." Youth and Society 1 (March).

STEEL, R. (1963) "Fortress America." Commentary (August).

STILLMAN, E. and W. PFAFF (1970) The Politics of Hysteria: Sources of Twentieth-Century Conflict. New York: Harper & Row.

TOFFLER, A. (1970) Future Shock. New York: Random House.

WHYTE, L. A. (1947) "Culturalogical versus psychological interpretations of human behavior." Amer. Soc. Rev. 12.

WILENSKY, H. L. (1961) "The uneven distribution of leisure: the impact of economic growth on free time." Social Problems 9 (Summer).

WIRTH, L. (1936) "Types of nationalism." Amer. J. of Sociology 41 (May).

Yankelovich, D., Inc. (n.d.a) Generations Apart: A Study of the Generation Gap Conducted for CBS News.

——— (n.d.b) Youth and the Establishment: A Report on Research for John Rockefeller and the Task Force on Youth.

15

IMPLICATIONS FOR THE FUTURE

DAVID GOTTLIEB

Much has been written about the behavior of American youth, particularly in the latter part of the past decade. The issues of student activism, racial unrest, drug abuse, counter-cultures, and contra-cultures have all received some empirical study and much in the way of national attention. Social scientists have sought to understand the dynamics of youth behavior and to note the relationships between the social structure of our society and the ways in which the young think and act. Presidential commissions have focused upon the behavior of college students, the problems of drug abuse, and juvenile delinquency.

Clearly, at the level of the federal government, there was recognition that youth had emerged and were a force with which to be reckoned. For the first time in our history, it was decided that there was a need to separate the White House Conference on Children into two distinct events—one dealing with children, the other with youth. Concern about how a national sample of youth would behave once brought together was a critical factor in selecting as the conference site a remote and isolated campground in Estes Park, Colorado.

Concerns and anxieties about the young were not limited to federal government agencies. On the contrary, at every level of government, in our schools, in industry, in the military, and even in penal institutions, adults expressed their apprehension and looked for strategies which might deter activism and confrontation. College students were appointed to the Board of Trustees, while others were invited to pass judgment on matters of faculty tenure, curriculum, budget, and campus life. In response to demands for youth involvement and relevance, governors and mayors, police chiefs, HEW organizations, and labor unions recruited young people to act as advisers. Regardless of the motivation or degree of sincerity, institutional leaders began to behave as if they believed that youth did have a legitimate right to some form of self-determination. Meanwhile, social scientists continued to study and speculate upon the condition of youth and society.

The following patterns or trends become apparent as one reviews the many, many contemporary pieces of literature and research which have dealt with youth behavior.

There are the "believers" and the "nonbelievers." The believers feel that, although there is evidence that previous generations have experienced some youth unrest, what we observe today is indeed unique. They endorse the notion of a distinct youth culture, or subculture, or counter-culture, or contra-culture, or consciousness culture. The nonbelievers feel that it has all happened before, that this, too, shall pass, and that kids are pretty much a carbon copy of their parents. The nonbelievers argue that youth are really not different; rather, there is an illusion of difference created by the mass media, the greater number of young people, and a societal willingness to be more tolerant toward bizarre behavior.

Then there are the "youth lovers" and "youth doubters." The lovers see in contemporary youth a much-needed element of honesty, sincerity, and commitment. The young are perceived as altruistic, indifferent to material gain, humanistic, and willing to "tell it and live it like it is," regardless of the consequences. The doubters are more likely to see youth as spoiled, overindulged, hedonistic, lacking in skills (social, occupational, and intellectual), and hardly able to take care of themselves, much less society.

The dramatic dichotomies presented in the portrayal of youth stem in part, I believe, from the kinds of youth behavior studied and discussed by social scientists. Generally, the tendency has been to deal with the more bizarre, far out, and colorful aspects of contemporary youth behavior. It seems that the combination of available research funds (frequently money made available in response to social crisis and allocated for social problem research) and the appeal of the more dramatic, the different, and the nonroutine, lead social scientists to the study of "deviant" youth behavior. Hence, we have stacks of papers on student activists and hippies but relatively little information about the transitional processes involved as students move from school to careers. More has been written about white youth than minority group youth; the emphasis in studies of minority groups has been on delinquency, militancy, and behavioral pathologies. Little empirical work is available which deals with the majority of Black, Chicano, and Indian adolescents who are neither junkies nor gang members. Only recently have we shown a more holistic interest in females, working-class youth, and ethnic groups. It is worth noting that the interest in these groups manifested itself when they began to demand equal time, and research funds were made available. The overkill on the extreme, activist, and deviant forms of behavior has done much to contribute to a distorted and unrealistic picture of American youth. It is no wonder that when talking about the young, emotions run high and dichotomous views prevail.

Additionally, in another aspect we have been quite selective (in fact biased) in the youth populations we have chosen to study. We have tended to concentrate upon white, male, fairly affluent college students. The reasons for our emphasis on the white middle-class student are not difficult to understand. First, these students represent a readily available study population since they are around the social scientists. Second, they are our children. Regardless of the motivating factors, I believe we know much more about college students than we do about any other segment of the youth population.

The emphasis on the age factor of this group has contributed to a popular view of youth as a monolith. As Simon, Gagnon, and Carns (1969) point out, there is more than one American; hence, more than one American youth. It hardly seems necessary to explain that the young are not cut from a common cloth. There are 40 million in this nation who are between the ages of 14 and 24; of these 40 million, college students are still a distinct minority. Obviously, the precise specification of whom we mean is essential when we talk about youth.

As indicated in the introduction to this reader, we intend to provide insights and information about different kinds of American youth. We also intend to say something about the potential status of different youth in the coming decade. This collection does not deal with each subgroup of the youth population. It does, however, represent a beginning—an attempt to identify the behaviors, needs, values, and aspirations of different kinds of American youth. As was also noted in the introduction, the task of making predictions is not a simple one. Not only is there significant variation among the young, but there is little in the way of empirical data. Hence, what are proposed by the various authors as being future trends are based upon a combination of hard data, speculation, "gut" feeling, and no doubt a bit of the authors' own personal preferences or hopes.

This final chapter is entitled "Implications for the Future." Not unlike my coauthors, my comments reflect my own familiarity with the research data, speculation, gut feeling, and my hopes for the future condition of youth and our society. In the way of hard data, and with the goal of providing some information about how the young see the future, the results of a national youth survey are presented below.

THE SURVEY METHOD

This study was conducted on behalf of the 1971 White House Conference on Youth by the Gilbert Youth Research Corporation. The total sample of 3,596 (1,828 males and 1,768 females) is a national one, representative of American youth between the ages of 14 and 24. Selected portions of the report, which was written in August of 1970, will be presented. The major emphasis will be upon the analysis of attitudinal change, and how attitudes compare with those of parents; current concerns and expectations for the future; and the projected condition of social institutions and society in the future.

Significant attitude and value changes have occurred in the past two years among the youth in this sample. Approximately *two-thirds* of them have experienced change in attitudes toward politics, religion, school, marriage and family, drugs, and the environment. The areas which produced the greatest proportion of change away from views held by parents were politics and religion. The number of those who believe they now hold views different from those of their parents is twice that of those who feel their views are similar to those of their parents. Changes were somewhat evenly split in the areas of drugs and marriage and family. Only regarding work is the change toward parents greater than the shift away from parents.

In all areas, the college youth show the greatest shift away from parental attitudes. Although fewer working youth have changed than have college student youth, the proportion of change away from parents is greater among them than is the proportion of change occurring within the high school youth, particularly in the areas of politics, religion, and school. While it might be expected that working youth have a lower percentage of change in the two-year period studied than do the college students, an interesting aspect is the significant change in a direction away from their parents. In all areas except work and drugs, about a third (or more) of working youth are less like their parents. Forty percent (40%) of working youth consider their attitudes less like those of their parents with regard to politics.

Whites have a greater proportion of away-from-parent change in all cases except work; nonwhites show a shift away from parents only in the areas of politics, friends, and marriage and family. Nonwhites have a greater percentage of shift *toward* parental attitudes than whites in *all* areas. As far as sex differences, in all areas except marriage and family and friends, a greater percentage of males than females experienced a change in attitude. Generally, males show a less-like-parents posture than do females.

Generally, the percentage less-like-parents is highest among the 17-18-year olds and decreases as the youth get older; the exceptions to this pattern are the areas of politics, drugs, and environment, in which the 19-21-year olds show the highest percentage of change away from parents. In all areas, the oldest youth are more likely than younger youth to indicate a shift toward attitudes held by parents. The pattern seems to indicate a high attitude difference with parents occurring at ages 17-18, a slight decline from ages 19-21, and then a more dramatic shift toward parental attitudes.

Each respondent was asked to project what he thought would be his main concern during the next five years. The variations between the different groups are minimal, the greatest deviation being the under-17 group's ranking of marriage and family in fourth place out of eight possible choices. Marriage and family is the most important topic (with work next) for all the groups except males under 17 years old and high school youth; these exceptions chose work as their main concern in the near future, with marriage not far behind. Friends, school, and environment follow, depending on who you are. Those not in school and those 22 and over place greater emphasis on their friends than those still in school. The nonwhites are concerned more with school than with friends, and more with religion than with environment. Politics is consistently the loser, except for males and college youth who think religion is even less important for them.

The notion that students should have no part in the governing of the academic community is definitely not endorsed by youth; less than five percent (5%) would accept this notion. The idea of student membership without voting rights on committees is hardly more acceptable; less than ten percent (10%) support this alternative. Over a third feel that students should have voting rights on committees, and more than half feel that students should have equal representation *as well as* the voting rights on committees. Thus, an overwhelming majority of youth (85%) feel that students should at least have voting rights on committees, and this is generally true for all groups. Females are actually more supportive of the highest form of participation than are males. Younger age groups favor this highest form of participation more than the older groups. There is virtually no difference between whites and nonwhites on any of these alternatives. Surprisingly, the college students are less supportive of equal representation with voting rights than either working youth or high school students. It is interesting to note how similar to the high school youth the working youth are in their choices.

YOUTH, EDUCATION, AND POVERTY

The sample was asked what they thought the emphasis of education would be in the next ten years. World affairs and science/technology were the first and second choices, but only a little over a quarter of the youth chose either. Three other choices were equally represented, with ethnic studies running lowest (12%). A greater percentage of males chose science rather than world affairs. Generally, world affairs loses status as a critical educational subject as youth get older, and their emphasis shifts to humanities. The 22 and over age group gives more support to the humanities than does any other group. There is no real difference between the racial groups except that a greater percentage of nonwhites think the emphasis will be on ethnic studies and cultural identity. The largest proportion of college students select ethnic studies and cultural identity. While the high school and working youth tend to choose human affairs, the college students choose science and technology.

Six alternatives proposed for solving the problems of youth in poverty were presented. No alternative received a majority, although "increased employment opportunities" clearly received the greatest support (37%). Both "more education" and "through their own initiative" were chosen by approximately a fifth of the sample; "less discrimination" by about ten percent (10%); and "more money" by about seven percent (7%). "Food programs" received an insignificant three percent (3%). There is no real difference between males and females. The 17-18 age group has the greatest percentage favoring increased employment opportunities of all the groups. It is interesting to note that, as the youth get older, there is an increasing percentage in favor of "through their own initiative"—poor youth solving the problem. Race, as might be expected, accounts for major differences. White and nonwhite youth are in agreement on two of the proposed alternatives: more education and more employment opportunities. Whereas twenty-two percent (22%) of the whites support "through their own initiative," less than nine percent (9%) of the nonwhites choose this alternative; nonwhites are more likely to favor less discrimination, food programs, and guaranteed incomes than are white youth. The same proportion of school and working youth select "employment opportunities." The proportion of high school youth who endorse less discrimination is twice that of the college and nonschool youth. The college youth are much more likely than other groups to favor more education as a solution. As might be expected, working youth are most likely to endorse "through their own initiative," while the college students are least likely to select this alternative.

Respondents were asked to select the statement which best described what they thought the institutions of society would become. Although no single alternative received a majority, there is no question that most youth believe youth-student activism will feel that while social institutions will become more receptive and sympathetic with what youth want, student activism will remain high, and our society will become more repressive, leading to a greater activism and possible revolution. Less than thirteen percent (13%) feel there will be a decline in youth activism. About a fifth of the respondents believe that there will be no great change in attitude or action toward youth.

Considering the sensitivity of the issue, it is significant that the majority in each youth category believe activism will continue at the present level or become more intense. However, some differences should be noted. The youngest respondents are most likely to believe our institutions will become more repressive, leading to an increase in youth activism. Differences between white and nonwhite youth are also apparent. Nonwhite respondents express more of a tendency to believe that our institutions will become more repressive in the years to come. Although they believe that institutions will become more receptive to youth, college youth also anticipate an increase in activism. High school students particularly see increased youth activism with increased institutional repression. A majority of working-class youth, though in fewer numbers than other groups, also anticipate an increase in youth activism regardless of institutional response.

In order to get some indication of future behavior, the following question was asked: "In the next five years, or when you are financially independent, which one statement describes what you think you will do?" "Working within the system to achieve authority and financial success," and "working within the system to improve the system" were each selected by at least one-third of the respondents. A fifth appear content to work within the system merely to support themselves. Seven percent (7%) indicated they thought they would "drop out of the system." Interestingly, half of those who anticipated dropping out plan on working from the outside in order to change the system. The high school and working youth have similar proportions selecting each alternative, but slightly more high school youth expect to drop out. The college students have the highest percentage of all groups who intend to work to improve the system; they also have the highest percentage indending to drop out. The nonwhites are next with the highest dropout intentions; over two-thirds of the dropout groups do not expect to work for change. The youngest respondents seem most content to merely support themselves, while older respondents are slightly more inclined to want to improve the system while working within it.

YOUTH, DRUGS, AND RACE

With regard to the drug abuse problem, "education in the schools" is seen as the most effective means by all groups. "Increased medical facilities" and "revision of the drug laws" are selected next, although nonstudents and those over 22 prefer "enforcement of current laws" more than either of these alternatives. Most groups rank legalizing drugs and peer pressure as possible solutions far below other alternatives. Males prefer revising the drug laws more than do females. The 19-21-year olds prefer revising the drug laws more than do other age groups. Nonwhite youth rank revising the drug laws lower in importance than whites, preferring the increasing of medical facilities as their second choice. The college students take the easiest line against drugs, seeing "enforcement of current laws" as the least desirable alternative. The high school youth take a stand somewhere between the college and working youth.

Over two-thirds of the sample feel that the use of illegal drugs will increase in the next ten years: forty-two percent (42%) think it will increase greatly; twenty-five percent (25%) expect a slight increase. Only a fifth believe it will decrease, and eleven percent (11%) think it will remain at the present level. There are no real differences between males and females. Of all the age groups, the under-17 group shows the largest proportion who feel there will be a great increase in the use of illegal drugs; the 17-18-year olds have the lowest proportion who feel there will be any increase. A greater proportion of whites than nonwhites feels there will be an increase; the nonwhites are much more likely than all other groups to believe that there will be a decrease in the level of illegal drug use. It is interesting to note that working youth, more than college students, foresee a great increase in illegal drug use. High school youth are least likely to predict any increase.

The respondents were asked in what manner their attitudes toward certain ethnic groups had changed during the past few years. The greatest change in attitudes was toward Blacks: nearly half say they have become more positive toward them, seventeen percent (17%) more negative. College students show the strongest positive change toward Blacks and toward most other ethnic groups. The oldest respondents, followed by working youth, indicate the largest amount of negative change. American Indians received the second greatest change in attitudes, most of which was positive. The Mexican-Americans received the next greatest change: twenty-six percent (26%) positive, eight percent (8%) negative. High school students, more than college students or working youth, show negative change. Generally, and with most ethnic groups, the oldest and the working youth have changed least in attitudes; nonwhites express greater negative change; and college youth more than others indicate positive change.

YOUTH AND COMMITMENT

Each respondent was asked to indicate agreement or disagreement with the following italicized statements. *Religion is not very important.* Nearly a quarter of all responding agree. The proportion of college students who agree is nearly twice that of the high school or nonschool youth. Nonwhites show less agreement than whites; the youngest and the oldest respondents are more likely to disagree than are those in the middle age groups. *Marijuana should be legalized.* Nearly thirty percent (30%) agree. The 19-21-year olds are the most supportive of the various groups. Whites are slightly more inclined to agree than are nonwhites. Nearly half the college youth agree, with working youth more likely to agree than the high school students. *The new lottery system for the draft is fair.* Nearly forty percent (40%) agree. As youth get older, agreement increases. Nearly twice the proportion of whites as nonwhites agree. Working youth indicate the highest support for the fairness of the new system. *People should show more respect for the flag.* Over half agree. Again, older youth are most likely to agree, as are whites. Working youth overwhelmingly agree (70%), whereas less than half the high school and only a little over a third of the college students agree.

More than half of all youth in this sample feel that *the*

U.S. should withdraw from Vietnam in the next six months.
College students are most in agreement, followed by working
youth and high school students. This item shows the least
amount of variation among the various age, race, and income
groups. A third of the youth believe that *all forms of military
draft should be abolished.* The only extreme difference
between the groups is that while half the college students
agree, a little more than a fourth of high school students and
working youth are in agreement. Less than a fifth of the
youth interviewed feel that *demonstrations are the best way
to get a point across.* High school youth and females are least
in agreement; nonwhites and college students are most in
agreement. What is significant is that over eighty-four percent
(84%) of all respondents feel that college students would
agree that demonstrations are the best way to get a point
across. It would seem that the visibility and rhetoric given to
demonstrations has greatly magnified the impression of
support of demonstrations by college youth.

Particularly interesting is that the majority of youth do
not believe that *everyone has a chance to get ahead in this
country,* nor do they believe that *racial discrimination is
disappearing.* This is true of working youth as well as school
youth, young and older of both races.

Nearly three-quarters of all youth agree that *women
should not be subordinate to men,* nonwhites being most
supportive of this statement.

Respondents were asked to rank what they saw as their
primary concerns and goals in selecting a career. All
subgroups, with the exception of college and nonschool
youth, rank these concerns as follows: (1) pays well; (2)
advancement potential; (3) regular hours; (4) relevance to
world problems; (5) security even if low paying; and (6) little
or no supervision. The college youth differ in that they rank
"relevance to world problems" as number three, and "security" last. Working youth rank security higher than the other
groups and are less concerned about relevance to world
problems.

Each respondent was asked to rank the importance to him of certain issues and problems facing youth. Education is ranked number one by all groups, with legal rights and responsibilities as number two by all groups with the exception of nonstudents, who feel that economy and employment are more important. This latter area of concern also tied for second place among the older age groups. For most of the groups, environment and employment concerns are third and fourth; race relations, and values and ethics are fifth and sixth; poverty, the draft, foreign relations next, with drugs always considered least important. Compared to the whites, nonwhites are less concerned about the environment, more concerned about race relations, and less concerned about issues of values and ethics. College youth are less concerned about economy and employment, and more concerned about the environment, and ethics and values than are the other groups.

The youth were asked to rank the importance of statements listed as motivations for U.S. involvement in Southeast Asia. "Preventing the spread of communism" received the greatest proportion of first choices in every grouping, with thirty-four percent (34%) selecting this explanation. "Protecting U.S. interests" and "insuring self-determination" were second and third in most ranking. "Honoring treaty commitments" was next, followed by "maintaining the balance of power" and "benefiting financially at home." Few differences were found among groups.

Finally, youth were asked in which of several situations they felt that the United States should be willing to commit troops to a conflict situation. Only one situation was chosen by a majority—"the U.S. being directly threatened by foreign aggression"—selected by fifty-nine percent (59%) of the respondents. "Honoring a U.S. defense agreement" was considered appropriate for troop commitment by a little less than half, followed by "when vital U.S. foreign interests are threatened." The other situations were chosen by a fifth to a third of the sample. All in all, youth appear to be extremely hesitant to have the United States become involved in actual troop commitments. Some generalizations can be made about the differences among the groups. On nearly all the issues, the older youth are more likely to support troop commitment than the younger ones. The nonwhites are less willing to support troop commitment than the whites. With two exceptions, the working youth have a consistently greater percentage who support troop commitment than either high school or college youth.

The results of this research would suggest that, while there are important differences in how youth view themselves and their society, there are important areas of consensus. Consensus occurs in the areas youth perceive as their most important concerns: in their feelings about the prevailing social and political climate with regard to youth behavior; and in their feelings about the involvement of youth in the operation of our institutions.

As previously mentioned, marriage and family, and work were viewed by both sexes and each age group (with the exception of males under age 17) as their primary areas of concern for the next five years. It was also noted that most respondents believe that youth-student activism will remain high or increase.

With regard to institutional responsiveness to youth, a little less than a third of the sample feel that while social institutions will become more receptive and sympathetic with what youth want, student actifism will remain high, and our society will become more repressive, leading to greater confrontation and possible revolution. Only a small minority (13%) anticipate a decline in youth activism. It is also interesting to note that, in addition to nonwhites, from whom it might be expected, it is the youngest respondents who are most likely to perceive our institutions as becoming increasingly repressive.

With regard to student involvement in the governance of

academic institutions, it was noted that almost half (49%) of all respondents believe that students should have "equal representation with other groups on committees having voting rights." Less than fifteen percent (15%) felt that students should either not participate in the governance of academic communities, or that their involvement should be limited to committee membership without voting privileges. Young and older respondents, as well as in-school and out-of-school respondents, agreed that students should be involved and should have voting rights.

Finally, it was also pointed out that the vast majority of respondents did not intend to "drop out" of the system, nor did they intend to work for change outside the system. On the contrary, ninety-four percent (94%) of all respondents anticipate working within the system. Of this group, a little more than a third say they seek to improve the system, a little more than a third seek to achieve authority or financial success, and about a fifth indicate that their primary goal is to work within the system "merely to support myself."

The responses of this national sample of youth should be of some satisfaction to both the lovers and the doubters of youth. Clearly, the youth appear to be more than reasonable in their goals and concerns. They do not express sentiments of despair, nor do they anticipate the need to destroy the social system. The results of this study, as well as the results of other studies, suggest that most young people believe that our society is confronted with social problems and problems of social injustice. Most believe that our system has the potential to provide meaningful, productive, and dignified life styles for all. There is little evidence of hatred or hostility toward this country. There is, however, disenchantment, frustration, and at times anger over our societal inability or reluctance to achieve our potential and to attain the national goals so often verbalized. There is also a strong desire on the part of many youth to make it different, to enhance the quality of life for all people.

The interaction between frustration, apprehension, and hope for the potential of our nation is more than adequately reflected in the preamble to the final report of the White House Conference on Youth (1971: 15-16). It is a statement written by the young and endorsed unanimously by all conference participants. It is an elegant and perhaps naive statement, but it does deal with what many youth feel are the problems, and it does represent what many young people seek for the future of our society.

To the People:

We are in the midst of a political, social and cultural revolution. Uncontrolled technology and the exploitation of people by people threaten to dehumanize our society. We must reaffirm the recognition of life as the supreme value which will not bear manipulation for other ends.

The approach of the two hundredth anniversary of the Revolution which gave birth to the United States of America leads us to reexamine the foundations of this country. We find that the high ideals upon which this country was ostensibly founded have never been a reality for all peoples from the beginning to the present day. The Constitution itself was both racist and sexist in its conception. The greatest blemish on the history of the United States of America is slavery and its evil legacy. The annihilation of Indians, genocide, exploitation of labor, and militaristic expansion have been among the important shortcomings which have undermined the ideals to which the people of this country have aspired.

It is time now finally to affirm and implement the rights articulated in the Declaration of Independence and the Constitution. Each individual must be given the full rights of life, liberty, and the pursuit of happiness; the Bill of Rights must be reinterpreted so as to be meaningful to all persons in our society. In addition the following rights are crucial:

The Right to adequate food, clothing, and a decent home.
The Right of the individual to do her/his thing, so long as it does not interfere with the rights of another.
The Right to preserve and cultivate ethnic and cultural heritages.
The Right to do whatever is necessary to preserve these Rights.

Governments and nation-states are created to secure and protect these rights. Through the acquiescence of its citizenery [sic], the government and other power structures of this nation have not fulfilled their responsibilities to the people, seeming instead to be concerned primarily with their self-perpetuation through serving the interests of the powerful at the expense of the people. In so far as any branch, agency, or member of the government or other power structure neglects its responsibility, it forfeits its legitimacy. We proclaim the following grievances:

Denial of equal opportunity has led to privation in the midst of plenty.

Repression has denied the free exercise of political rights in a "free society."

The system of justice lacks legitimacy for vast segments of the people, particularly minority groups and the poor.

Free cultural expression is discouraged in a supposedly pluralistic society.

Appeals to chauvinism, nationalism and militarism smother the individual's right to conscientious free choice of action and belief.

A war which is abhorrent to the majority of Americans and which inflicts inestimable anguish on a foreign people continues.

The government and the people have allowed economic and political power to be concentrated in institutions which are not responsive or answerable to the people, resulting in the waste and destruction of human and natural resources, and the failure to meet the people's needs.

The fear of youth identifying with adults and vice-versa, the fear of people identifying with themselves, the fear of people identifying with their race, the fear of people identifying with a country—all create a climate of fear which permeates this nation.

Internal divisiveness has contributed to a loss of national purpose.

The recommendations which follow we submit to the people as a realistic, positive, fundamental, minimal program for the redress of such grievances and the recognition of these Rights.

We are aware that "commissions," "conferences" and "reports" have often been used as a mechanism to divert the attention and energy of the people, in the guise of furthering "communication." This Conference shall not be so used.

Youth has been seeking reform of political and social institutions. Evidently these institutions are threatened by the basic insecurity inherent in change. The result has been repression which has transformed our struggle for reform into a struggle for survival.

We must recognize that change is not restricted to the realm of history, but is an ongoing process, the central dynamic of life. We recognize further that while youth is often most receptive to change, they are not alone in desiring it. We affirm our kinship with persons of good will of all generations. This affirmation stems from our appreciation of the indivisible nature of liberty.

We are aware of our responsibility to fight for the rights of all people. We recognize that we in the United States of America have strayed from the fundamental tenet of this nation, that the government is responsible to the people, in whom power resides, and that the people are therefore fully responsible for the policies and actions pursued in their name.

We, as have so many before us, dedicate ourselves to struggle and sacrifice for the realization of the ideals embodied in the program we have set forth.

Out of the rage of love for the unimplemented principles we here assert, we challenge the government and power structures to respond swiftly, actively, and constructively to our proposals. We are motivated not by hatred, but by disappointment over, and love for, the unfulfilled potential of this Nation.

REFERENCES

SIMON, W., J. H. GAGNON, and D. CARNS (1969) "Working class youth: alienation without an image." New Generation (Spring): 15-21.

White House Conference on Youth (1971) Report. Washington, D.C.: Government Printing Office.

ABOUT THE CONTRIBUTORS

DAVID GOTTLIEB is a sociologist at the University of Houston.

DONIVAN J. WATLEY is senior research psychologist at The Educational Testing Service in Evanston, Illinois.

DORIS Y. WILKINSON is a sociologist at Macalester College.

HAROLD L. SHEPPARD is a sociologist and senior study director with The Upjohn Institute in Washington, D.C.

ELIZABETH BRALY SANDERS is a sociologist at Pennsylvania State University.

LAUREN LANGMAN is a social psychologist at Loyola University in Chicago.

NATHAN HARE is a sociologist and publisher of *The Black Scholar*.

NED L. GAYLIN is in the Department of Family and Community Development at the University of Maryland.

JOEL FORT, M.D., is a psychiatrist and director of Fort Help in San Francisco.

JOHN H. GAGNON is a sociologist at the State University of New York at Stonybrook.

WILLIAM SIMON is a sociologist with the Institute for Juvenile Research in Chicago.

GLEN ELDER is a sociologist at the University of North Carolina, Chapel Hill.

JERALD G. BACHMAN is a psychologist and senior study director at the Survey Research Center, University of Michigan.

WILLIAM P. KUVLESKY is a sociologist at Texas A&M University.

LUIZ R. SIMMONS is director of the Narcotics Research Program at the Institute for the Study of Health and Society in Washington, D.C.